WOMEN AND ROMANCE FICTION IN THE ENGLISH RENAISSANCE

This book traces the progress of Renaissance romance from a genre addressed to women as readers to a genre written by women. The Elizabethan period saw a boom in the publication of romances by male authors. Many of these, Helen Hackett argues, were directed at an imagined female audience, advertising to male readers the voyeuristic pleasures of fictions supposedly read in women's bedchambers. Yet within a hundred years this imagined audience gave way to real women romance-readers and even women romance-writers. Exploring this crucial transitional period, Hackett examines the work of a diverse range of writers from Lyly, Rich and Greene to Sidney, Spenser and Shakespeare. Her book culminates in an analysis of Lady Mary Wroth's *Urania* (1621), the first romance written by a woman, and considers the developing representation of female heroism and selfhood, especially the adaptation of saintly roles to secular and even erotic purposes.

HELEN HACKETT is Senior Lecturer in English Literature at University College London. She is author of *Virgin Mother, Maiden Queen: Elizabeth I and the Cult of the Virgin Mary* (1995) and *Writers and Their Work: 'A Midsummer Night's Dream'* (1997). She has published articles on Lady Mary Wroth's *Urania* and other Renaissance literature by or about women.

WOMEN AND ROMANCE FICTION IN THE ENGLISH RENAISSANCE

HELEN HACKETT

CAMBRIDGE
UNIVERSITY PRESS

PUBLISHED BY THE PRESS SYNDICATE OF THE UNIVERSITY OF CAMBRIDGE
The Pitt Building, Trumpington Street, Cambridge, United Kingdom

CAMBRIDGE UNIVERSITY PRESS
The Edinburgh Building, Cambridge CB2 2RU, UK www.cup.cam.ac.uk
40 West 20th Street, New York, NY 10011–4211, USA www.cup.org
10 Stamford Road, Oakleigh, Melbourne 3166, Australia
Ruiz de Alarcón 13, 28014 Madrid, Spain

First published 2000

Printed in the United Kingdom at the University Press, Cambridge

Typeface Baskerville 11/12.5pt *System* 3B2 [CE]

A catalogue record for this book is available from the British Library

ISBN 0 521 64145 4 hardback

Contents

Acknowledgements

It is a great pleasure to record my thanks to the many kind friends and colleagues who have assisted and supported this project in many different ways. My greatest debts are to Paul Cobb, Josie Dixon, Katherine Duncan-Jones, Lorna Hutson, Dennis Kay, Jeri McIntosh Cobb, the late Josephine Roberts, Paul Salzman, Sue Wiseman, Henry Woudhuysen and Amelia Zurcher. Others who have helped include Gavin Alexander, Ros Ballaster, Anne Barton, Catherine Bates, Philippa Berry, Julia Briggs, Pippa Brill, Anne Button, Jocelyn Catty, Hero Chalmers, Kate Chedgzoy, Danielle Clarke, Kate Clarke, Audrey Cotterell, Alexander Davis, Paul Davis, Lindsay Duguid, Clara Farmer, Margaret Patterson Hannay, Elizabeth Heale, Margaret Healy, Tom Healy, Katharine Hodgkin, Leo Holloway, Raphael Lyne, John Kerrigan, Paulina Kewes, James Knowles, Tim Langley, Alison Light, Gordon McMullan, Robert Maslen, the late Jeremy Maule, Steven W. May, Kathy Metzenthin, Charlotte Mitchell, Abbey Onayiga, Melanie Osborne, Kathryn Perry, Mary Price, Neil Rennie, Yvonne Reynolds, Jennifer Richards, the late Gareth Roberts, Richard Rowland, Corinne Saunders, Oonagh Sayce, Suzanne Scholz, Leah Scragg, Alison Shell, Elaine Showalter, Alan Stewart, John Sutherland, Peter Swaab, Karen Tan, Alison Thorne, Ann Thompson, Suzanne Trill, David Trotter, Yoshiko Ueno, Amanda Vickery, Keith Walker, Valerie Wayne, René Weis, Helen Wilcox, Richard Wilson, Christopher Wheeler, Sarah Wintle and anonymous readers for Edward Arnold and Cambridge University Press.

I am grateful for interest and feedback from audiences at the Cambridge Renaissance Research Seminar, the 1992 European Society for the Study of English conference at the University of East Anglia, the *Voicing Women* conference at the University of Liverpool, the London Renaissance Seminar, the *Renaissance Man/Renaissance*

Woman conference at the University of Newcastle, the conference on *Shakespeare's Late Plays* also at the University of Newcastle, the Renaissance drama research seminar at the University of Oxford, the Renaissance research seminar at the University of Reading, the graduate seminar at the Roehampton Institute and the Middle English I seminar and the staff–graduate seminar at University College London. Parts of Chapter 9 first appeared in ' "Gracious be the issue": Maternity and Narrative in Shakespeare's Late Plays' , in Jennifer Richards and James Knowles (eds.), *Shakespeare's Late Plays: New Readings* (Edinburgh University Press, 1999), pp. 25–39.

The many library staff who have given unstinting assistance include those of the Bodleian Library, the British Library, the University of London Library and University College London Library, where the wonderful John Allen must be singled out for special mention. I am also grateful to the Brown University Women Writers Project for supplying a text of the *Urania* in the dark period before Josephine Roberts's superb editions, and to the Newberry Library in Chicago for a microfilm of the *Urania*'s manuscript sequel. Staff at UCL's Education and Information Services Division and Prospects Careers Service helped to solve computer problems.

As ever, I warmly thank all the staff and students of UCL English Department for being such a vibrant intellectual community.

Steve, Eddie and Marina Hackett have had to live with this project for a long time – in two cases, for their lifetimes – and I give them heartfelt thanks for putting up with it and letting me give it time which might otherwise have been theirs. I am also grateful to the wonderful staff of Fortis Green Nursery, without whom none of this would have been possible.

My grandmother, Anne Rooke, has passed on to me her pleasure in reading and a little of her tenacity, without which this book might not have been written. It is dedicated to her, with thanks, admiration and much love.

Abbreviations

DNB	*Dictionary of National Biography* on CD-ROM (Oxford: Oxford University Press).
OED	*Oxford English Dictionary* (2nd edn) on CD-ROM (Oxford: Oxford University Press).
STC	*A Short-Title Catalogue of Books Printed in England, Scotland and Ireland 1475–1640*, comp. A. W. Pollard and G. R. Redgrave, 2nd edn, rev. W. A. Jackson, F. S. Ferguson, and Katharine F. Pantzer, 3 vols. (London: Bibliographical Society, 1976–91).

A note on the text

In quotations from primary sources, the use of i/j and u/v has been modernised, printers' contractions have been silently expanded, and obvious printers' errors have been silently corrected. All references to Shakespeare are to *The Norton Shakespeare*, eds. Stephen Greenblatt et al. (New York and London: W. W. Norton, 1997) unless otherwise stated.

Introduction

> The importance of a new class of readers, composed of women from the middle ranks of society, deserves attention, because the influence of feminine opinion, an influence which has grown continually more powerful in English and American literature, began to be felt in the sixteenth century . . . Since women in general have never subscribed to realism, romance in strange opera lands and love stories with happy endings found favour with the Elizabethans even as with feminine readers today.[1]

So wrote Louis B. Wright in 1935, in his eminent study of Elizabethan popular reading which laid the groundwork for much subsequent scholarship. How true, though, is the story he tells, of a rising Elizabethan female readership craving romance?

In the first place, many others concur that the last quarter of the sixteenth century saw a 'fiction explosion'.[2] Much of that fiction is little known today, although in recent years it has begun to receive more critical attention.[3] It can require some acclimatisation from the modern reader, since it operates not by the familiar principles of the novel, but in the fantastical, non-naturalistic mode designated by the term 'romance'.[4] It tends to be concerned, for instance, with the adventures of elaborately named knights and ladies in exotic lands and/or in periods of distant mythologised history. Robert Greene's *Pandosto*, the source for Shakespeare's *The Winter's Tale*, is a typical example; it tells the story of the King of Bohemia, his daughter Fawnia and her lover Dorastus, Prince of Sicilia, set in some unspecified past age when perplexed rulers were inclined to consult the Oracle at Delphos. Another example is *Amadis de Gaule*, the popular Spanish romance, recounting the chivalric exploits of the eponymous knight and his secret love for Oriana, daughter of an ancient king of Britain.

These fictions usually also involve supernatural interventions, amazing coincidences and twists of fate, amidst a general ambience of the marvellous and wondrous; and their style is highly rhetorical, aiming primarily at the display of prowess in verbal artifice rather than the realistic simulation of natural speech and of psychology which we have come to expect of the novel. In *Pandosto*, for instance, Fawnia, who has been brought up as the daughter of simple shepherds and does not yet know that she is a princess, laments her unworthiness of Dorastus in a far from rustic or uneducated style:

> Unfortunate Fawnia, and therefore unfortunate because Fawnia! thy shepherd's hook sheweth thy poor state, thy proud desires an aspiring mind: the one declareth thy want, the other thy pride. No bastard hawk must soar so high as the hobby, no fowl gaze against the sun but the eagle: actions wrought against nature reap despite, and thoughts above fortune disdain.

So she goes on for a lengthy paragraph.[5]

Renaissance romances can be long and highly digressive, often consisting of many strands of narrative; Philip Sidney's *New Arcadia* and Edmund Spenser's *Faerie Queene* are obvious examples. These two romances underwent ongoing processes of revision and expansion by their authors and were left unfinished at their deaths, features which suggest open-endedness and the potentially infinite self-generation of the narrative. A similar effect is conveyed by the amplitude of the very popular cycles of chivalric romances translated from Spanish and Portuguese, of which *Amadis de Gaule* was one, along with *Palmerin* and *The Mirror of Knighthood*. *Amadis* inspired in its original Spanish no fewer than eleven sequels chronicling the exploits of the titular hero's descendants through seven generations. The *Palmerin* cycle, beginning with *Palmerin d'Oliva*, ran to four sequels and five generations, including *Primaleon*, concerning Palmerin d'Oliva's son, and *Palmerin of England*, concerning Palmerin d'Oliva's great-nephew.[6] The adventures of such descendants often echo those of the original protagonists, creating what can seem like an endlessly circling spiral of narrative, and presumably catering to a reading public with an appetite for more and more of the same. The Iberian cycles seem to be an early example of the market as a generator and shaper of narrative: commercial success encouraged a fertility of narrative which in turn was based upon the fertile progeneration of each central fictional dynasty. Primaleon the fictional heir was synonymous with *Primaleon* the book; volumes begat sequels just as heroes begat heirs.

Since Wright, the popularity of Renaissance romance has frequently been attributed to a rise in female literacy. This theory is often accompanied by suggestions that romance gave prominence to female characters; that it was especially concerned with love, courtship and other private and personal areas of life which might be classified as 'feminine'; and that women have a special affinity with escapist fictions. Margaret Spufford, in her invaluable study of popular fiction and its readership in seventeenth-century England, accepts that chivalric romances were 'the favourite reading of women to whom the romanticized love of the chivalric works appealed'.[7] Linda Woodbridge, in her feminist study of *Women and the English Renaissance*, states that prose fiction from the 1560s onwards was 'obviously slanted towards female readers', and that romance authors like Robert Greene 'obviously hoped to tap into the enormous resources of the female reading public'.[8]

However, one fact about Renaissance romances which is immediately striking and which might complicate ideas of them as 'women's literature' is that they were all written by men – with the two notable exceptions of *The Mirror of Knighthood*, which was translated from Spanish by Margaret Tyler (1578), and the *Urania* (1621), which was written by Mary Wroth. The present study aims to examine the relationship between women and romance in the English Renaissance in detail and in a number of different senses, including not only the relationship between romance and a female readership, but also the related subjects of the representation of women in romances, and what happened when these two remarkable women, Tyler and Wroth, made their singular interventions into the genre. It aspires to be a feminist study, although it participates in the process of debate which has always characterised feminist criticism, and I may therefore sometimes differ from some other feminist critics. I begin by looking further at the question of the readership of romance.

CHAPTER I

The readership of Renaissance romance

RENAISSANCE ROMANCE AS WOMEN'S READING

Various kinds of evidence support the view of Louis Wright and others that the commercial success of Renaissance romances was attributable to a new female readership. Many Elizabethan and Jacobean romance authors included in their works dedicatory prefaces and incidental narrative asides which specifically addressed 'gentlewomen' readers, that is, women of middle rank. John Lyly began *Euphues and his England* (1580), the sequel to *Euphues: the Anatomy of Wit*, with an epistle 'To the Ladies and Gentlewomen of England', beseeching them to 'take the pains to read it, but at such times as you spend in playing with your little dogs', and to have 'Euphues . . . as often in your hands, being but a toy, as lawn on your heads, being but trash'.[1] Barnaby Rich included a similar dedication 'To the right courteous gentlewomen' in *Rich's Farewell to Military Profession* (1581), a collection of romance-type stories, explaining that he had turned away from military pursuits in favour of the more fashionable entertainment of ladies. His title page declared his tales to have been 'Gathered together for the onely delight of the courteous Gentlewomen . . . for whose onely pleasure thei were collected together'.[2] Robert Greene informed 'Gentlewomen' readers of *Penelope's Web* (1587), another collection of romance tales, that it was aimed at 'discovering [i.e. revealing, publicising] the vertues of your sex'.[3]

By the early seventeenth century, foolish female readers of romance had become favourite subjects for satirists and moralists. A Chambermaid in the 1615 edition of Sir Thomas Overbury's *Characters* 'reads *Greenes* workes over and over, but is so carried away with the *Myrrour of Knighthood*, she is many times resolv'd to run out of her selfe, and become a Ladie Errant'.[4] Thomas Powell in 1631 gave the following instructions for how to educate 'a private Gentlemans daughter': 'In stead of Song and Musicke, let them learne Cookery and Laundrie. And in stead of reading Sir *Philip Sidneys Arcadia*, let them read the grounds of good huswifery.'[5]

Some modern critics have surmised that Renaissance romance appealed to women readers because of protofeminist narrative ingredients, like frankness about sexual matters, and the centrality of independent female characters. Tina Krontiris argues that chivalric romance, in particular, constituted an 'oppositional genre':

> First, by its portrayal of daring heroines the romance often encouraged women to ignore social restrictions . . . Secondly, by its construction of an ideal world, the romance . . . could make the female reader critical of her position in the real world . . . Thirdly, romances tended to provide experiences unattainable for women in actual life. Amazons and warrior women are found primarily in romantic fiction.[6]

It is noteworthy that feminist critics like Krontiris and Caroline Lucas have wholeheartedly adopted Wright's view that Renaissance romance was primarily women's reading. We can deduce several reasons for this. For one thing, the relative invisibility of women on the literary and historical scenes in the period makes it refreshing and heartening to come across apparent evidence of female activity, and moreover activity which may have had a significant shaping influence on the kind of literature written and the way it evolved. For another, this model is attractive because of its connotations of female pleasure and subversiveness. Much of Wright's evidence for female romance-reading takes the form of admonitions by moralists and educationalists *against* the suitability of the pastime for daughters and wives, like that of Powell quoted above. This suggests that women chose romances for their reading matter in the face of strong disapproval, with their own enjoyment defiantly in view, in preference to the devotional texts, herbals and books of household management otherwise available to them. All of this indicates an encouraging female independence of spirit. Moreover, this apparent disreputability of Renaissance prose romances in their own time, combined with the fact that in our time they tend to be less well known and less studied than the poetry and drama of the period, also lends to discussion of them an exciting sense of challenging the literary canon and conventional hierarchies of 'high' and 'low' culture.

However, a problem with most of these kinds of evidence of women's reading – whether prefaces by romance authors, mocking satires, or moralising prohibitions – is that they are themselves literary texts. As such, they were composed for various kinds of rhetorical effect, and cannot be claimed as authoritative proof of what women were actually reading. In addition, the assertion that romances foreground positive female characterisations and must therefore have appealed to women depends upon highly subjective, and possibly anachronistic, definitions of what is 'positive'. Indeed, some other kinds of evidence may unsettle the idea that romance was especially popular with women.

REAL WOMEN READERS

It is questionable whether the female readership did indeed possess the 'enormous resources' that Linda Woodbridge claims. On the contrary, according to David Cressy, ninety-five per cent of women in 1550 were illiterate, a figure which did not decline much by the time of the Civil War, when he estimates ninety per cent.[7] However, these figures are based on ability to write a signature, and it is very likely that the ability to read was a more widespread attainment. Keith Thomas regards Cressy's statistics as 'a spectacular underestimate',[8] and Paul Salzman, citing E. H. Miller, estimates fifty per cent literacy by 1600; he relates this to statistics showing that the period 1558 to 1603 produced three times as much published fiction as the period 1475 to 1558, and he regards women as playing an important part in this new reading public.[9] Overall, though, it has to be confessed that solid evidence as to the size of the female readership remains frustratingly elusive; as Cressy resignedly acknowledges, 'Unfortunately, reading leaves no record'.[10]

A few individual women of the late sixteenth and early seventeenth centuries did leave records of their reading habits. On the whole, these tend not to provide a picture of widespread romance-reading, and the evidence for the Elizabethan period is especially thin. We know from Margaret Tyler's 1578 translation of *The Mirror of Knighthood* that at least one Elizabethan woman was reading romances, and doing so with enjoyment and close attention. However, the diary of Lady Margaret Hoby for the period 1599–1605, which records extensive reading, refers almost exclusively to the Bible and devotional works.[11] Lady Grace Mildmay, in her journals for 1570–1617, similarly displayed a predominant concern with godliness, combining this with a special interest in medicine which led her to spend much time reading herbals. She appears to have taken to heart the warning given in her youth against the seductive dangers of dubious books: she was advised 'to take heede of whom I received gifts, as a book wherein might be some fine words whereby I might betray myself unawares . . . for that wicked companions would ever presente treacherous attempts'.[12] Jacqueline Pearson, in a survey of women's reading between 1500 and 1700, admits that evidence of women's recreational reading is extremely hard to find, especially earlier in the period. She may be right to suppose that 'women tended not to record recreational reading because they had absorbed the conservative anxiety about it',[13] but this remains impossible to prove.

In the next generation, the journals of Lady Anne Clifford (1590–1676) for the period 1616–19 detail works read to her by her servants which do include romances, namely *The Faerie Queene* and the *Arcadia.*[14] Indeed, such was her admiration for Spenser that she commissioned his memorial in Westminster Abbey and composed the epitaph herself.[15] Her 'Great Picture' of 1646, a triptych whose side-panels show her both as a girl and as a middle-aged woman surrounded by her books, also displays the *Arcadia* and Spenser's works among the reading matter of her youth, along with *Don Quixote* and *'Godfrey of Boloigne'*, a translation of Tasso's *Gerusalemme Liberata.* On the other side, the reading of her maturity includes John Barclay's *Argenis* (1621), a political *roman à clef* in romance form.[16] Even in later life, she does not appear to have laid the *Arcadia* aside: a surviving copy of the 1605 edition bears notes in her handwriting, including, on the verso of the title page, 'This Booke did I beegine to Red over att Skipton in Craven aboutt the Latter=ende of Januarey and I made an ende of Reding itt all ower in Apellby Castell in Westmorland the 19 daye of Marche folloing, in 1651.'[17]

There are some other examples of women of aristocratic families whose reading included romance. Most prominent are the women of the Sidney family. Mary Sidney (or, to use her married name, Mary Herbert, Countess of Pembroke) evidently had a close knowledge of both the *Old* and *New Arcadias*, the former of which her brother Philip described as written 'only for you, only to you',[18] and the latter of which she supervised through its publication in 1593. Her niece, Lady Mary Wroth, displayed detailed knowledge of the *Arcadia, The Faerie Queene* and other romances in her own 1621 *Urania* (see chapter 10 below). These Sidney women might be regarded as unrepresentative, however, because of their membership of a distinctively literary and romance-oriented family. Two other women of the early seventeenth century, Lady Elizabeth Southwell in 1605 and Lady Arbella Stuart in 1610, donned masculine disguise to elope with their lovers, suggesting by their translation into real practice of a conventional romance trope their familiarity with the genre.[19] In 1601 Mary Fitton, one of the Queen's ladies-in-waiting, was rumoured to have adopted male disguise to make clandestine visits to the chambers at court of her lover William Herbert, Earl of Pembroke.[20] These cross-dressers, though, were scandalous, far from typical cases. In general, aristocrats and courtiers such as these last three, the Sidneys and Lady Anne Clifford may well have enjoyed more licence to read secular works than did women in less privileged circumstances, and may also have enjoyed more licence to admit to such reading. They do not furnish evidence of a sizeable female romance-readership.

In any case, in both Anne Clifford's diaries and portrait the named romances form only a fraction of the reading matter catalogued. Graham Parry comments that the library depicted in the portrait of the young Lady Anne consists primarily of stoical works of philosophy and religion, and that it is debatable whether this 'genuinely reflected Anne's mood as a young woman of fifteen'.[21] This reminds us that the Great Picture is very much a statement of the public identity which she wished to project, and although she includes 'high' courtly romances like *The Faerie Queene* and the *Arcadia*, she does not include, say, works by Robert Greene or Barnaby Rich which presented themselves as catering to female tastes. However, the range of works shown is in other ways very broad, encompassing religion, moral philosophy, history, classical literature, languages, geography, botany, poetry and architecture, and giving no particular prominence to romance. Similarly, works dedicated to women of the Russell family over the period 1570–1620 included the likes of Robert Greene's *Penelope's Web*,[22] but also embraced religion, geography, history, travel, modern languages and Montaigne's *Essays*.[23] The letters of Lady Brilliana Harley (*c.* 1600–43) to her son Edward, which often discuss books exchanged between them, include a reference to Bishop Francis Godwin's *The Man in the Moon* (1638), a narrative of a fantastic voyage, which she compares to *Don Quixote* (endearingly spelled 'Donqueshot'). Again, though, these references to romance-related fictions are relatively isolated among more numerous mentions of books of devotion, history and topical debate.[24]

As we move towards the mid seventeenth century, we do find more numerous examples of more extensive female romance-reading. Mary Rich, Countess of Warwick (1624–78), born Mary Boyle, was apparently addicted to romances in her youth; her father, Richard Boyle, first Earl of Cork, presented her with the *Arcadia* when she was twelve and encouraged her romance-reading, but admonished his sons against such frivolity.[25] One copy of the *Urania* by Lady Mary Wroth is three times inscribed 'Dorothy Long her booke'.[26] By the 1650s we find Dorothy Osborne an avid devourer of the new monumentally proportioned French heroic romances like *Cléopâtre* (1646–57) by Gauthier de Coste de la Calprenède, and her favourite, *Artamène, où le Grand Cyrus* (1649–53) by Madeleine de Scudéry. She is breathlessly eager to discuss their plots and characters, her 'old acquaintances', in the letters she exchanged with Sir William Temple.[27] By 1664, Margaret Cavendish could include in a list of the kinds of works commonly written by women not only 'Devotions', 'Receits of Medicines' and 'Complemental Letters', but also 'Romances'.[28]

Such evidence as these individual women provide is unquestionably fragmentary, but does point towards certain conclusions. Significantly, it strongly suggests that ideas of a large Elizabethan female readership for romance are exaggerated. Nevertheless, by the mid seventeenth century female romance-reading, and even writing, seems to have become accepted as fairly unremarkable. Some process of growth in the female romance-readership must have taken place between these two points, possibly by the gradual dissemination of romances from privileged aristocratic readers to their female servants and to socially aspiring women of the gentry and trading classes. Wright and his followers tend to put together material from, say, the 1580s and the 1630s as if they are all part of the same scene, but it looks as if we need to be careful to distinguish between different moments in a period of transition and process.

ROMANCE AS A FEMININE GENRE

In particular, we need to ask why, in the 1580s, when, as far as we can tell, the female romance-readership was not at all extensive, authors like Lyly, Rich and Greene were blatantly addressing their fictions to women readers. This disparity draws our attention to the fact that all that we can certainly deduce from such textual evidence is that these authors wished their works to be *perceived* as directed at gentlewomen. It appears that some sort of connection was developing between women and romance which had less to do with actual women's reading habits than with cultural perceptions of romance as 'women's reading' and cultural constructions of romance as a feminine genre.

In fact, even before the Elizabethan fiction boom, romance had been associated with imagined female readers. This originated as concern as to the dangers which might ensue if literate women got hold of romances. Early in the sixteenth century, the works in this category were mainly popular chivalric romances like *Guy of Warwick* and *Bevis of Hampton* which had been in circulation for centuries and were beginning to appear in printed form. Juan Luis Vives, the Spanish humanist, wrote a tract on the education of girls at the instigation of Catherine of Aragon for the instruction of her daughter Princess Mary.[29] He listed romances, including 'Arthur, Guye, Bevis', and 'in my countre in Spayn Amadise', as being 'fylthe and vitiousnes . . . playne and folysshe lyes'. He elaborated: 'though they were never so wytty and pleasant, yet wold I have no pleasure infected with poyson: nor have no woman quickened unto vice. And verely they be but folisshe husbandes and mad, that suffre their wives to waxe more ungratiously subtyle by redyng of such bokes.'[30] The Protestant reformer Heinrich Bullinger also expressed disapproval of romances in *The Christian State of Matrimony*, translated by Miles Coverdale in 1541. He advised for the education of daughters:

> let them avoyde idlenes, be occupyed ether doing some profytable thynge for youre familie, or els redynge some godly boke, let them not reade bokes of fables of fonde and lyght love, but call upon God to have pure hertes and chaste . . . Bokes of Robyn hode, Beves of Hampton, Troilus, and such lyke fables do but kyndle in lyers lyke lyes and wanton love. (fo. 75r–v)

Bullinger voices a fundamental anxiety which accompanied the humanist educational programme: those of the unlearned who were given literacy in order to read godly books had also become equipped to read books of the opposite moral character.

Such pronouncements are based on three premises: that romances exercise undue freedom concerning erotic matters; that women are especially susceptible to the charms of such erotic entertainments; and that the consequent effect of romance upon women will be to make them sexually unruly. This may tell us less about what women liked to read than about how male moralists constructed and evaluated their categories of 'romance' and 'women'. As Michael McKeon observes, 'From Dante on the fear that women's morals will be corrupted by reading romances is quite conventional, and its articulation . . . may provide evidence less of the rise of the reading public than of the persistence of anxiety about women.'[31] 'Women' and 'sexuality' were clearly closely associated categories in these condemnations of romance, but in a paradoxical fashion: in so far as women embodied sexual attractions for men, romance was identified with women as itself a form of eroticised pleasure; yet in so far as women's own sexuality was regarded as wayward and in need of restraint, romance was regarded as something to be kept from women.

These cultural constructions further produced an inverse position whereby for an author to declare that his book was designed for the pleasure of women was in effect for him to advertise his wares to readers of both sexes as racy, lightweight and fun. Aristocratic patronage of literary works seems to have declined markedly in the late sixteenth century, forcing the development of marketing techniques by printers, booksellers and writers. Prefatory materials like epistles to women readers need to be read in this context: they are designed to attract the potential buyer browsing in the congested marketplace of St Paul's Churchyard.[32] In the cases of Lyly, Rich and Greene, intrinsic to their dedications to women readers is the presentation of their works as toys and playthings to be enjoyed in hours of delinquency from duty. Significantly, all of them set these epistles to women alongside dedicatory epistles to male readers; they clearly expected to have male readers to whom a flirtatious address to women readers would announce that titillating reading pleasures were to follow.

This may include a suggestion of voyeuristic pleasures: to read a book of courtship narratives which would 'normally' be read by a woman is at once to read about women's erotic secrets, to spy upon the imagined woman reader's private communion with her erotic book and to penetrate the private space of a woman's bedchamber or closet where she is supposed to indulge in such reading. Thus Lyly declares in his epistle to women readers that 'Euphues had rather be shut in a lady's casket than open in a scholar's study',[33] while Rich in his epistle to women explains that he has taken up romance writing because 'I see now it is lesse painfull to followe a Fiddle in a gentlewomans chamber: then to marche after a Drumme in the feeld.'[34] Greene informed gentlemen readers of *Penelope's Web* that 'I was determined at the first to have made no appeale to your favorable opinions, for that the matter is womens prattle, about the untwisting of Penelope's Web' (the book depicts Penelope and her ladies telling one another stories while they unweave her web in her chamber by night in order to keep her suitors at bay). However, he changed his mind on 'considering that *Mars* wil sometime bee prying into *Venus* papers, and gentlemen desirous to heare the parlie of Ladies'.[35]

For such rhetorical purposes it was clearly in the interests of the male author to exaggerate the extent and enthusiasm of his female readership. Rather than reading their addresses to women literally as evidence of real women's reading habits, it seems that we need to read them *literarily*, as part of the fictions which they frame and punctuate. The imagined woman reader may even be construed, on closer inspection, as a man in drag. As Maureen Quilligan points out, Sidney's *Defence of Poesy* indicates that male readers were habituated to reading as women in order to judge the rhetorical effectiveness of erotic writings by fellow men.[36] Sidney complains that 'truly many such writings as come under the banner of unresistible love, if I were a mistress, would never persuade me they were in love: so coldly they apply fiery speeches'.[37] The male reader may adopt a female persona in order to assess male writing apparently addressed to women, and to enjoy metaphorical access to women's bedchambers and other spaces of courtship.

WOMEN AND THE ORAL TRADITION

The cultural construction of romance as having a special affinity with women was based not only upon ideas about women's reading, but also upon ideas about women as storytellers. As we have just seen, *Penelope's Web* claimed to give men access to the kinds of tales which women tell one another in private. The stories of Penelope's ladies are described as 'merrie chat' designed to 'beguyle the night with prattle'; they are entertainments which enliven time which would otherwise pass slowly.[38] The activity of narration is also closely identified with the archetypal feminine activities of spinning and weaving: one of Penelope's maids is described as 'applying as well her fingers to the web as her tongue to the tale', while later when Penelope takes her own turn at storytelling her maids listen 'setting their hands to the Web, and their eares to hir talke' (pp. 155, 162). The 'endlesse web' of cloth (p. 233), whose ravelling and unravelling makes time stand still and seems able to go on forever, becomes in effect a metaphor for the generation of a potentially limitless thread of female story.[39]

In fact the word 'text' derives from the Latin word for weaving, *texere;* and further classical myths present women who literally wove narratives, such as Philomel and Arachne.[40] Their stories combine positive and negative aspects of spinning or weaving metaphors for female storytelling. Philomel was able to tell the truth about her rape, even though her tongue had been cut out, by depicting it on cloth; female weaving is thereby represented as equivalent to a female voice, and as a vivid means of communication. Arachne defeated Minerva in a weaving contest by her depiction of the many affairs of the gods, associating female storytelling with the capacity to draw upon an abundant fund of story. The idea of making an intricate narrative fabric from a thread also suggests skill in plotting. On the other hand, though, thread connotes linearity and a tendency to run on and on, such that the metaphor can represent women's narration as the undirected, unlimited and unthinking flow of a 'natural' facility. This is emphasised by Minerva's punishment of Arachne: she metamorphoses her into a spider, an image which does invoke the intricate structure of a web but also reduces spinning, and the female narrative for which it stands, to the status of a spontaneous bodily emission. Webs could also have sinister associations with the weaving of magic, an occult feminine art.[41]

The idea that women were especially liable to tell idle and foolish tales was well established by the sixteenth century and was already described in the phrase 'an old wives' tale' In *Amadis de Gaule*, the heroine Oriana, on being parted from her newborn baby, fears that his wetnurse might 'sit gossipping with her neighbours, telling vaine tales and fruitlesse fables'.[42] In Marlowe's *Dr Faustus*, the protagonist scoffs at Mephistopheles's talk of hell and damnation with the words 'Tush, these are trifles and mere old wives' tales'.[43] Alinda in Thomas Lodge's *Rosalynd* refers to foolish popular assumptions as 'but old wives' tales'.[44]

George Peele's play *The Old Wives' Tale* (*c.*1593) is, just as its title suggests, grounded upon this idea of the fantastical women's story.

Three pages named Antic, Fantastic and Frolic who are lost in a wood are taken in by a smith and his wife, Madge, whom they address as 'gammer'. They entreat her to tell them a story:

ANTIC Methinks, gammer, a merry winter's tale would drive away the time trimly. Come, I am sure you are not without a score.

FANTASTIC I'faith, gammer, a tale of an hour long were as good as an hour's sleep.

FROLIC Look you, gammer, of the giant and the king's daughter, and I know not what. I have seen the day, when I was a little one, you might have drawn me a mile after you with such a discourse.[45]

Madge accedes to their request with the words 'So I am content to drive away the time with an old wives' winter's tale' (lines 98–9), accepting their evaluation of her story as merely a little better than doing nothing. However, she puts up some slight resistance to their accompanying evaluation of it as equivalent to a sleep: she asks 'that you will say hum and ha to my tale, so shall I know you are awake' (lines 110–11). Her story begins: 'Once upon a time there was a king or a lord or a duke that had a fair daughter, the fairest that ever was; as white as snow and as red as blood; and once upon a time his daughter was stolen away, and he sent all his men to seek out his daughter . . .' (lines 113–17). Madge narrates in this style for a while, then the characters appear on stage to act out the tale, but with periodic interruptions from the pages and Madge to remind us of the oral narrative frame of teller and audience.

Peele achieves dramatic evocation of the oral tradition in several ways. First, the interruption of the narrative by questions from the pages and explanations by Madge depicts the audience participation characteristic of a tale told 'live' and in a circle. Secondly, Madge is shown actively making choices between formulaic motifs which she puts together to construct a plot. The motifs are common to both fairy-tale and printed literary romance, like the beautiful princess, the lost child and the quest. Their familiarity is part of their entertainment value; originality is not a measure of worth in this context. Madge's ongoing selection suggests that she is rummaging in a bottomless chest of such motifs. The indecisions, muddles and loops in her narratorial style also evoke a spontaneous oral delivery: she frequently interrupts herself with phrases like 'O Lord, I quite forgot! . . . O, I forget!' which provide occasions for elaborations and digressions (lines 122–8).

Margaret Spufford has further examples from the seventeenth and eighteenth centuries of women's involvement in various oral traditions like ballad singing and the sharing of bawdy tales and jokes, as well as fairy tales and folk tales.[46] Such evidence often takes the form of affectionate reminiscences of childhood pleasures, just as Frolic in *The Old Wives' Tale* nostalgically recalls 'when I was a little one'. John Clare (born 1793), for instance, remembered that in his rural childhood 'the old women's memories never failed of tales to smooth out labour; for as every day came, new Giants, Hobgoblins and Fairies was ready to pass it away'.[47]

These depictions and recollections are no doubt partly a reflection of real life: since women were less educated and literate than men, their storytelling was likely to take oral forms and to be relatively 'foolish'. Equally, it was usually women who looked after children, and who would therefore seek to occupy them with stories; and the boring yet often communal nature of women's tasks like weaving and spinning would lend themselves to simultaneous storytelling. All the same, I think we can surmise that the association between women (especially old women) and oral fantastical stories became an entrenched cultural construction for several other reasons. First, it might be called a fantasy of maternal origin, for the following reasons. The combination in fairy tales of simplicity, familiarity and fantasy means that they are readily identified with a vaguely remembered past, a primitive time of beginnings, something which can be sunk back into comfortably but from which the individual must move on; all of these qualities make them readily identifiable with a child's relationship with its mother. Secondly, the idea of these stories as unstructured, boundless and indeed oral, conceptualises them almost like a biological flow – something which just pours out; and women have historically been identified with the fluxes of the body, especially mothers who personify bodily sources of production. Thirdly, we can see the association of fantastic stories with women as an example of the kinds of parallel binary oppositions which have historically configured patriarchal culture.[48] Even before the advent of print, oral culture was the culture of the unlearned and was therefore 'low': the hierarchical oppositions learned/unlearned and high/low map onto the further hierarchical opposition male/female.

Moreover, an entrenched idea of women as purveyors of recreational narrative can also be traced through to 'high' culture and printed literature. The participation of women in group tale-telling was central to several influential courtly models for Elizabethan fictions, such as Boccaccio's *Decameron* (1349–51), in which seven young ladies and three young men divert each other with stories while on a pastoral retreat from plague-ridden Florence; or Castiglione's *Il Cortegiano* (*The Courtier*, 1528) a dialogue presided over by the Duchess of Urbino in which women contribute equally with men to the game of *questioni d'amore*, or questions of love. In the vernacular, the *Canterbury Tales* showed female narrators among the male ones. What is significant about these examples too is that they show women as deliverers of oral, not written, narratives; and the purposes of those narratives are to fill in idle time, implying their entertaining qualities, but also, crucially, associating them with the idleness for which they substitute. All sorts of sources and influences, then, showed women as storytellers in such a way as to connect them with stories which were diverting but also foolish and pointless, and this connection was in turn invoked in male fiction-authors' characterisations of their works as stories for women.

'WOMAN' AS SIGN

Various feminist critics have shown over recent years how texts which appear to be about women, or addressed to women, do not necessarily give us documentary evidence of the nature of women's lives. Lisa Jardine's 1983 book, *Still Harping on Daughters*, for instance, challenged the assumptions of earlier feminist critics that the prominent and active heroines of Shakespeare and his contemporaries could be regarded as evidence of a Renaissance emancipation of women. Instead she argued that:

> the strong interest in women shown by Elizabethan and Jacobean drama does not in fact reflect newly improved social conditions, and greater possibility for women, but rather is related to the patriarchy's unexpressed worry about the great social changes which characterise the period – worries which could be made conveniently concrete in the voluminous and endemic debates about 'the woman question'.[49]

Women were symbols of the property and power held and exchanged by men, whether as daughters deployed in marriage alliances, or as wives and mothers whose chastity ensured the perpetuation of the name and estate of the male head of the family. Expressed anxieties about women who pursued their own wills and sexual desires, and about the difficulty of detecting their 'impurity', were therefore homologous with anxieties about the instability of male economic and social status and of *masculine* identity.

A number of other critics, including Nancy J. Vickers, Linda Woodbridge, Eve Kosofsky Sedgwick and Patricia Parker, have drawn attention to ways in which Renaissance texts which appear to be about women may tell us more about masculine anxieties.[50] Texts which use women as their subject matter may do so in order to display masculine rhetorical prowess in working variations on a conventional theme, to construct a relationship of what Sedgwick calls 'homosocial exchange' between male author and male reader, and to define a masculine subject position in opposition to the feminine other. For instance, Vickers shows how in Shakespeare's *Rape of Lucrece* the heroine is described in terms of 'fragmentation and reification', such that, in short, 'this text explicitly dedicated to the celebration of a woman' ultimately provokes the question 'Is there a woman in this text?'.[51] Although 'woman' as sign is endemic in Renaissance texts, this may be to the exclusion of women as beings with their own subjectivities.

This critical attention to 'woman' as sign has many kinds of relevance to Renaissance romance. Parker shows how the expansiveness and digressiveness of romance narrative, and the pleasurable distraction from duty which it represented, were associated with the lability and seductiveness of the female body. This was expressed metaphorically in attacks on romance by writers like Roger Ascham and Stephen Gosson, who described Italianate fictions as full of 'the enchantments of Circe';[52] and was also a shaping concept within romance narratives, as evil but alluring enchantresses like Spenser's Acrasia deflected virtuous knights from their quests, thereby extending and diffusing the narrative.[53] Wendy Wall, in her study of the construction of the role of author during the Elizabethan expansion of print culture, finds that writers contending with the 'stigma of print' and striving to legitimate publication often metaphorically feminised the text as a means of asserting their masculine authority. We have seen how the language of romance prefaces feminised and eroticised the text; Wall explores in detail how the relations of author, and reader, to the text were mediated in 'a gendered and sexualised language – replete with figures of courtly love, cross-dressing, voyeurism, and female desire'.[54] Meanwhile Lorna Hutson offers a sophisticated analysis of the new 'economies of friendship' between men which developed in the sixteenth century's post-feudal age of humanism, commerce, careerism and print culture, and of the ways in which they crucially depended upon 'fictions of women'. She suggests that Elizabethan fiction

> is primarily concerned with the emergence of textual communication as the new medium in which manhood is to be tried . . . its preoccupation with lengthy speeches of courtship made to women, rather than lengthy descriptions of combats between men, may have less to do with the anticipated pleasure of women readers than with the displacement of masculine agency from prowess to persuasion.[55]

All these recent contributions to feminist critical debate encourage us to look at women in Renaissance texts less as mirror-images of women in real life than as figures who stand for something metaphorically, and are being used for some rhetorical and ideological purpose. Hence neither addresses to women romance-readers, nor moralistic or satirical characterisations of women as romance-readers, constitute proof that the female reader of romances had a material existence. In fact it would be possible to argue that the female audience addressed in romance dedications and narrative asides was a phenomenon entirely imagined in the texts and projected by the authors, with no real existence at all.

This would be a pretty depressing conclusion. In general, the kinds of feminist criticism which attend illuminatingly to 'woman' as cultural sign can sometimes have the simultaneous gloomy effect of returning real women to invisibility and re-erasing female action from the historical scene. We have hardly any women authors of romance in the Renaissance; to follow through these kinds of arguments to their furthest extents would be to leave us hardly any female readers either. In terms of the narrative or dramatic content of texts, it can be bleak to learn that what look like stories of women making their own choices in love are less about female agency than about the operations of masculine persuasive power. In terms of the readership of romance, it would be disheartening to think that no women disobeyed the prohibitions of moralists and indulged in the private and *risqué* pleasures of romance-reading, and influenced the fiction market in the process.

Of course, the fact that we would like to think that Renaissance women read romances is by no means legitimate grounds for asserting that they did so. However, evidence for a case that *no* Elizabethan women read romances is ultimately no more substantial than the evidence that numbers of them did read them. Indeed, it is counter-intuitive to argue that there was no female romance-readership at all: the fact that male authors could refer to a female readership as a recognisable phenomenon suggests that it did exist on some scale, even if they exaggerated it; and the established female romance-readership of the mid seventeenth century must have had its origins somewhere. I suggest that we attempt to sustain a sense that textual material does have some extratextual reference, while simultaneously paying heed to the literary (as opposed to literal) nature of textual evidence.

Lori Humphrey Newcomb's study of the reading history of Robert Greene's *Pandosto* is helpful in mapping out a middle course between ideas of the maidservant romance-reader as either a real person or a complete fiction.[56] She cites the edition of Overbury's *Characters* quoted above, in which a chambermaid's reading of Greene and *The Mirror of Knighthood* makes her yearn to be a lady errant. Newcomb points out that these works would have been too expensive for a servant; *Pandosto* became no cheaper over the period from 1585 to 1615 ('The Romance of Service', p. 128). The maid was most likely to have obtained a copy by borrowing it from her mistress. The satire therefore expresses anxieties about both the extension of literacy and new, less stable structures of service based less on feudal loyalty than social mobility and economic aspiration. Hence the chambermaid's longings for greater scope are ridiculed in order to rewrite 'the legitimate ambitions that induced the young to go into service as the foolish fantasies of an oversexed and overreaching female' (p. 127). The designation of certain cultural materials as degraded and the assignation of them to women and servant readers attempted to reinforce wavering social boundaries (p. 123). Thus the maidservant romance-reader could be simultaneously a real phenomenon *and* an ideologically loaded literary construction.

Piecing together all the diverse evidence gathered in the present chapter, it seems plausible to surmise that some female romance-readership did exist in the Elizabethan period. At the same time, though, ideas of the profusion of women romance-readers, and of their frivolity and credulity as readers, are exaggerations and caricatures with clear rhetorical purposes, probably constructed by male authors implicitly addressing a male audience.

CHAPTER 2

Renaissance romance and modern romance

RENAISSANCE ROMANCE AS POPULAR CULTURE?

The readership of Renaissance romance was often constructed not only as female but also as middling in class. Lyly, Rich and Greene described their imagined readers as 'gentlewomen': that is, of the gentry class, a notch below the nobility, but able to live without recourse to manual labour. Later, as we have seen, Overbury's *Characters* and other satires identified the chief readers of romances as maidservants. Going along with such middling class designations, romance was often denigrated as a 'low' genre both by the moralists who condemned it, and by many of the authors who wrote it and who presented their works as toys and trifles. Lyly even used the term 'trash' in his prefatory epistle to *Euphues and his England* (pp. 200–1).

Taking such representations at face value, modern critics often draw casual comparisons between Renaissance romance and modern forms of popular culture. Sheldon P. Zitner, seeking to understand Lord Herbert of Cherbury's enthusiasm for romance, suggests 'Perhaps we are dealing with a half-secret intellectual indulgence – like television.'[1] David Margolies speculates that 'Fiction may well have been regarded by the Elizabethans in the same way as cinema early in this century', as a vulgar and ephemeral amusement.[2]

In particular, the idea of Renaissance romance as women's reading is often bound up with suggestions that it is directly comparable with modern romantic fiction. As we have seen, Louis B. Wright asserted that 'the Renaissance woman, like her modern sister, found in fiction the literature of escape which the strenuousness of her life demanded', and that 'since women in general have never subscribed to realism, romance in strange opera lands and love stories with happy endings found favour with the Elizabethans even as with feminine readers today'.[3] A. C. Hamilton has described Emanuel Forde, a successful romance author of the 1590s, as an Elizabethan Barbara Cartland.[4] Although recent feminist critics like Caroline Lucas and Tina Krontiris do not, of course, repeat Wright's ascription of the success of romance to innate female silliness, they do tend to perpetuate his assumption that Renaissance romance is a 'women's genre' like modern romantic fiction and of interest to feminist critics for this reason.

The idea that sentimental escapist fiction and women go together has become deeply entrenched over the centuries, and is traceable through such diverse works as George Eliot's essay 'Silly Novels by Lady Novelists', Ian Watt's account of the part played by a newly leisured female readership in *The Rise of the Novel* in the eighteenth century, and the discussion of 'chick movies' and 'guy movies' in the 1990s film *Sleepless in Seattle.*[5] Rather than take this connection for granted, it might be as well to attempt some precision regarding the specificities of different periods and genres. When we refer to 'romance' in the context of modern fiction, we mean narratives which are predominantly, or indeed exclusively, concerned with love and courtship, and usually directed towards a happy ending in marriage. They are stories which are overwhelmingly woman-centred, presenting events from the heroine's point of view, and being almost exclusively authored by women, and aimed at women readers. Although, or perhaps because, this genre is hugely popular and clearly gives immense pleasure to its readers, it is pejoratively branded as 'trash'.

As their shared label of 'romance' implies, Renaissance romance and modern romance do have in common some escapist, artificial and formulaic qualities, and a shared interest in plots of courtship. However, there are also some problematic differences. I have already mentioned the fact that Renaissance romances were almost exclusively written by men. Besides this, the categorisation of Renaissance romance as popular requires some qualification. As I mentioned in relation to Peele's *Old Wives' Tale*, printed literary romances did share some motifs with oral folk tales and fairy tales. However, we have also seen that the prefaces in which romance authors deprecated their works as trifles were designed for rhetorical effect. They served as advertisements of a text's playful and entertaining qualities; and moreover, courtly modesty was conventional to the Renaissance authorial preface. This is not to say that their authors necessarily regarded the ensuing works as inconsequential and disposable. Arthur Kinney asks why authors like Lyly, Sidney and Nashe 'put their more important and more sustained efforts in fiction, a genre we now place considerably lower than poetry and drama on our scale of Renaissance literary forms? The answer, of course, is that for the Elizabethans (and for their Henrician and Continental counterparts) fiction was a genre of high calling.'[6] According to Kinney, romance was the forging-house of humanist poetics. R. W. Maslen, too, contends that the prose fiction authors of the 1570s 'were as serious as they were playful', and that their works are 'witty, and daring, and innovative'.[7]

The disparity in evaluations of romance, both by Renaissance writers and by modern critics, arises partly from the vast range of works encompassed by the term 'romance'. At one end of the social and literary scale were cut down chap-book versions of old-established chivalric romances like *Guy of Warwick* and *Bevis of Hampton* which aimed at readers of limited income and education. At the other end of the scale, works like the *Arcadia* and *The Faerie Queene* clearly had high literary ambition, and were produced in lavish formats for an illustrious courtly audience. Moreover, individual romances could shift their positions in the cultural hierarchy over time. The *Arcadia*, for instance, was extremely mobile in its cultural status. Its origins were of course impeccably élite; in 1588, at which date it had circulated in the select milieu of manuscript but had not yet been published in print, Abraham Fraunce's *Arcadian Rhetoric* used illustrations from it as models of elegant expression. Francis Meres, in his panegyrical survey of vernacular English literature in *Palladis Tamia*, 1598, censures *Amadis de Gaule*, *Palmerin*, *Bevis of Hampton*, *Guy of Warwick* and a litany of other chivalric romances (fo. 268), while placing the *Arcadia* in an utterly different category as an 'immortal Poem . . . in Prose' comparable to Xenophon's *Cyropaedia* and Heliodorus's *Aethiopica*.[8] However, by 1631, for Wye Saltonstall *Amadis* and the *Arcadia* occupy precisely the same category, as the kinds of romances read by young girls to supply erotic fantasy. He describes a 'Mayde' (i.e. a young virgin), who 'reades now loves historyes as *Amadis de Gaule* and the *Arcadia*, and in them courts the shaddow of love till she know the substance'.[9] Two years later William Prynne condemned 'Arcadiaes, and fained Histories that are now so much in admiration'.[10] By 1672, when Francis

Kirkman revived the Iberian chivalric romance *The Honour of Chivalry* and used his preface to promote the now unfashionable and debased genre, he stated that such fictions had been supplanted 'by an other sort of Historyes, which are called *Romances*, some whereof are written originally in English, as namely, that Incomparable Book of its time called, *The Countess of Pembrokes Arcadia*'.[11] Even as he acknowledges that the *Arcadia* is more recent and more admired, he places it in the same cultural slot and suggests that readers who enjoy it will also enjoy his own more rusty literary offering.

No doubt the mobile status of romance owed much to the genre's relative novelty and relative lack of classical models and strict formal rules. Much writing within the genre, like the *Arcadia*, was innovative and experimental, testing the possibilities of the form. Its malleability opened liberating opportunities to authors, but at the same time gave rise to ambivalence and uncertainty surrounding its literary status.

It is therefore an over-simplification to categorise all Renaissance romance merely as trash; and it is a further over-simplification to assume that it was women's reading simply because we are accustomed to the idea that women and trash go together. It is true that it is often in representations of Renaissance romance as 'low' that women readers are foregrounded. Interestingly, though, even 'high' examples of the genre give special prominence to women. Sidney's *Arcadia* was of course dedicated to his sister the Countess of Pembroke and gave its heroines at least as much attention as its heroes. Spenser's *Faerie Queene* both addressed and multiply represented Queen Elizabeth. Sir John Harington's translation of *Orlando Furioso* (1591) was produced in a splendid and costly format, and contained a prefatory defence of poetry which laid claim to high seriousness; yet it was said to have been undertaken because Harington's translation of an erotic episode to amuse the ladies of the court did not amuse the Queen, who banished him from court until he had translated the whole work.[12] This example neatly sums up the mixed properties of much Renaissance romance: it was courtly (high) yet entertaining (low), an innovative literary work (high), yet composed in a period of delinquency from serious public affairs (low); and in both its 'high' and its 'low' aspects it sustained an association with 'feminine' subject matter of love and courtship and with female readers. In short, Renaissance romance did not have to be popular to be regarded as a feminine genre, and we should be wary of assuming either that it was trashy because women read it, or that it was read by women because it was trashy.

COURTSHIP AND COURTIERSHIP

As we have seen, a number of Renaissance writers present romances as 'feminine' in genre not only because they are presumed to address women readers, but also because their plots concern matters of love and courtship. Modern comparisons between Renaissance romance and modern romantic fiction often rest upon a similar assumption that courtship narratives are of special interest to women because courtship is an activity of the 'feminine sphere'. Ann Rosalind Jones, summarising ways in which feminists might understand the appeal of traditionalist Mills and Boon romances for a mass female readership, argues that 'the concentration on courtship . . . [is] an affirmation of the one period of women's lives when social consensus puts their concerns at centre stage'.[13] Likewise for Ann Barr Snitow, the appeal of modern romance is explicable by its celebration of women's 'one socially acceptable moment of transcendence', while another recent study of the genre finds in it a 'reversal of the common view of history, allowing the usually marginalized female sphere to dominate'.[14]

This model rests on an assumption that courtship is a period when women can enjoy a temporary supremacy as men are obliged to woo them and are rendered subservient to female choice. Such a model, however, would obviously need some modification to fit a Renaissance context, when women may not have exercised even such fleeting power in courtship. There are some examples from the period of couples who married for love, like Philip Herbert and Lady Susan de Vere; but there are many other examples of arranged and less than successful marriages such as those of Lady Mary Sidney to Sir Robert Wroth; of her cousin William Herbert, Earl of Pembroke, to Lady Mary Talbot, daughter of the Earl of Shrewsbury; and of Lady Anne Clifford to Richard Sackville, Earl of Dorset.[15] Evidence from both historical and literary research suggests that marriages were a matter of negotiation between parents or guardians in which the chief imperative was to make financial and social connections advantageous to the dynasty. Marriage was primarily a property transaction in all classes which held any property, which extended down as far as the yeomanry; daughters and wives were merely a part of that property. Although many parents were reluctant to proceed without their children's consent, and although their authority in courtship-choices was coming under increasing pressure from the gradual development of what Lawrence Stone has called 'affective individualism', when push came to shove many women had little or no say in the selection of their partner.[16] Courtship was not, therefore, for most Renaissance women, a period in their lives when they could enjoy being deferred to and exercising freedom of choice. Moreover, just as the large and excitable female readership for Renaissance romance can be argued to be a fiction serving the interests of male writers and readers, so the assumption that courtship plots indicate an appeal to a female readership in this period has been shown to be open to challenge, because of the connection between courtship and courtiership as *masculine* fields of endeavour.

As martial prowess became less important as a means of male self-advancement, skills of rhetoric and courtiership came increasingly to the fore. An important model for this was Baldassare Castiglione's *Il Cortegiano*, 1528, translated by Sir Thomas Hoby as *The Book of the Courtier*, 1561. This fictional dialogue among members of the court of Urbino set out the attributes of the ideal courtier, which included not only military and sporting gifts but also intellectual and social ones. The last of *The Courtier*'s four books was wholly devoted to discussion of the proper way to love. Thus courtiership, in the sense of the pursuit of social and political ambition, and courtship, in the sense of wooing a mistress, were increasingly complementary and intertwined arts, as their shared etymology implies, and were especially linked by their mutual dependence upon successful self-promotion through the exercise of persuasive rhetoric.[17]

It has been widely recognised that in Elizabethan poetry the discourses of love and politics became almost interchangeable: Petrarchan love-poets wrote as servants seeking promotion in the favour of their mistresses, while panegyrists of the Queen expressed their fealty in an erotic language of devotion.[18] Similarly, in prose fiction, heroes who were shown practising the arts of wooing in the private, erotic sphere were exempla of skills of verbal persuasion and the pursuit of personal goals which were transferable to the public sphere of courtly ambition. Thus the *Treasury of Amadis of France*, 1567, a selection of excerpts from *Amadis de Gaule*, declared itself to be a means 'whereout men may learne to be noble oratours, wise and prudent counsellors, excellent Rhetoricians, expert captains, amorous companions, fervent & honest lovers, secrete messengers'.[19] Extracts from the Spanish romance were presented here as a conduct book, offering models of courtly deportment, which equally encompassed love and statesmanship.

Women inevitably figured largely in such fictions as the objects of the heroes' suits, but this prominence of women could be not so much an attempt to appeal to women readers, as a by-product of the display of masculine arts for the interest of a male readership. Lorna Hutson argues persuasively that 'the centrality of women to the plots of this newer "romantic" fiction is a direct consequence of its increasing devotion to the representation of *masculine* social agency as "civil" rather than martial, and as celebrating victories of mental readiness rather than physical courage'.[20]

However, just as I argued for the retrieval of the existence of some female readership, so I propose that we do not wholly discard the idea that plots of courtship had particular appeal for women. Even if such narratives were generated by an intention to entertain male readers rather than women, this is not to say that women who got hold of them could not take pleasure in their centrality of female characters. Indeed, since it appears that women were not always allowed much freedom of choice in courtship, fictions which celebrated an ingenious young man's winning of a bride against her father's wishes could also provide women readers with a fantasy of rebellion against patriarchal dictate, and the satisfaction of being valued as a prize. Again both the pontifications of moralists and romance authors' invitations to readers assumed that stories of love and courtship had a special appeal for women, and again I suggest that we sustain the idea of some extratextual reference for this. Just as in relation to the question 'who read romances?' the rhetorical exaggeration of the female readership need not mean that no female readership existed, so in relation to the question 'how were romances read?' an awareness of how courtship narratives served masculine interests need not preclude acknowledgement of the simultaneous use of them to serve female pleasures. To quote Hutson again, the authorial intention behind romance 'may have less to do with the anticipated pleasure of women readers than with the displacement of masculine agency from prowess to persuasion',[21] but a published text is set free from authorial intention and becomes open to a variety of reader responses. Indeed, as we shall see, a number of romance authors expressed anxiety as to how their works might be misinterpreted or misappropriated, and this could include their potentially subversive appropriation by women readers.

FEMALE HEROISM

The pleasures of romance for Renaissance women readers have been seen not only in terms of plot – a concentration on courtship narratives – but also in terms of character – the assumed presence within such plots of autonomous heroines who are able to fulfil their own desires. As we have seen, Krontiris locates the appeal of romance for women in the presence of 'daring heroines . . . Amazons and warrior-women'.[22] Caroline Lucas, too, while acknowledging that these fictions 'reinforce patriarchal prescriptions for female behaviour', argues that they 'simultaneously offer women a version of themselves as far more independent, powerful and significant than they would have experienced themselves in any other area of their lives'.[23] Romance is therefore assumed to have provided escapist pleasures for women as a space of wish-fulfilment fantasies. The chambermaid in Overbury's *Characters* who was inspired by *The Mirror of Knighthood* to become a lady errant and 'run out of her selfe' may be cited as a supportive case; the surface mockery of her foolishly literal-minded reading may be seen as symptomatic of an underlying anxiety as to the liberating and exhilarating ideas which romances might put in women's heads.[24]

However, even a fairly limited survey of Renaissance romances will find numerous directly contrary examples of heroines presented in ways which we might expect (or hope) to have been uncongenial to female readers. Robert Greene's *Penelope's Web*, for instance, might appear female-oriented in several respects: its title page promises 'a Christall Myrror of faeminine perfection'; its three dedications include one to Margaret Clifford and Anne Dudley and one 'To the Courteous and Courtly Ladies of England' (pp. 141–3, 146–7); and its substance concerns stories told to one another by Penelope and her female companions. However, the purport of those stories is to propound 'three especiall vertues, necessary to be incident in every vertuous woman . . . namely Obedience, Chastitie, and Sylence' (title page) – hardly a celebration of female autonomy and self-fulfilment. Lucrece, who was raped then killed herself to save her husband from the slur on his honour, is one of the heroines held up as an example (p. 157), and Penelope relates a story in the

Patient Griselda genre concerning a nobly suffering heroine named Barmenissa (pp. 168–92). Suzanne Hull remarks of *Penelope's Web* that 'even their escape literature reminded women that they must be obedient, chaste and silent'.[25]

What we often find in Renaissance romances is both the repression of female agency and, beyond this, the infliction of extreme torments upon female victims. From numerous further examples one could select, from *The Faerie Queene*, the forceful capture of Acrasia and brutal destruction of her Bower, the torture of Amoret by Busirane, and the attempted devouring of Serena by cannibals;[26] or, from the *Arcadia*, the bloody death of Parthenia, and the sadistic torture of the princesses Pamela and Philoclea.[27] In all these episodes the infliction of pain or humiliation on a female body is dwelt upon in detail, with fascination, or even with relish. Violence and degradation serve either as a punishment of female characters who are transgressively dominant and sexual, like Acrasia, or as a test of heroines who prove their virtue through passive stoicism and noble self-denial, or even, as in the very popular and oft-retold story of Lucrece's case, through self-deletion.

Thus if we accept that the popularity of romance was at least partly attributable to its success with a female readership, we need to address the question of what kinds of reading pleasure women could have found in such antifeminist plots and images. Caroline Lucas invokes the idea of 'resistant reading', a phrase coined by Judith Fetterley to signify the capacity of women to read texts 'against the grain', resisting the male author's designs upon them in order to find pleasures in the text which subvert its patriarchal didacticism.[28] Applying this to George Pettie, Rich, Greene and Sidney, all romance authors who explicitly address imagined female readers, Lucas argues that although they offer the woman reader 'a variety of often inconsistent, self-contradictory and self-destructive roles . . . crucially, she can refuse to adopt them . . . By recognizing the more oppressive designs these texts have on us, and by disengaging from them, women can instead revalue the romances as important domains of women's independence and power.'[29] Similarly for R.W. Maslen transgressive figures like Pandora in Geoffrey Fenton's *Certain Tragical Discourses*, who induces her own abortion, or Lucilla in Lyly's *Euphues*, who outdoes the protagonist in duplicitous wit and erotic infidelity, are supreme exponents of the arts of policy and rhetoric who may have helped to encourage women writers to venture into print, despite the fact that such female figures are narratorially condemned and stringently punished for their behaviour within their stories.[30] According to this model a woman reader could choose to ignore the retributions inflicted upon unruly women within the texts and instead just enjoy the unruliness.

Unfortunately this solution does not quite resolve all aspects of the problem. For instance, what do we do with the fact that even a female author, Mary Wroth, included scenes of the sadistic abuse of the female body in her romance? And must we rule out all the numerous heroines of the Lucrece or Patient Griselda type as offering no pleasure to female readers? It is insufficient merely to find examples of women characters in Renaissance romances whom we as modern feminist critics recognise as strong and attractive and assume that these constituted the appeal of the texts to women readers in the past.

Indeed, modern feminist critics have found difficulties not only with this kind of material from the past, but also with modern romantic fiction, which is similarly preoccupied with libidinous heroes who threaten female chastity and heroines whose mission is to defend that chastity at all costs. This is a specific issue on which comparisons between Renaissance romance and modern romantic fiction could prove fruitful, since feminist critics of both genres face the challenge of trying to work out what women find to enjoy in antifeminist narratives. At first feminist critics dealt with modern romances simply by roundly condemning them for offering bad role models and false consciousness: Germaine Greer declared that the romance stereotypes of 'the characterless, passive female' and the masterful hero were 'invented by women cherishing the chains of their bondage'.[31] More recently, however, critics like Tania Modleski, Janice Radway and Alison Light have moved beyond merely dismissing and ridiculing romances and their readers to recognise that these conservative narratives clearly offer pleasures to women, and to seek to understand what these pleasures might be.[32] Radway in particular offers an analysis which seems to have transhistorical application: she argues that the very act of reading a romance, almost regardless of what it contains, absents a woman from the demands of her husband and family and offers her a private space of fantasy and pleasure,[33] a model which strikingly echoes Renaissance representations, like Lyly's, of romance-reading as an illicit and almost masturbatory act of female self-pleasuring which takes place behind closed doors.

In general, these less unsympathetic attempts to understand the pleasures of romance have been called 'diagnostic' or 'symptomatic', often using psychoanalytical terms to assess how romances speak to the traumas and confusions experienced by women under patriarchy.[34] Modleski is representative of this approach when she argues that the 'omissions, distortions and conservative affirmations' of modern mass-market fictions for women reflect their readers' anxieties and speak profoundly even to those who would call themselves feminists:

> We cannot rest content with theories which would attribute the texts' popularity to the successful conspiracy of a group of patriarchal capitalists plotting to keep women so happy at home that they remain unwilling to make demands which would greatly restructure the workplace and the family. Such changes are frightening to *most* of us, for they involve an entire reorganization not just of our social lives, but of our psychic lives as well.[35]

If we accept that the dominance of patriarchal ideology was probably even more rigid in the sixteenth and seventeenth centuries than it is today, and that women of that period would inevitably have internalised such ideology, then it becomes incongruous to expect them to have chosen Amazons and warrior-women as their heroines.

Renaissance texts of all kinds voiced an incessant preoccupation with feminine silence, chastity and obedience, and texts written by Renaissance women often declared their allegiance to these ideals. Attacks on women, which were numerous, and included John Knox's *First Blast of the Trumpet against the Monstrous Regiment of Women* (1558) and Joseph Swetnam's hugely popular *Arraignment of Lewd, Idle, Froward and Unconstant Women* (1615), charged the female sex with loquacity, promiscuity and insubordination. The responses of men who wrote defences of women, and of women themselves who braved the impropriety of publication, often did not challenge the terms of the debate but instead simply held up counter-examples of chaste matrons and virginal martyrs.[36] It appears that many Renaissance women would have found disturbing and alienating a female character who, in Lucas's words, exercised 'independence and power', and would have concurred in the judgement that a female figure who pursued her own desires without restraint was licentious, dangerous and even evil; whereas female characters who exercised patience in the face of extreme suffering offered less troubling models of female heroism.

It has long been recognised that women writers in the Renaissance tended to choose their genres in negotiation with, rather than in opposition to, patriarchal constraints; hence their tendency to write and translate religious works, which could be justified by their godly purpose.[37] Similarly we can imagine Renaissance women readers responding to heroines who combined qualities like strength and even defiance with some degree of conformity to patriarchal definitions of virtuous femininity. Just as religion could offer women licence and scope for self-definition and self-expression, so saintly qualities like constancy and endurance could embody female strength without threatening the security of conventional gender roles. In particular, heroic chastity, which a modern feminist might distrust as a means of repressing women's desires and preserving patriarchal lineage, could become a form of immovable female resolution against masculine threats, and a feminine means of defining boundaries of selfhood. Andrea Dworkin, for instance, has argued that the unswerving dedication to virginity of mediaeval saints such as Margaret, Catherine and Joan of Arc can be regarded as an anti-patriarchal political statement: 'This was a rebel virginity harmonious with the deepest values of resistance to any political despotism . . . virginity was an active element of a self-determined integrity, an existential independence . . . dangerous and confrontational because it repudiated rather than endorsed male power over women.'[38]

What we can find in some Renaissance romances is a bending or stretching of definitions of chastity, so that it means not so much a refusal of sex and denial of desire, but truth and constancy in love, proved and tested by saint-like endurance in the face of apparently insurmountable obstacles and extreme hardships. As we shall see, this may even extend in some cases, such as the Spanish and Portuguese chivalric romances, as far as sanctioning sex outside wedlock, and *still* representing a heroine as pure and virtuous, as long as she remains faithful to her destined beloved through all vicissitudes.

A full account of female heroism in romance, then, needs to look beyond warrior-women to the more numerous figures who suffer nobly in the cause of love and are praised for their chastity, however flexibly defined. Indeed, as we shall see, a heroine's adoption of masculine dress could often be represented not as signifying competition with men or the exercise of masculine freedoms, but as a form of self-humiliation, bespeaking a love so strong that the heroine will become a servant and submit to hardships of travel and battle in its cause. Rather than imposing stereotypical modern feminist definitions of heroism we need to reconstruct iconographies of martyrdom and sanctity which have become relatively alien to us (although even in recent times, the definition of female heroism in terms of an ability to suffer beautifully and strike saintly poses in secular contexts persists in aspects of the adulation of figures like Princess Diana).

In mediaeval literature, female saints and courtly-love mistresses were frequently addressed in virtually indistinguishable terms,[39] while female saints' lives recorded the bodily ordeals of virgin martyrs in ways which strikingly deployed potentially erotic material in the cause of holiness.[40] After the Reformation the iconography of sainthood continued to have wide currency in the literary representation of women, but, mediated through conventions like Petrarchism, became primarily secular, with idealised love taking over from religious devotion as the holy cause. Indeed, as I have discussed elsewhere, through the late sixteenth century specifically Catholic terminology in which a lover venerated his mistress as his saint, with all the trappings of shrines and incense, became increasingly fashionable in Elizabethan courtly poetry.[41] Such iconography persisted while being emptied of its original spiritual significance and was turned, almost iconoclastically, to secular, erotic and even arguably blasphemous uses. In Renaissance romances, as we shall see, heroines often adopt the behaviour of saints in the cause of love. An idea of 'erotic sainthood' might be a useful way of understanding the forms of female heroism found in these fictions, and the nature of their appeal to women.

As we have seen, analogies between Renaissance romance and modern romantic fiction depend upon a characterisation of Renaissance romance as a popular genre of courtship narratives offering escapist pleasures to women readers; yet each one of the terms of this equation is debatable. This is not to say that I want to throw out completely both the general comparison and its constituent elements, especially the existence of various kinds of association between romance and women. I hope that the issues I have outlined will become clearer as I go on to look in detail at examples of Renaissance romance, beginning with the novellas of the 1560s and 1570s.

CHAPTER 3

Novellas of the 1560s and 1570s

WILLIAM PAINTER'S *PALACE OF PLEASURE*, 1566 AND 1567

The story of Elizabethan fiction can be said to begin with this work, a collection, as the 1566 title page has it, of 'Pleasaunt Histories and excellent Novelles, selected out of divers good and commendable authors'. 'Novelle' here is usually rendered in modern English not as 'novel' but as 'novella'. This term designates stories which are relatively short: each of Painter's tales is only a few pages long, and some are even less than two pages. Novellas could also be more domestic and contemporary in setting than romances and tended to make greater claims to documentary truth; Painter refers to his stories not only as 'Novelles' but also as 'histories' and 'newes', both terms which imply some degree of factuality.[1] Nevertheless, novellas often depicted marvellous and heroic events, and shared with romances an interest in matters of courtship. As the origin of the term novella implies, the genre was especially associated with Italian authors, including Boccaccio and Bandello, although Painter's sources also range among Greek, Latin, English and French authors, including one woman, Margaret of Navarre (1492–1549), author of a collection of tales of love named the *Heptameron*.

The first volume of 1566 was sufficiently successful to inspire a sequel the next year and imitations, and the *Palace* became a fertile source for later Elizabethan and Jacobean drama. It is a compendium of many diverse kinds of story, not just tales of courtship: it includes not only the rape of Lucrece, and the source stories for *All's Well That Ends Well*, *The Duchess of Malfi* and *Romeo and Juliet*, but also the source stories for *Coriolanus* and *Timon of Athens*.[2]

The first volume of 1566 does not announce any particular intention to appeal to women readers. The prefatory address 'To the Reader' does mention women readers, but last and least (sig. *4v);

and the aristocratic dedicatee is not only male, but decidedly martial: he is Ambrose Dudley, Earl of Warwick, explicitly addressed in his post as General of the Royal Ordnance and Armoury. We are told on the title page that Painter was a clerk in the same body, and both this and the dedication present his writing of the *Palace* as a complementary activity to loyal military service. The opening story of the volume is in the genre of military history, recounting the war between the Romans and the Albans as told by Livy. The volume conforms readily to Lorna Hutson's theory of Bandellian fictions as secular exempla which provide male readers with models for self-advancement in whatever predicaments daily life might present: a prefatory listing directs the reader who wishes to succeed in such-and-such a situation to turn to such-and-such a tale (sigs. ¶¶3v–4v).

The prefatory material of the volume creates expectations that, like the first story, the narrative content will not be particularly female-oriented. Painter declares that he will show the heroism or tyranny of princes, and the admirable deeds of 'noble Gentlemen', alongside 'the vertuous minds of noble dames, the chaste hartes of constant Ladyes . . . the milde sufferance of well disposed Gentlewomen' (sig. ¥3v). In practice, however, the tyranny or heroism of male characters is often manifested by their behaviour towards women, while extremes of sexual virtue or vice are frequently personified by female characters. The raped Lucrece is eulogised for her self-destruction of her 'polluted' body (fo. 6); in the fifth novella, Appius rapes Virginia, and, though the man betrothed to her still wishes to marry her, her father, 'to save the shame of his stocke, killed her with a Bochers knife' (fo. 13r).

Thus women and their sexual morality are central to a number of the stories, but this is by no means to say that the stories have protofeminist qualities. Virginia, for instance, is merely the object of the actions and interests of her ravisher, her betrothed and her father. Her passivity is so extreme that she never even speaks: the only reaction imputed to her is when she is seized by Appius, and even then she seems incapable of voicing alarm on her own behalf: 'The maide [i.e. Virginia] beeyng afraied was amazed, and the Nursse that waited upon her, cried out' (vol. I, fo. 13v). Most of the narrative is taken up with the political and martial conflicts consequent upon this assault; the moral drawn at the end is that: 'Thus upon the filthie affeccion of one nobleman, issued parricide, murder, rebellion, hatred, deprivyng of magistrates, and greate mischiefes succedyng one in an others necke. Whereupon the noble and victorious citie, was like to be a praie to forren naccions' (vol. I, fo. 19v). The rape of an individual woman is of consequence because it makes the whole state metaphorically vulnerable to 'rape' in the form of penetrative assaults by invaders.

Other stories in the 1566 volume also foreground women while clearly addressing masculine interests. The twenty-third novella is a philosophical discourse from Aulus Gellius on the benefits of breast-feeding (an example of the diversity of Painter's material), but even here the opposition to wetnursing is grounded upon concern as to the health and character of the male child and the preservation of the father's stock: 'truely the condicion of the Noursse, and nature of the Milke, disposeth almoste the greater parte of the Childes condicion, whiche (notwithstanding the fathers seede, and creacion of the bodie and mynde, within the mothers wombe) dooeth now in the beginnyng of his nourriture, configurate and frame a newe disposicion in him' (fo. 47v). The fifty-sixth novella, 'A straunge punishment', taken from Margaret of Navarre, concerns an adulterous wife whose husband punishes her by making her shave her head, hanging her lover's skeleton in her chamber and making her drink from his skull. The wife bears all of this patiently and confesses the gravity of her fault, but the husband is only persuaded to show mercy when a visiting traveller points out that if they have no children his patrimony may be lost to his enemies.

These look like clear examples of narratives in which women are prominent only as the objects of masculine actions and the vehicles of masculine interests. Nevertheless, some aspects of the second volume of 1567 suggest that the success of the first volume was perceived to have been based on its inclusion of stories of women, and possibly on some consequent popularity with women readers. Whereas the 1566 volume opened with the battle between Rome and Alba, the 1567 collection begins with a story of the Amazons. Painter explicitly presents this as a feminine counter-image to the opening of volume I, and as striking a feminine keynote for volume II: 'The maners and qualities of [the Amazons], bicause they were women of no common spirite and boldnesse, be thought good in the front of this second volume to be described: bicause of divers womens lives plentifull varietie is offered in the sequele' (fo. 5r). The ensuing stories do indeed lay less emphasis on wars and the fortunes of states.

Painter also begins explicitly to address imagined female readers in this second volume. At the end of the third novella, 'Timoclia of Thebes', he asks, 'What say ye (good Ladies) to the heart of this noble Gentlewoman, that durst be so bold to stone this caitife wretch to death, and for wrong done to hir bodie till that time untouched[?]' (fo. 11r). Not only this, but he stresses Timoclia's vigour and enterprise in inflicting retribution upon her defiler:

> A simple woman voide of helpe, not backed with defence of husbandes aide, doeth bring a mightie captaine, a strong and loftie lubber, to enter into a cave, and when she sawe hir best advauntage, thacked him with stones, untill he groned forth his grisly ghost. Suche is the might and prowesse of chastitie. No charge too burdenous or weightie for such a vertue, no enterprise too harde for a mynde so pure and cleane. (fo. 11r)

Timoclia's physical and moral strength is attributed in conventional fashion to the sanctity of chastity, but her aggressive retaliation, combined with the explicit address to female readers, forms a distinct contrast to stories from the first volume of extremely passive heroines like Virginia and Lucrece. Moreover female heroism seems to have become of central interest, rather than being a sub-plot to the fortunes of states.

However, what may be seen as a 'feminisation' of narrative in the 1567 volume is accompanied by more strident moralising. Painter gives didactic and somewhat harsh expositions of the moral of each novella: for instance, the story of the Duchess of Malfi reveals 'what matche of mariage Ladies of renowme, and Dames of Princely houses ought to choose', while the examples of Romeo and Juliet disclose not only 'the hartie affections of two incomparable lovers', but also 'what secret sleightes of love, what danger either sort incurre which marry without the advice of Parentes' (sigs. ***i.r–ii.r). It looks as if Painter is anxious to prove that just because he is writing about women's doings in love, and has some expectation of being read by women, does not mean that he is providing women with examples of disruptive or improper behaviour.

This combination of a 'feminisation' of narrative with a desire to be seen to be respectably tough on unruly women can sometimes produce muddles and self-contradictions. The fifteenth novella of 1567 concerns Euphimia of Corinth, and begins with a lengthy disquisition in praise of 'Constancie in Honeste love':

> as the mynd is constant in love, not variable, or given to chaunge, so is the bodie continent, comely, honest and pacient of Fortunes plagues . . . The blustering blastes of parents wrath, can not remove the constant mayde

from that which she hath peculiarly chosen to hir selfe . . . A goodly example of constant and noble love this history ensuing describeth. (fo. 101r)

At this point it looks as if Painter is praising female constancy in love as a quality which can combine limited female autonomy with conventionally admirable qualities of resolution and truth. However, only a few sentences later Euphimia's constancy to her lover leads her to marry him in the face of her father's express disapproval. The virtue of constancy to one male figure – a lover – is now abruptly overruled by the higher claim of constancy to a different male figure – a father. Euphimia's constancy is immediately transformed from a heroic quality to a punishable offence: '*Euphimia* fondly [i.e. foolishly] maried against hir fathers wil, and there fore deservedly afterwards bare the penaunce of hir fault: And albeit she declared hir selfe to bee constant, yet dutie to loving father ought to have withdrawen hir rashe and headie love' (fo. 101v). The condemnation of her filial disobedience goes on at some length, and when Painter returns to the narrative he shows Euphimia suffering retribution when her husband turns against her. Again the narrator turns to a female audience: 'Howe thinke you faire Ladies, was not thys a faire rewarde[?] . . . Here is a lesson for yong Gentlewomen' (fo. 109). A further long homily follows on the wisdom of submitting to parental wishes.

The escalation of Painter's moral didacticism can be attributed to more than just an expectation of a female readership. In the 1566 volume Painter was already anxious to assert the worth and seriousness of his stories, repeatedly and emphatically stating an intention to teach by entertaining. His declared purpose was to show the dangers of wantonness, even though in the process his stories might concern 'pleasaunt discourses, merie talke, sporting practises, deceytful devises, and nipping tauntes, to exhilarat the readers minds', and may even 'intreat of unlawfull Love, and the foule practises of the same' (vol. 1, sig. ¥3v). Whether sincerely or otherwise, he makes a case for teaching through entertainment, although it is not unlikely that the popularity of his book was based on the entertaining revelation of 'unlawfull Love' more than on the supposed moral lessons.

Certainly in 1567 Painter's prefatory material seems defensive, as if the 1566 volume had gained a reputation for impropriety. This time he loftily places the writing and reading of 'histories' alongside such illustrious fields of knowledge as theology, philosophy, rhetoric, music and astronomy. He is especially anxious to refute any charge that reading fiction is an idle pursuit; instead it is a means of 'shunning the petulant monster Idlenesse' (sig. *ii.r). Painter ascribes to Cicero (in turn quoting Publius Scipio) the saying '[t]hat he was never lesse idle, than when he was idle', meaning that rest from duty is both necessary and virtuous, and concurs that 'when labour resteth him selfe in me, and Leisure refresheth other affaires, nothing delights more that vacant time, than reading of Histories in such vulgar speche, wherin my small knowledge taketh repast' (sigs. ii.v–iii.r). Reading stories, then, is claimed as an appropriate activity for Painter's hours of rest from his duties at the Armoury, a manly, serious and respectable pursuit. The author of *The Institution of a Gentleman* (1555) had warned that 'idlenes is the Mistres of wanton appetites, and the portres of Lustes gates'.[3] Painter rebuffs such suggestions that idleness, including the reading of novellas, is a seductress who both beguiles men with her feminine charms, and infects them with femininity by ensnaring them in her world of folly and sensuality. Mars seduced by Venus was conventionally depicted, as in Botticelli's painting, as having discarded his weapons and become oblivious of the world beyond her bower. Painter asserts, on the contrary, that retreat into a world of leisure, of fiction and of relations with women is a valuable resource from which to return refreshed to masculine responsibilities.

Thus in so far as Painter aims to provide entertainments for leisure time which provide secular *exempla* of the management of situations in private life, his stories give prominence to women. In so far as such stories might be feared to appeal to women by offering exciting examples of female waywardness, Painter is anxious to be seen to draw morals which condemn and constrain female independence. At the same time, a concern that such stories might be regarded as effeminising and morally debilitating for male readers intensifies the impulse to moralise. An anxiety to moralise idleness manifests itself as the moralisation of women.

GEOFFREY FENTON'S *CERTAIN TRAGICAL DISCOURSES*, 1567

A mark of Painter's success is the appearance in the same year as his second volume of this anthology of novellas taken from Belleforest's *Histoires Tragiques*, a French translation of Bandello which Painter too had used as a source. The presentation of Fenton's volume confirms the perception that Painter's success had been mainly based on his inclusion of stories about women and love. George Turberville, in a prefatory commendatory poem, describes Fenton's subject matter as 'lovynge Ladyes haples haps';[4] and Fenton himself states in the Argument for his first story (the source for Thomas Heywood's *A Woman Killed with Kindness*), that he will not write of the historic deeds of princes, 'but I have in presente intente to discover unto you the mervellous effects of love' (fo. 1r).

At the same time, Fenton adopts an even more rigid moral stance than Painter. Fenton's volume contains fewer stories than Painter's, in longer form – there are only thirteen stories in its 306 folios – and this amplitude arises largely from his addition of lengthy moral disquisitions to his source material. Belleforest himself had added moral expansions to Bandello's largely amoral tales; Fenton in turn expands, adding even longer didactic interpretations and also elaborate rhetorical flourishes.[5] Moreover, Fenton makes no use of Painter's repeated argument that pleasure can be a means of teaching, and instead represents his stories simply as didactic *exempla*.[6] Each of them is surrounded by a rigid didactic apparatus: each one begins with an argument and an introductory moral disquisition, and is accompanied by marginal *sententiae*. Fenton's previous translations included theological works, giving him an established public image as an upright and pious writer.[7]

As with Painter, we can see the emphasis on morality as generated by a desire to cater to a market for stories of erotic matters while disclaiming any impropriety. Wantonness is shown as a warning against its dangers; Turberville states that the stories teach the reader 'to flee the darte / Of vyle deceytefull Cupids bowe that woundes the lovers harte' (sig. **i.r). This produces narratives of retribution with a tragic tone and structure, as described in Fenton's title. The volume emulates not only Painter but also the most recent major exercise in tragic writing, the hugely popular *Mirror for Magistrates* (1559, 1563), a collection of verse tragedies by several authors in which historical figures recounted their downfalls. The *Mirror* was presented as exemplary didactic material against the tyranny of princes; Fenton may be seen as attempting a complementary anthology concerning correct conduct in private rather than public life, which inevitably involves more female-centred material.[8]

This interest in tragedy means that the stories present much female suffering: not only 'lovynge Ladyes haples haps', but further 'theyr deathes, a[n]d deadly cares' (sig. **i.r). At the same time, the combination of love-matters and morality produces a recurrent preoccupation with female chastity. The dedicatory epistle advertises 'to a woman, what stoare of examples are there to instructe her in her dutie, eyther for the maried, to kepe her fayth to her husband with *Lucretia*, or the unmaried to defende her virginitye with *Virginya*' (sig. *ii.v). The duty of both these paragons ended somewhat discouragingly in death. As we have seen, Painter had described female virtue in terms of 'vertuous minds . . . chaste hartes' and 'milde sufferance' (vol. 1, sig. ¥3v); Fenton takes this martyr-like transcendence of bodily weaknesses a stage further, stating in his dedication that: 'heare maye bee seene suche patternes of chastetye, and maydes so assured and constant in vertue, that they have not doubted rather to reappose a felicitye in the extreme panges of death, then to fall by anye violent force into the daunger of the fleshelye ennemye to theyr honour'.[9]

The volume has a female dedicatee, Lady Mary Sidney, mother of Philip, Mary and Robert. She is herself represented as an exemplary heroine; Fenton claims that his admirable female protagonists are all merely personifications of Lady Sidney's manifold virtues (sig. *iii.r). Fenton addresses 'your Ladyship' again at the end of his first story, inviting her and other imagined readers to pass judgement on the events described (fo. 36r–v). He often interrupts the narrative to address and indeed berate female readers as a group, as in a long moral digression on the beauty of female chastity which interrupts the first story: 'the Croune of immortal glorye, attendes youe Ladyes, who by withstandynge thassaultes and importunities of the fleshe, do give to your selfe the true title of honest women . . . wherewith wishyng you al no lesse desier to lyve wel, then the most of you are gredy of glory, I leave you to the remorce of your owne consciences' (fo. 17v). When in the third story a villainness named Pandora induces her own abortion, Fenton invites 'vertuous Ladyes' both to 'tremble at the remembraunce of the inordinate crueltye of this cursed mother' and to 'open the conduits of their compassions, weping on the behalfe of the torment wherin unnaturally she plunged the innocent impe which nature had formed of the substance of her selfe' (fo. 76r).

As in the latter example, Fenton's moral pontifications often sit somewhat queasily alongside the sensational matter being moralised.

We are told in lurid detail how, after attempting other brutal methods, Pandora completes her abortion by leaping from the top of a coffer, 'having her eyes sonke into her head, her stomacke panting, and her face all full of black bloud' (fo. 76v). The foetus lies in a basin feebly breathing. Fenton pauses to assert his difficulty in transcribing this shocking material, but in effect to heighten the tension and tighten his grip upon the appalled and enthralled reader: 'Certenlye good Ladyes my harte abhoring no lesse the remembraunce of this bychfoxe, then my spirite trobled with tremblinge feare at the contynuance of her crueltye, gives such impediment to my penne, that it is scarce hable to discribe unto you, the laste act of her rage' (fo. 77v). After this build-up comes the final outrage: Pandora beats the baby 'with all her force againste the walles, painting the postes and pavements in the chamber with the bloodde and braynes of the innocent creature neweborne' (fo. 77v). While claiming to present a deterrent example to women of the wages of sin, Fenton succeeds in creating the thrills of a video nasty.[10]

Fenton also adds to Belleforest military metaphors for erotic acts and obscene innuendos borrowed from Aretino.[11] His incessant moral assertions can be seen as hypocritical attempts to justify his actual role as a purveyor of sex and violence, a strategy backed up by efforts to shift the responsibility for any immoral reading on to the reader. Another prefatory commendatory poem, by John Conway, compares Fenton to a bee labouring to collect nourishment, admonishing: 'Good reader yet beware, least Spyder lyke thou take / By cancred kinde a spightfull stynge, whence he did honye make.'[12] The conclusion to the volume abjures any improper intent:

> as I have seamed in some places to enterlarde this profane tra[n]slation with certeyne testimonies oute of sacred recordes, So I hope the same will the rather defende th'integritie of myne intente againste all objections . . . I wishe that as in writynge thies tragicall affaires, I have founde the falte of mine owne life, that also the reste of the younglinges of our countrey, in reding my indevor, maye breake the slepe of their longe follye, and retire at laste to amendement of lyfe. (fo. 306r)

R.W. Maslen regards both Fenton and Painter as simply unable to cope with their material, confused by their own 'conflicting responses' of 'excitement and suspicion'.[13] Alternatively it may be that they were consciously using moral disquisitions hypocritically, to deflect criticism for exploiting the commercial appeal of morally dubious reading matter. At the same time, though, such authorial attempts to dictate how their texts should be received implicitly acknowledge the difficulty of regulating interpretation of a story once it is in circulation. Their homilies to the imagined reader, particularly the imagined female reader, can be understood simultaneously as voicing an anxiety as to how women might use the tales, and enabling men to enjoy stories of women and love while being reassured that the stories have been made safe against giving women dangerous ideas. For all these reasons, the address to women and the strident assertion of moral rectitude are symbiotic at this stage in the history of Elizabethan fiction.

REACTIONS TO NOVELLAS

The response of the educationalist Roger Ascham to the fashion for Italianate novellas indicates that Painter and Fenton were certainly not able to control their readers' responses to the extent of convincing them of their moral propriety. Ascham had already vituperated 'bookes of fayned chevalrie' of 'our fathers tyme' in *Toxophilus* (1545, sig. A1r), and he returned to this theme in *The Schoolmaster* (1570). He regarded the older chivalric romances as celebrating 'open mans slaughter [*sic*], and bold bawdrye', and deplored '[w]hat toyes, the dayly readyng of such a booke, may worke in the will of a yong jentleman, or a yong mayde, that liveth welthelie and idlelie'. However, an even worse genre had now appeared, namely: 'fonde bookes, of late translated out of Italian into English, sold in every shop in London . . . there be moe [*sic*] of these ungratious bookes set out in Printe within these fewe monethes, than have bene sene in England many score yeare before'. These are 'bawdie bookes', designed 'to intice the will to wanton livyng,' which 'open, not fond and common wayes to vice, but . . . sutle, cunnyng, new, and diverse shiftes, to carry yong willes to vanitie, and yong wittes to mischief, to teach old bawdes new schole poyntes' (fos. 26v–27v).

For Ascham these new Italianate books are full of 'the inchantments of *Circes*' (fo. 26v). Along with other fashions imported from Italy, he fears that they degrade and debilitate the men they enslave, just as '*Circes*, by pleasant inchantmentes, did turne men into beastes'. He personifies the pleasure which they offer as a seductress who, 'by licentious vanitie, that sweete and perilous poyson of all youth', corrupts 'all those, that yeld up themselves to her' (fo. 25r).

For him they are gendered as feminine in that they concern erotic matters, and in that they represent a form of idleness. Thus Ascham was especially concerned with their emasculating influence upon male readers. Another educationalist, however, Edward Hake, expressed alarm at the effect of erotic fictions upon young girls. In *A Touchstone for this time present . . . Whereunto is annexed a perfect rule to be observed of all Parents and Schoolmasters, in the training up of their Scholars and Children in learning* (1574) he lamented the depravity of the age, and especially the laxness of the typical girl's education: 'Eyther shee is altogither kept from exercises of good learning, and knowledge of good letters, or else she is so nouseled in amorous bookes, vaine stories and fonde trifeling fancies, that shee smelleth of naughtinese even all hir life after.'[14]

At this stage, then, both the authors of secular fictions and the commentators upon them were voicing concern as to their moral effects upon both male and female readers. It was not long, however, before authors began to turn these connotations of male delinquency from duty and female erotic pleasure into attractive selling points. R.W. Maslen comments that Ascham counter-intentionally provided fiction writers

> with an intriguing storyline. It is the story of themselves: of a group of well-educated and headstrong young men, idle through no fault of their own, with a flashy control over language and a finger on the pulse of fashion . . . who insinuate themselves by verbal charm and sexual charisma into the domestic life of an unsuspecting nation.[15]

It was a storyline swiftly taken up and developed by writers like George Gascoigne and George Pettie.

GEORGE GASCOIGNE'S *THE ADVENTURES OF MASTER F.J.*, 1573

The prefatory material to this volume openly flaunts its inconsequentiality. Its (probably fictional) editor, 'H.W.', describes its contents, in his preface 'To the Reader', as 'these trifles', of which 'the wiser sort would turn over the leaf as a thing altogether fruitless'.[16] Even at the end, in place of any didactic interpretation or conclusion, the narrator simply shrugs 'It is time now to make an end of this thriftless history' (*Master F.J.*, p. 80).

The volume is presented as a compendium of private papers gathered by one G.T., loaned to his friend H.W., and published by H.W. against G.T.'s instructions that he 'should use them only for mine own particular commodity' (p. 3). One function of this framing device is to disclaim direct authorial responsibility for publication and to present the enclosed material as 'really' a collection of manuscripts, thereby evading the ungentlemanly 'stigma of print'.[17] It also, however, enables Gascoigne to present his narrative tantalisingly as a disclosure of private and true events. When Painter described his novellas as history or news, he was not only making a high claim for them as truthful, but also offering his readers the lower pleasures of spying into the secrets of public figures and speculating as to their real identities, which were often only half revealed: one story concerned the love of a king of England for the Countess of Salisbury, another the actions of a king of Naples.[18] Gascoigne further implies that his story is based on events which are not only true but also recent and in England. He sets his readers' curiosity working by withholding his protagonists' full identities, while simultaneously accentuating the erotic content of the narrative and thereby intensifying its voyeuristic pleasures.

G.T.'s 'papers' consist of poems and letters exchanged between F.J. and a lady named Elinor whom he courted 'once in the north parts of this realm' (*Master F.J.*, p. 6). G.T. has supposedly ordered these in their proper sequence and linked them together with an explanatory narrative. The pretext for the volume, then, is an anthology of verses and letters too well composed to be concealed. Each poem is followed by a short critical appreciation; the framing device which recesses Gascoigne as author enables him to point out the aesthetic qualities of his own verses. However, the narrative expands from being merely a frame for the poems to become arguably the chief interest. The plot is as follows: F.J. woos Elinor; she at first seems reluctant, then yields; another lady, Frances, seeks to aid F.J. and warns him of Elinor's inconstancy; then Elinor's previous lover returns, and she indeed drops F.J. Elinor, we are told in parenthesis some way into the story, is also married (p. 27).

This summary illustrates that not a great deal happens in terms of event; the substance of the narrative concerns dilemmas and predicaments in which F.J. must deduce how to act and, above all, what to say in order to further his interests. It can thus be read as a narrative of a young man's education in courtiership. F.J.'s wits and resourcefulness are tested against bewilderments, frustrations and problems of interpretation. Elinor's letters to him are sometimes dissimulations actually penned by her other lover who is also her secretary; Elinor herself often gives him cryptic and ambiguous responses which suspend and disempower him; and Frances often deals in hints and riddles in order to make discreet and testing disclosures of her inside knowledge. Sometimes the ladies seem to collude to make fun of F.J. The peak of his success as a wooer is a night which he spends with Elinor in the gallery adjoining her chamber, where he comes to her in his nightgown and carrying his 'naked sword', an occasion for much innuendo (p. 30). Immediately after this, Frances, who has observed these nocturnal manoeuvres, steals the sword from his chamber while he is sunk in post-coital slumber. When F.J. finds his sword missing and realises that someone knows he has slept with Elinor, he is distressed by a gallant concern for his lady's honour; she, however, is largely unperturbed, and simply arranges, magisterially, for the sword to be retrieved. The episode gives a sense of F.J. being foolishly cast adrift with an inappropriate code of honour, one less sophisticated than that by which the ladies are operating (pp. 30–6).

As in this particular episode, so throughout *Master F.J.* the women exercise considerable power, and pursue their sexual desires in a relatively uninhibited way. Frances, although F.J. resists her pursuit, is unmistakably motivated by a desire to supplant Elinor as his mistress. Elinor not only quite clearly consummates her relationship with F.J. during the night in the gallery, but subsequently makes a nocturnal visit to his chamber in her nightgown to assure him of her affection. He swoons with pleasure, and, 'returning to life, the first thing which he felt was that his good mistress lay pressing his breast with the whole weight of her body, and biting his lips with her friendly teeth' (pp. 59–60). Yet F.J. is always clearly the protagonist, the centre of the action and of the narrative point of view: these active and controlling women function as tests and challenges to him, as domesticated equivalents of the enchantresses and combatants with whom the knightly heroes of chivalric romances had to contend. His mission is 'manfully and valiantly to repress faintness of his mind' in the combats of love (p. 74).

The testing and controlling role of women is ritualised in the game of *questioni d'amore* which is played at several points in Gascoigne's text. This courtly pastime derived from Castiglione, and involved a company of both sexes who took it in turns wittily to set out love-problems on which a nominated arbiter would then pass judgement. The ladies make F.J. preside, and the game thereby becomes another means for them to set him puzzles and dilemmas. It is also an occasion for inset narratives which can have bearing on the main narrative. Frances contributes a 'history' which she presents as 'done indeed of late days, and not far distant from this place' (p. 67); it concerns the triangular relationship between a woman, her lover and her husband, culminating in the ending of the affair. Since, like the lover in the story, F.J. has befriended Elinor's husband, it has direct relevance to his current predicament, but he dull-wittedly fails to notice this, and indeed passes judgement that the husband's 'losses abounded above the rest, and his injuries were uncomparable', at which Frances understandably 'smile[s] in her sleeve' (p. 73).

Frances's story acts as a *roman à clef* within a volume which is itself presented as a *roman à clef.* Besides the opening hints at veracity, others are scattered through the text; one participant in the *questioni d'amore,* for instance, is a gentlewoman 'whom I have not hitherto named, and that for good respects lest her name might altogether disclose the rest' (p. 53). These hints at real locations and identities serve to intrigue and titillate the reader. At the same time, disclosures which are only partial, providing clues and fragments of information rather than statements and confirmations, are shown as endemic to the role of a courtly lover like F.J. His aim is to advance his suit without revealing it to curious onlookers or risking direct rebuff, and in this, like Gascoigne as author, he must make use of verbal codes and dissimulations. Thus when Elinor asks F.J. who composed a love song he has performed, he replies that it was addressed by his 'father's sister's brother's son' to 'a niece of an aunt of yours' (p. 28). When F.J. achieves success as Elinor's lover, we are told that he composed many verses which he did not show to G.T., who acknowledges that the lover who is 'charged with inexprimable joys, and therewith enjoined both by duty and discretion to keep the same covert, can by no means devise a greater consolation than to commit it into some ciphered words and figured speeches in verse' (p. 41). Courtly versifying at this point in the narrative becomes almost a verbalisation of sexual effusion, and its privacy becomes almost masturbatory:

> for a man to record unto himself in the inward contemplation of his mind the often remembrance of his late received joys doth as it were ease the heart of burden and add unto the mind a fresh supply of delight . . . F.J. swimming now in delights did nothing but write such verse as might accumulate his joys to the extremity of pleasure. (p. 41)

The reader is thus tantalisingly invited to imagine more verses of a more *risqué* kind which were too private for F.J. to disclose.

Indeed, the descriptions of sexual acts in *Master F.J.* themselves involve further forms of narrative tantalisation performed through simultaneous disclosure and concealment. The fiction of the privacy of the text as an intimate exchange between G.T. and H.W. is used as a pretext for frankness, yet just enough inexplicitness is sustained to provoke the reader's imagination. In the gallery scene, for instance, 'G.T.' interjects:

> Were it not that I know to whom I write, I would the more beware what I write. F.J. was a man, and neither of us are senseless, and therefore I should slander him, over and besides a greater obloquy to the whole genealogy of Aeneas, if I should imagine that of tender heart he would forbear to express her more tender limbs against the hard floor. Sufficed that of her courteous nature she was content to accept boards for a bed of down, mats for cambrike sheets, and the nightgown of F.J. for a counterpoint to cover them. (p. 30)

The depiction of erotic acts and the claim to contain true-life secrets are interdependently voyeuristic, offering the reader textual pleasures which are intensely sexualised.

However, Gascoigne's hints at real referents seem to have been almost too successful, such that the text was construed as scandalous. In the preface to the second edition of 1575 Gascoigne protested that the story was not based on real events; but even so he revised it, transposing the action to Italy, and retitling it *The Pleasant Fable of Ferdinando Jeronimi and Leonora de Velasco, translated out of the Italian riding tales of Bartello.*[19] He also added a more moralistic conclusion, condemning Elinor for her contagious 'wicked lust' and inconstancy, and stating that the 'fable' had an instructive purpose as an 'ensample to warn the youthful reader from attempting the like worthless enterprise'.[20]

The transposition to Italy and the attribution to the non-existent Bartello both make use of the current fashion for Italianate, Bandellian fiction. In fact several elements of the 1573 text already show Gascoigne's knowledge of Italian literary models which had not yet achieved wide influence in England. There are a couple of points where F.J.'s poetry imitates Petrarch,[21] but the most pervasive allusions are to Ariosto.[22] Ludovico Ariosto's *Orlando Furioso* first appeared in Italy in 1516; in common with a number of earlier romances, the story was set during the wars of Charlemagne, but elements like its allusions to Virgilian epic, the depiction of Orlando's frenzied love-madness, a fantastic voyage to the moon and an ironic indeterminacy of tone, confounded existing generic definitions, producing a new form usually called romantic epic or epic romance.[23] Although writing within a less fantastic and epic setting, Gascoigne was perhaps seeking to introduce to the more domestic and contemporary world of the novella an Ariostan tonal fluidity and sophistication.

It is also striking that a couple of his Ariostan allusions link F.J. with Bradamant, Ariosto's female warrior, possibly implying F.J.'s effeminisation in his plight of disempowerment by love (pp. 28, 51). Susan C. Staub has pointed out the irony in the gallery scene discussed above where F.J.'s success in achieving sexual union with the elusive Elinor is accompanied by Frances's theft of his sword, 'a symbolic emasculation'.[24] Staub goes further to argue persuasively that Frances, as voyeur of F.J. and Elinor's love-making, is a personification within the fiction of the troubling figure of the woman reader and her ungovernable responses to the text; she thereby embodies Gascoigne's anxieties about his published work travelling beyond the hands of 'H.W.' and his like. At the same time, however, the combination of the effeminisation of F.J. and the dominance of sophisticated women with titillating framing devices seems to serve primarily to invite the male readers personified by H.W. to join the male protagonist in experiencing the pleasures and thrilling dangers of a holiday in the 'feminine' world of sexuality. Gascoigne innovates in embracing and promoting the pleasures of the supposedly effeminising qualities of erotic fiction. In the process, self-determining and sexually active female characters are present, but more as tests and rewards for the male hero and reader than as heroines offered for women to identify with and enjoy.

GEORGE PETTIE'S *A PETITE PALACE, OF PETTIE HIS PLEASURE*, 1576

As Pettie's Painter-like title implied, he reverted to the novella format; his work contains twelve tales mainly from classical sources, including the rape of Virginia as already related by Painter and Fenton. However, Pettie also incorporated some of *Master F.J.*'s features. Like *Master F.J.*, his volume has a prefatory apparatus which presents it as a pirated publication of private papers exchanged between male intimates. 'G.P.' writes to 'R.B.' that it is at his request that he has set down 'certaine of those Tragicall trifles, whiche you have heard mee in sundrie companies at sundrye tymes report', and importunes:

> I pray you only to use them to your owne private pleasure, and not to impart them to other, perchaunce to my prejudice, for that divers discourses touch neerely divers of my nere freindes: but the best is, they are so darkely figured forth, that only they whom they touch, can understand whom they touch: yet to avoide all captious constructions, I pray you in any wise let them bee an object onely for your owne eyes.[25]

Here again the publication of a claim to privacy invites the reader to indulge in voyeurism.

However, unlike *Master F.J.*, the *Petite Palace* precedes this with an address by R.B. 'To the gentle Gentlewomen Readers'. He asserts that he 'woulde have onely Gentlewomen' as his audience, and that he has disobeyed G.P. to publish out of 'service to your noble sexe . . . I care not to displease twentie men, to please one woman' (sig. A2r). Thus, from the outset, to Gascoigne's titillating promise of half-disclosed secrets is added a flirtatious direct address to female readers. Indeed, the text itself is personified as virile and amorous in an epistle from the printer to the readers, in which he professes to have cut out over-sensitive material, but hopes he has not 'gelded to[o] mutch' (sig. A4r). Whereas in Gascoigne the male character F.J. attempts to deploy literary skill as a medium for seduction of a female character, in Pettie's *Petite Palace* the text itself is presented as a potential masculine seducer of the women whom it solicits as readers.

The first story is of Sinorix and Camma, and opens with a long moral eulogy of the unity of man and wife in marriage very much in the vein of Painter or Fenton. The ensuing tale relates how Sinorix, governor of Siena, lusted after Camma, the impeccably chaste wife of a gentleman named Sinnatus. When all his seduction attempts failed, Sinorix had Sinnatus murdered; Camma then married Sinorix, but killed both herself and him by drinking a poisoned pledge. At one point in her tribulations, Camma invokes the examples of the Countess of Salisbury and the Duchess of Savoy, an allusion to Painter, who relates their stories; Pettie openly acknowledges the anachronism of putting such allusions into the mouth of Camma, who is supposed to live in ancient times, but uses this as a means of implying that 'Camma' is a front for an identifiable contemporary personage (sig. A3r and p. 14).

The story ends with Camma taking leave of her orphaned children, at which point the narrator turns to address his female audience. However, although this concluding disquisition is a Fentonesque gesture, it begins with a far from Fentonesque sentiment:

> Now I would wish you blazing starres, which stande upon your chastity, to take light at this lot, to take heed by this harme: you see the husband slaine, the ruffian [i.e. the hired murderer] fled, the lover poysoned, the wife dead, the freinds comfortles, the children parentlesse. And can the preservation of one simple womans chastitie, countervaile all these confusions? (p. 23)[26]

The blame for this over-valuing of chastity is put on female excessiveness: 'it is naturally incident to women to enter into extremities' (*ibid.*). Camma should have used reason, courtesy and delays to calm Sinorix down. Then Pettie suddenly changes tack:

> But howsoever my words run, I would not you should take them to tend altogether to her dispraise, for as I must condemne her crueltie, so can I not but commende her constancie, and chastitie, and thinke her worthy to bee compared to *Lucrece*, *Penelope*, or what woman soever that ever had any preheminence of praise for her vertue. (p. 23)

In the citing of the commonplace examples of Lucrece and Penelope and the lack of effort to think of any more it is possible to detect a cultivated weariness, an accentuation of the fact that the narrator is going through the conventional motions. Finally he seems to give up with a shrug and turn the verdict back to the reader: 'Therefore Gentlewomen I leave it to your judgements to give sentence, whether be more worthy reprehension, hee or she' (p. 24). The effect is a parody of the moral disquisitions of Painter and Fenton, combining their sermonising form with a joky redundancy and unreliability of content.

The same structure is employed in the ensuing stories: a sententious opening peroration is followed by the plot, then a whimsical and morally ambiguous address to female readers. Thus the second story, of Tereus and Progne, closes: 'It were hard here gentlewomen for you to give sentence, who more offended of the husband or the wife, seeing the dooinges of both the one and the other neere in the highest degree of divelishnesse . . . I thinke them both worthy to bee condemned to the most botomles pit in Hell' (p. 38). On the one hand the female reader seems to be given a certain amount of power to draw her own judgement and is even deferred to as an authority;

on the other hand, to be drawn into making such judgement is shown as futile and laughable, the act of a gullible dupe. Meanwhile, Pettie's tone towards these imagined female readers becomes steadily more intimate and flirtatious. When the characters Admetus and Alcest embrace, he writes: 'hee aptly ended his talke upon her mouth, and they entred into sutch privy conference, their lips beeing joyned most closely together, that I can not report the meaninge of it unto you, but if it please one of you to leane hitherward a litle I will shew you the manner of it' (p. 110). This takes the direct address to the female reader to an unprecedentedly graphic level, as Pettie invites the reader to picture him leaning out from the printed page to steal a kiss. Again, the printed text is being personified as a virile potential seducer.

The narrator's self-undermining gestures towards moralism, and his flirtation with the female reader, increasingly merge together. At the end of the story of Amphiarus and Eriphile, Pettie writes:

> I knowe not what effecte my wordes will take, for that I know not how you courtlye dames accounte of my cunninge: but before mine owne face I am able to assure you this, that the girles of our parish thinke that welch *Sir Richard* him selfe [i.e. the village priest] can not make a better preache then I can: but it may be you wil thinke me over saucy with my lisping lips to prefer [i.e. put forward] persuasions to them, who are as voyde of folly every way, as my selfe of wit any way. (p. 79)

In other words, Pettie aspires to the same success with the girls as he has observed his local priest enjoying. His closing comment of the final story strongly implies that the real purpose of didactic exposition is covert seduction:

> But I could preache better to you in a more pleasant matter, I wil leave this text to maister parson, who while he is unmaried I warrant you will disswade you so earnestly from sutch idolatrous doting on your husbands, that hee will not sticke to tell you beesides that you ought to have no respect of persons, but to love an other man or him selfe so well as your husbandes. (p. 224)

The pun on persons/parsons implies that preachers want women to lay aside the 'respect' for them which causes them to regard them as sexually out of bounds, and instead to admit them as their lovers. Hence, by implication, preaching authors like Painter and Fenton stand exposed as hypocrites: their sermonising to women is really an attempt to inveigle themselves into intimacy with them.

Caroline Lucas professes outrage at Pettie's tone towards female readers, describing it as sexual harassment.[27] She is especially critical of his narration of the story of Pygmalion, where a long misogynistic diatribe is followed by an apology and another request for a kiss: 'for my part, I am angry with my selfe to have uttred it, and I shall like my lisping lippes the worse for that they have bene the instrumentes of sutch evill, neither shall I think them savory againe, untill it shall please some of you to season them with the sweetenesse of yours' (p. 200). Lucas finds Pettie's 'outrageous suggestion that a kiss . . . will "make everything alright", and his choice of humour at this juncture' offensively inconsiderate of the sensibilities of women readers.[28] But this is to take literally both Pettie's self-characterisation and his representation of his audience as female. Our only evidence that his readership consists of women is his own construction of this imagined readership within the text. It is reasonable to suppose that these kinds of novella-type morally framed stories had found some recognised success with women readers in order for Pettie to assume his readers' recognition of the phenomenon. However, it also seems possible that his playful manipulation of the implied gullibility of the female readership, his irreverent jokes about the real motives of those who preach to women and his pose as a practised seducer, are all performances for male readers in his audience. Lucas herself points out features of Pettie's text which suggest an underlying expectation of a male readership, such as his incidental use of the pronouns 'our' and 'us' to refer to men, and phrases like 'when wee once arrive to mans estate'.[29]

The satirical nature of Pettie's address to female readers means that men are thereby exempted from ridicule, even though they are reading 'effeminate' material. Just as in *Master F.J.* H.W. stood for a male readership, so here 'R.B.', that is, a close male friend, is supposed to be the 'true' intended reader; the joky address to susceptible female readers is framed by an intimate convivial exchange between male author and a male reader who is implicitly taken more seriously, as a friend and equal. As Paul Salzman comments: 'The *Petite Palace* has, in effect, two audiences: the gentlewomen created by the narrator, cajoled by him, and spun around by his ambiguous moralizing until they are dizzy; and an invisible audience of fellow young wits, enjoying Pettie's dexterity, his sleight of hand.'[30] It is worth recalling that the prefatory letter from G.P. to R.B. presents the stories as texts of oral performances by Pettie 'in sundrie companies at sundrye tymes'; he also, in the same prefatory letter, describes himself in Latin as a reformed libertine. A male audience are offered a collection of model narratives which their teller has previously found efficacious in his dealings with women. At the same time, the text's promise as a *roman à clef* to give hints and clues of sensational real-life events is enhanced by its claim to offer voyeuristic disclosure of how women read in private: it purports to allow the male reader to look over an imagined woman reader's shoulder and discover what kinds of pleasures she derives from her intimate engagement with a printed book.

Sharon Stockton has pointed out that Pettie's stories are 'narratives of social mobility' which 'depend upon noblewomen marrying down, against their fathers' wishes'.[31] In Pettie's scheme such women therefore have to be both sexually available to the socially aspirant suitor, but also chaste once marriage has been achieved and they become emblems of their husbands' social status. Stockton locates in this another reason for the moral ambivalence surrounding female behaviour in Pettie: 'The gentlewomen are beseeched [*sic*] to consider adultery and to remain chaste, to be the active suitors in affairs of the heart and to be the passive recipients, to disobey fatherly authority and marry "for love" and to follow parental guidelines for marriage' (p. 57). The fact that, as critics have noted, Pettie adds to stories like 'Germanicus and Agrippina' and 'Icilius and Virginia' expansive accounts of the courtship of young lovers not found in his sources, may be attributed less to a desire to cater to women's reading tastes than to an interest in the successful deployment of rhetorical persuasion by young men in pursuit of their own social and sexual advancement.[32] This central narrative trajectory of male self-promotion through wooing can be traced not only through the anthologised fictions, but also through the framing characterisation of the author and his relationship with his imagined readers.

In the preface to his 1581 translation of Guazzo, Pettie claimed that he did not authorise publication of the *Petite Palace*, and disparaged it as a trifling work. Even here, though, in what he self-consciously advances as a quite different, more reputable kind of work, he asserts the chief purposes of men's writing and reading to be the cultivation of masculine attributes in the private as well as the public sphere. Authors, he says, should not subscribe to fashionable modesty about their own scholarship, since without it no man can serve his prince or fulfil other public gentlemanly offices, and, 'To come lowest of all, can you so much as tell your Mistresse a fine tale, or delight her with pleasant device, being unlearned?'[33] It seems plausible that the intended function of the *Petite Palace* is as much to display and share Pettie's manly prowess in delighting the ladies with pleasant devices as it is simply to entertain the women it claims to address.

The fashion for novellas, then, moved through several phases. Painter began with no particular interest in a female audience or in feminine stories, but the increased 'feminisation' of his sequel suggests that he perceived stories about women which were seen to address women as being commercially successful. At the same time, a desire not to be seen to be corrupting women, and an anxiety about the association of secular fiction with effeminising idleness, prompted increasing moral intervention. Fenton took further both the address of stories about women to women, and the accompanying moral didacticism. Gascoigne turned the effeminising triviality of stories about women into a selling point, and combined this with voyeurism into erotic secrets and with sexually active female characters in order to intensify the seductive appeal of the text to male readers. Pettie integrated Gascoigne's voyeurism with parody of the moralising address to women in order to make the author's dialogue with imagined female readers itself an entertainment for male readers.

CHAPTER 4

Spanish and Portuguese romances

Besides Italian or Italianate novellas, another very popular and influential form of imported fiction came from Spain and Portugal. These were chivalric romances, of which there were three major Iberian cycles in the sixteenth century. *Amadis de Gaula* had its first known Spanish edition in 1508, and was known in England by its French title of *Amadis de Gaule*. *Palmerin* first appeared in 1511, and the *Mirror of Knighthood* (*Espejo de Principes y Cavalleros*) had its inception somewhat later than the others, in 1562.[1] Their scale was vast: the *Amadis* cycle ran through seven generations of one dynasty, from Amadis's father Perion to his great-great-great-grandson Rogel of Greece;[2] while *Palmerin* had five volumes which covered five generations of the dynasty, from Palmerin d'Oliva's father Florendos to his great-great-grandson Flortir (Book IV) and his nephew's son Palmerin of England (Book V).[3] This proliferation of sequels resulted in multiple authorship. *Amadis* was begun by Garcí Ordóñez (or Rodríguez) de Montalvo, but taken over by others. The authorship of the early books of *Palmerin* is obscure, while the four volumes of *The Mirror of Knighthood* had three different authors.[4]

John J. O'Connor, in his detailed study of *Amadis* and its influence, asserts that 'The romance of chivalry is a literary genre that was as close to the hearts of sixteenth-century readers as it is distant from ours.'[5] It is true that these romances appear alien to a modern sensibility if judged by the novelistic criteria of naturalism and of a narrative structure which has a clear beginning, middle and end. However, if we compare them with some popular modern genres they may begin to look a little less unfamiliar. For instance, post-Tolkien sword-and-sorcery sagas are very successful today, and share with the sixteenth-century romances fantastic and/or archaic settings, a central concern with deeds of combat, supernatural interventions and an extended narrative structure of successive sequels.

In terms of narrative structure there are further distinct parallels with another popular modern narrative medium, television soap opera. *Amadis*, which ran to twelve volumes in Spanish and twenty-one in the French version, is described by O'Connor as 'a story so fluid that it promised to go on forever' (*Amadis*, p. 85). Similarly, it is often remarked that soap operas 'have a certain open-ended quality and could, potentially at least, run for ever'.[6] Christine Geraghty develops this idea as follows: 'Soaps can run (potentially) forever and their lack of resolution can make them aimless and repetitious. One way of handling the problem of repetition is to make it enjoyable, to give the audience a sense of familiarity with setting and characters so that to return to them is pleasurable.'[7] Compare O'Connor:

> No alert reader can wade through many books of *Amadis* without being aware of the recurrence of themes, episodes, and motifs . . . The repetition or parallelism in *Amadis* is so constant that it represents a habit of composition and indeed establishes an underlying unity. . . . The repetitions set up mnemonic echoes in the reader and help give an impression of purpose and form that is belied by the rambling structure of the work.[8]

Both soap opera and the Iberian romances use the family as a structure which offers both continuity and variety, as children grow to adulthood and lost relatives are rediscovered. Both genres also exhibit responsiveness to their audience. The recycling of popular elements can take precedence over narrative consistency: when Amadis was killed off in Book VIII there was widespread public distress and he was brought back again in the next volume,[9] a striking prefiguration of the death of Bobby Ewing in *Dallas* and his notorious resurrection in the shower after viewing figures dropped.

Of course I am not suggesting any direct connection between modern soap operas and sixteenth-century Iberian chivalric romances, but merely that some of the narrative principles of soap opera as a long-running, audience-responsive and open-ended medium may be more helpful in understanding these romances than are ideas about the literary novel like Frank Kermode's sense of an ending or Peter Brooks's narrative desire with an impetus towards climax and release.[10] In the seventeenth century the Iberian romances also seem to have come to prefigure the cultural evaluation of soap opera as trashy entertainments for women, as I shall discuss.

This chapter will concentrate on the English translations of the Iberian romances, and will discuss four intertwined topics. The first of these is their content, especially how they represent female sexuality. They tend to be more liberal in this than was most native English prose fiction; as we have seen, even an author like Robert Greene, who is often thought of as a writer for women, produced works which propounded the virtues of silence, chastity and obedience. The second topic is how their readership is addressed and constructed in the translators' prefaces; and the third is how their readership is represented in external sources like drama and satire, which is often quite a different matter. Finally I will consider how female heroism is represented, and what we can infer about what kinds of heroinism might have appealed to a female readership.

MARGARET TYLER'S TRANSLATION OF *THE MIRROR OF KNIGHTHOOD*, 1578

The story of the Iberian romances in English begins with a collection of extracts from *Amadis* (*The Treasury of Amadis of France*, 1567), but continues, strikingly, with a translation by a woman, Margaret Tyler, whose version of *The Mirror of Princely Deeds and Knighthood* appeared in 1578. Frustratingly, we know nothing else about Tyler apart from the information from her dedication of the *Mirror* that she had been a servant in the household of the parents of Lord Thomas Howard.[11]

The plot is a fairly typical one for the Iberian romances. The King of Hungary is at war with Trebatio, Emperor of Greece, and the King's daughter, Briana, is secluded at the monastery of the river (in fact a religious community of women) where she is to marry Prince Edward of Britain. Trebatio falls madly in love with Briana on merely hearing of her beauty; he ambushes and kills Prince Edward and assumes his identity in order to marry Briana. Briana has been ordered by her parents not to consummate the marriage until the war is over, but when Trebatio vaults into her private garden she is unable to resist the force of his passion. Trebatio is carried off by an enchantment and spends twenty years in sexual enslavement to Lindaraza. Meanwhile Briana gives birth to twin boys, Rosicleer and Donzel del Febo (the Knight of the Sun), who grow up to be chivalric heroes. Rosicleer embarks on his own secret affair with Olivia, daughter of the King of Britain, while the Knight of the Sun rescues his father Trebatio, enabling his reunion with Briana.

In contrast to the didactic emphasis on chastity in authors like

Painter or Fenton, Briana is at no point condemned for breaking her father's prohibition on sexual relations with Trebatio. Her behaviour is somewhat mitigated by the attribution of all the initiative to the unstoppable male libido, though even this was not enough to sustain Lucrece's purity in her story. Here, however, both Briana's and Trebatio's status as paragons survives intact.

The climactic consummation scene is fraught with sexualised topography which suggests an intention to titillate the reader. Trebatio vaults into Briana's garden using two spears, 'rearing them up against the wall with the blunt ende upwards' (fo. 11v). When Briana protests that the garden has never been entered by a man before, he replies: 'I have lodged my heart in your excellent beautie, and well maye the body lawefully enter where the heart is harboured. Let not therefore my entrie, good madame, seeme straunge unto you.' He embraces her and draws her down to the ground with him in a pleasant hedged bower of scented flowers 'neere unto the well'. Briana is deflowered before she can make any resistance, but is credited with some respectable reluctance: 'the beautiful princesse now became a wife somewhat against her will, but when she sawe no remedy to that which was past, she conforted hir selfe in that he was hir lawfull husband, and therefore she pardoned him his boldnesse in troubling her' (fo. 12r). Her modesty affords verification of both her purity and Trebatio's virility. At the same time, since she conceives her twin sons in this union, male desire is implicitly figured as a power which begets the heroes of the future, and thereby as a force of destiny which both Trebatio and Briana are powerless to resist. In the background of the scene lies the tradition of the conception of heroes by supernatural rape in mediaeval Arthurian romance. Indeed, there is a close analogue in Malory's *Morte Darthur*, where Uther Pendragon desires Igrayne, wife of the Duke of Tyntagil. Three hours after the death of the Duke in battle, Uther is magically transformed into his shape by Merlin, and lies with the deceived Igrayne, who conceives Arthur.[12] Behind this tradition in turn lie the conceptions of heroes in Ovid by divine rape; and arguably even the impregnation of the Virgin Mary, a submissive handmaiden, by the Holy Spirit, to conceive Christ.[13]

Briana also serves as a personification of chastity in so far as she is the antithesis of Lindaraza, the seductress-enchanter who leads Trebatio astray. In this episode Trebatio has his desires more readily satisfied, but at the cost of the loss of initiative and predominance.

Whereas he had to vault over Briana's wall, at Lindaraza's castle he is reduced to a state of bewilderment and meekly led by a damsel through a series of courts and rooms to the inner chamber where her mistress awaits. Whereas at the monastery of the river he used his weapons, both military and sexual, to achieve penetration of Briana, at Lindaraza's castle he is disarmed by her maidens; and whereas at the monastery he was shown to a separate bedroom even after marrying Briana, Lindaraza herself takes him 'to hir owne lodging . . . where was a riche and stately bedde, and there unclothed by hir gentlewomen both of them went to bed' (fo. 17v). In some ways this is a masculine wish-fulfilment fantasy, as the Knight of the Sun recognises when he comes to rescue his father: 'The Emperour *Trebatio* leaned his heade uppon the white and delycate breasts of *Lyndaraza* with suche shewe of pleasure therein that the young *Greke* feelyng thereby in himselfe that which all men have, coulde have bene content wyth the others roome' (fo. 144v). However, the dominance of the sexual woman renders it an emasculating temptation which, for all its pleasures, must be resisted and escaped. At both Trebatio's and the Knight of the Sun's first encounters with Lindaraza, she is compared to the sirens who sought to lure Ulysses and his followers away from their quest. Briana's reluctantly compliant sexuality is legitimated by the providential purpose of the progeneration of heroes; Lindaraza's blatant sexuality is a deviation from both masculine heroic destiny and feminine propriety.

Most of the incidental female characters in the *Mirror* are of a somewhat feeble type exemplified by Clarinea, who is carried off by a giant. She 'cried out so loud that it was great pitie to heare hir', alerting Prince Brandizel to her plight; she swoons, then wakes as the giant drops her to fight Brandizel, then swoons again (fo. 154r–v). However, another heroine represents a contrasting type: the Amazon. Near the end of Tyler's translation, three knights encounter Claridiana as she hunts a boar (fo. 150r–v). Significantly, she is dressed less like a warrior woman than a nymph of Diana, in a green velvet hunting costume with her golden hair hanging down. The knights express themselves amazed at 'your beautye being a Ladye huntresse as if you were *Diana* which in lyke attire was wont to hunte the forrests'. This not entirely unfeminine appearance at her first entry prevents Claridiana from being perceived as too mannish or unnatural, as was often the case in representations of Amazons as armed, warlike and gynocratic.[14] However, once she is established as a sympathetic figure, no doubt is left that she is a warrior as well as a huntress: her mother was the Queen of the Amazons, and at a tournament at Trabisond 'the great prowesse which the Princesse *Claridiana* shewed were suche that every man was amazed at them' (fo. 153r).

Tyler's *Mirror* thus contains a variety of forms of femininity: there are some conventional depictions of female passivity; there is some relative frankness about female sexuality tempered by an emphasis on masculine dominance and the patriarchal cause of dynastic progeneration; and there is the presentation of an Amazon tempered by emphasis on her femininity. Even so, Tyler felt it necessary to preface her translation with an epistle to the reader which constitutes a defence both of the work and of her own temerity as a woman writer (sigs. A3r–4v).[15]

TYLER'S EPISTLE TO THE READER

Tyler is self-conscious that the *Mirror* might be seen as 'unseemly for a woman to deale in' because it is 'a story prophane, and a matter more manlike then becometh my sexe'. However, she locates its arguably inappropriate masculinity in its martial, not its sexual, character, possibly a purposeful manoeuvre to distract attention from its provocative sexual content. Thus she declares that 'The chiefe matter therin conteined is of exploits of wars', and admits that she may be seen as 'bolde to intermeddle in armes, so as the auncient Amazons did, and in this story Claridiana doth, and in other stories not a fewe'. This statement at once acknowledges that Amazons are controversial models for a real woman to emulate, while implying that the presence of 'not a fewe' of them in stories offers precedents for women to take an interest in deeds of war. However, Tyler is careful to distinguish herself from the Amazons; she is merely a cheerer-on of the martial deeds of men, who wants to inspire her individual dedicatee, Lord Thomas Howard, to 'mayn-teine your auncestours glorye', and all readers 'in thy princes and countries quarrel to hazard thy person and purchase good name'. It is notable that in these passages she seems to expect her readership to be chiefly male.

However, Tyler also argues for the suitability of chivalric romances for female readers and for female translators like herself. She points out that men dedicate to women works in all kinds of genres including stories of war,

> And if men may & doe bestow such of their travailes upon gentlewomen, then may we women read such of their works as they dedicate unto us, and if we may read them, why not further wade in them to the serch of a truth . . . why not deale by translation in such arguments, especially this kinde of exercise being a matter of more heede then of deep invention or exquisite learning.

She charges those who would oppose her translation and publication with élitism. She imagines educated male critics who 'could wel alow the story in Spanish, but they may not afford it so chepe, or they would have it proper [i.e. exclusive] to themselves. What natures such men bee of, I list not greatly dispute, but my meaning hath beene to make others partners of my lyking.' She thus appropriates the humanist argument that vernacular translations are praiseworthy because they make learning more accessible, and extends it to more entertaining texts. Male readers were indeed more able than female readers to become acquainted with continental fictions even without English translations: Gascoigne, for instance, must have known *Orlando Furioso* in the Italian (see pp. 47–8 above), and *Amadis de Gaule* was read by Sidney and others in its French translation before its first publication in English in 1590. Tyler's epistle is therefore implicitly an argument for women to be allowed to read romances as well as to emulate her in translating them.

Tyler's translation of the *Mirror* was hugely successful, but despite her rallying-cry to other female readers and translators there is no evidence that it or the other Spanish romances were particularly associated with women readers in England at this date. The assumptions that Tyler pits herself against, that chivalric romance was 'manlike' matter, seem to have remained in place for some time. The popularity of her translation generated a number of sequels by other English translators, but all these translators were male, and for some years their prefatory material continued to emphasise the purpose of inspiring martial heroism in male readers.[16] The printer of the second part stated that he had been 'importuned by sundry Gentle*men* . . . to procure' a translation of this sequel.[17] It was not until 1598 that the translator of *The Seventh Book of the Mirror of Knighthood* pointed out that 'I have in many places addrest my speech, and directed the Historie as it were particulerly to one or to more Ladies or Gentlewomen'; but even then he described this as 'onely an immitation of my Author' and couched this as an explanation to male readers.[18] No other woman entered the field of romance as a writer until Mary Wroth's publication of the *Urania* in 1621. Tyler's translation is an impressive example of early female romance writing and of an assertion of female freedom of choice in reading matter, but it is also an isolated and idiosyncratic case.

ANTHONY MUNDAY'S TRANSLATIONS OF IBERIAN ROMANCES

The other Iberian romances began to reach an English-reading audience in the 1580s and 1590s, when Anthony Munday translated several volumes of the *Palmerin* cycle, the first two books of *Amadis* and other similar works such as *Palladine of England*.[19] There are three characteristics of Munday's translations which might lead us to expect them to be aimed at women readers. First, he invokes the convention of the idle 'winter's tale', as associated with the old wives' tale: *Palmerin d'Oliva* (1588) is 'a freendly companion for the long evenings, and a fit recreation for other vacant times' (sig. *iii). Secondly, writing the translations is itself presented as a recreation for vacant times: at the end of *Palladine of England* (1588) Munday apologises for 'want of my attendance to reade the proves, beeing called away by matter of greater importance; and whereto I am bound by dutie of mine office' (fo. 92v). The title page describes him as a messenger of the Queen's chamber. The idea of diversion from public duty, as in Painter's presentation of his translations as made during intervals in his work at the Armoury (see pp. 34 and 38 above), or, as we shall see, in Sidney's depiction of the *Arcadia* as composed during recreational absence from court (see pp. 101–2 below), could imply delinquency and in turn effeminisation. Thirdly, Munday's translations are blatantly commercial. The above remark about the proofs gives the impression of his churning out volumes at speed; each volume contains an advertisement for the next;[20] and Munday presents them as disposable commodities, qualities often associated, as in Lyly, with women's reading matter. Munday's epistle to the reader in *Palmerin d'Oliva* explains that he has divided the multi-volume original into even smaller sections for affordability and novelty, since 'such are affecions now a daies, that a booke a sennight olde, is scant worth the reading' (sig. *iii.v).

Despite these factors, though, Munday did not for some time seem particularly aware of a female market and did not direct his earlier translations at women. *Palmerin d'Oliva* (1588) was dedicated to Edward de Vere, Earl of Oxford; *Palladine of England* (1588) was dedicated to the Earl of Essex, 'in respect of your owne love to Chivalrie' (sig. *iii.v), stressing the martial aspects of the narrative. Both volumes carried closing addresses to 'Gentlemen' readers, as did the first volume of *Amadis* (1590?).[21] By 1609 a new edition of Munday's translation of *The first part of Palmerin of England* carried the insinuating subtitle 'Wherin gentlemen may find choyse of sweete inventions, and gentlewomen be satisfied in courtly expectations', and a dedication 'To the Ladies and Gentlewomen of England', but this was a departure from the presentation of his earlier volumes.[22]

FEMALE SEXUALITY IN *AMADIS DE GAULE*

Amadis was arguably the most influential of the Iberian romances in England, where it appears to have been known even before Munday's translation of *c.*1590 in its French translation by Nicholas de Herberay and others (1540–81). It has even greater frankness about sexuality, especially female sexuality, than does the *Mirror*.[23] Whereas Briana is a somewhat reluctant and passive partner for Trebatio, and active female desire is displaced on to the dubious figure of Lindaraza, the central and virtuous heroines of *Amadis* are driven by fierce and physical passions. As the story opens Elisena, princess of Little Britain, is known as '*the lost Virgin in Devotion*' because of her religious habits and her aversion to marriage. However, when she sees King Perion of Gaul, she not only falls in love at first sight but is desperate for physical union, demanding of her maid and go-between Darioletta, 'when will the hower come, that I shall holde betweene mine armes, my Lord whom thou hast given me?' (fo. 4v). Whereas Trebatio has to vault into Briana's garden, Elisena, accompanied by Darioletta, who is herself aroused by envy of her mistress's imminent pleasure, makes her own way through a secret garden door to Perion's chamber, where Amadis will be conceived (fo. 5v).

Later, Perion is on his travels and spends a night at the house of the Count of Zealand, where he is woken by the host's daughter holding him to the bed: 'Why Sir? quoth she that thus maistred him, take you no pleasure in me who am alone with you?' (fo. 191v). She describes herself as 'one that freely gives her selfe to you', and Perion 'pass[es] the night with her in such sort, as her hot dessire was quallifyed, and at that instant she conceived with child: the King little thinking thereon, for the next morning he tooke his leave' (fo. 192r). The child will be Florestan, a hero of later volumes in the series. Extramarital sex thus provides more heroes to people the narrative; and the lady's role as progenitor of a hero represents her 'hot dessire' as a force of destiny of which she is merely the pawn.

The central couple, Amadis and Oriana, differ from the many characters around them who move swiftly from love at first sight to consummation. They are brought together aged twelve and ten when Amadis, not yet known as Perion's son, enters Oriana's service, and they fall in love as they grow up together. There is a long delay between mutual declarations of love (at fo. 22v) and consummation (at fo. 171r). Even so, this is not because of any strict devotion to virginity on Oriana's part. She promises Amadis that she will find a way 'to yeeld us content . . . whatsoever happen, be it hate of father, mother, kinred, and freends: for we may not thus procrastinate our joy, and groane under the weightie burden of desire, the flame whereof climeth so high, as the martirdome of our hearts may easily be discovered' (fo. 147r). It is striking how love is accorded primacy over all other claims, and how this is expressed in religious language, as I will discuss further shortly.

The consummation finally takes place after Amadis rescues Oriana from abduction by an enchanter. As they travel through the country-side, Amadis points out their opportunity, and Oriana concurs, 'because her payne was equall with his, and had not he begun the motion, her selfe would have sollicited the same' (fo. 170r). She only asks 'that you will carefully manage our enterprise, by keeping it from knowledge or suspect' (fo. 170v). They lie down on a mantle on the grass, where '*Amadis* forgetting his former bashfulness, seeing Fortune allowed him so queint a favour, let loose the reynes of amourous desire' – with a salacious pun here on 'queint', meaning either 'ingeniously contrived', or 'a woman's private parts'.[24] He proceeds

> with such advantage, as notwithstanding some weake resistance of the Princesse, she was enforced to proove the good and bad together, which maketh freendly maydens become faire women. Daintie was the good grace and subtiltie of *Oriana*, in shaddowing her surpassing pleasure, with a delicate and femenine complaint of *Amadis* boldnes, shewing in countenance such a gracious choller and contented displeasure. (fo. 170v)

Unlike the *Mirror*, this narrative permits female sexual pleasure, but still primarily as a proof of the hero's virility – hence the emphasis on his force; and Oriana, to indicate her essential virtue, still has to show an ability to conceal her enjoyment.

THE RECEPTION OF THE IBERIAN ROMANCES

These fictions seem to have been regarded by their Elizabethan readers in a diversity of ways. The fashionable status of *The Mirror of Knighthood* in the years immediately after its publication is suggested by allusion to it in John Lyly's courtly romance *Euphues and his England* (1580). Euphues, as a visitor to England, claims that the chastity and beauty of the native ladies made him think that 'some strange enchantment altered my mind. "For it may be," thought I, "that in this island either some Artemidorus or Lisimandro or some odd necromancer did inhabit" ' (p. 428), both names from the *Mirror.* Meanwhile, Sidney characterised *Amadis* as a book enjoyed by soldiers which 'wanteth much of a perfect poesy', yet borrowed from it the Amazon disguise of Pyrocles and other elements of the *Arcadia.*[25] Elizabeth I was sometimes eulogised as 'Oriana'.[26] Yet in about 1588, when John Charlewood sought a licence for the translation of *Palmerin of England*, the Stationers' Company granted it only on condition 'that if there be anie thing founde in the booke when it is extante worthie of Reprehension that then all Bookes shall be put to waste and Burnte'. Similar conditions were placed on the second part of *The Mirror of Knighthood* and on *Amadis.*[27] In 1598 Francis Meres included in a list of books 'hurtfull to youth' *Amadis de Gaule*, *The Mirror of Knighthood*, *Palmerin d'Oliva*, and several of their sequels.[28]

However, as the century turned the Iberian romances were increasingly regarded less as dangerous than as old-fashioned, ridiculous and *déclassé.* In Munday's translations the Iberian romances were already aiming at an audience less aristocratic than that addressed by the French translations or by recent original English romances like the *Arcadia.* This slide down the class scale continued, and became the premise of a whole play in Francis Beaumont's *The Knight of the Burning Pestle*, *c.*1607, a burlesque of the Iberian romances in which an apprentice called Rafe becomes the eponymous knight and a Grocer Errant. The apprentice, his grocer-employer and the grocer's wife are all shown as avid and credulous romance fans.

A few positive references to the Iberian romances are found in writers like Fynes Moryson and Lord Herbert of Cherbury,[29] and the personae of Amadis and Oriana continued to be used in courtly panegyric.[30] However, the predominant seventeenth-century attitude to the genre was disdain, especially after the appearance of Shelton's English translation of *Don Quixote* in 1612 and 1620, which William Vaughan regarded as serving 'to reclaime a riotous running wit from taking delight in those prodigious, idle, and time-wasting *Bookes*, called the *Mirrour of Knighthood, the Knights of the Round Table, Palmerin de Oliva*, and the like rabblement'.[31] Their absurdity and the folly of their readers becomes almost a cliché in stage comedy; Ben Jonson, for instance, disparaged them in both *The Alchemist* (1612)[32] and *The New Inn* (1629).[33]

IBERIAN ROMANCES AS WOMEN'S READING

The categorisation of the Iberian romances as idle, foolish and lower-class frequently translated into the attribution of their popularity to ignorant women readers. In *The Anatomy of Melancholy*, Robert Burton castigated both the ignorant English rural gentry and self-indulgent male 'inamoratoes' as readers of chivalric romances, but he also associated the romances with 'silly Gentlewomen' who are 'incensed by reading amorous toyes, *Amadis de Gaul, Palmerin de Oliva, the Knight of the sunne* [i.e. *The Mirror of Knighthood*], *&c.*'.[34] In *Eastward Hoe*, 1605, a goldsmith's daughter who has been deserted by Sir Petronel Flash asks, 'Would the Knight o'the *Sun*, or *Palmerin of England*, have used their Ladies so?' Her maid takes up the theme: 'Or sir *Lancelot*? Or sir *Tristram*?'.[35] Their different choice of comparisons may be meant to suggest a subtle gradation of class: the maid reads older chivalric romances, while her mistress is slightly more up-to-date in favouring the Iberian romances, though even this preference confirms her place in the middling trading class rather than the aristocracy.

However, many later examples presented the Iberian stories as distinctively the reading of servants; and it was usually the naive literal-mindedness of women readers which was mocked. As already discussed in chapter 1 above, the 1615 edition of Sir Thomas Overbury's *Characters* included a satirical portrait of 'A Chamber-Mayde' who 'reads *Greenes* workes over and over, but is so caried away with the *Myrrour of Knighthood*, she is many times resolv'd to run out of her selfe, and become a Ladie Errant' (sig. ¶4v) – her desire to turn escapist fantasy into reality is turned into mocking *double entendre*. In Massinger's *The Guardian*, 1633, a paid confidante tells her mistress:

> Seek no more president:
> In all the books of *Amadis de Gaul*,
> The *Palmerins*, and that true Spanish story
> *The Mirror of Knighthood*, which I have read often,
> Read feelingly, nay more, I do believe in't,
> My Lady has no parallel.[36]

Again, the uncritical absorption of the romances as offering truth or reality is ridiculed. A poem by William Browne (1591–1645) shows a 'vaine inconstant dame' (line 93) in her closet with her chambermaid:

> Op'ning a Paper then she showes her wytt,
> On an Epistle that some foole had wrytt,
> Then meeting with another which she lykes,
> Her Chambermayds great readyng quickly strykes
> That good opynion dead, and sweares that this
> Was stolne from Palmerin or Amadis.[37]

Here the lover is exposed as deriving his words of courtship from the fiction favoured by mere chambermaids, and the mistress is exposed as foolish for having been impressed by him; the 'great reading' of the maid ironically equips her with superior knowledge in such matters.

It is important to note that these satirical representations of women as readers of Iberian romances all date from the seventeenth century. The association of the romances with women is part of their progressive decline in cultural status, deploying the familiar connection between women and trash. It is at this point that parallels to modern soap opera become most striking: as Jane Root has commented, the fact that 'soap operas are seen as female has helped to bring the whole form into disrepute'.[38] This provokes a question: were the Iberian romances merely '*seen as* female'; or were they, like soap operas, not only culturally constructed as women's trash for ideological reasons, but also in fact enjoyed by a female audience? As with the whole question of romance as women's reading, as discussed in my opening chapters, it seems reasonable to assume that the female readership came gradually to exist while also being exaggerated for rhetorical and satirical purposes. What is notable about the Iberian romances is that, unlike English Elizabethan fictions by Pettie, Lyly, Rich and Greene, their early editions evince no intention, feigned or otherwise, to appeal to a female audience. If they did indeed become the favourite reading of women, then they must have done so by gradual processes, perhaps being dumped on maidservants as they were discarded by more élite readers, perhaps being actively appropriated by women counter to the intentions of the original translators and publishers, perhaps a little of both.

IBERIAN ROMANCES AS PATRIARCHAL FICTIONS

Many things in the Iberian romances confirm the sense that they were not originally generated by a motivation to entertain a female readership. Even aspects which might look protofeminist from a modern perspective can be understood in context as reinforcing patriarchal social structures. The relative sexual freedom enjoyed by heroines is a means whereby the virility of a male hero can be displayed and carried forward into the next generation, and an opportunity for semi-pornographic entertainment for the male reader. For example, during the consummation scene in *Amadis*, the reader is invited to share the hero's male gaze upon Oriana: 'Heere-upon, carelessly spreading her armes abroad, as though she slept in deed, and by reason of the exceeding heat, leaving her gorget [collar, bodice] open, two little alabaster bowles lively shewed them-selves in her bosome, so faire and sweetly respiring, as Nature never shewed more curious workemanship' (fo. 171r).

The protection of damsels-in-distress from violence is prized less because of sympathy with the plight of female victims than as a measure of masculine chivalry and nobility and as part of the preservation of patriarchal order. Although Trebatio is himself arguably the rapist of Briana, we are told that he is especially fierce in the punishment of rapists because 'his saying was, that it quenched the naturall love betweene father and mother, sister and brother, betweene kiffe and kinne: that the bastard broode seldome came to good purpose: that it was partly the sinne of *Sodomy*,[39] etc.' (*Mirror*, fo. 164r–v). The primary imperative throughout is the preservation and perpetuation of masculine lineage.

There is considerable gender-fluidity in the romances, in the presence of both Amazons and of male heroes in temporary female disguises. *The Mirror of Knighthood*, the romance which made the chambermaid in Overbury's *Characters* want to become a lady errant, seems to have become especially notable for its Amazon characters, which include not only Claridiana, who is particularly prominent in the third part of the first book (1586?), but also Archisilora, Queen of Lira.[40] In the later volumes their presence is offered as an attraction: the openings of the seventh, eighth and ninth parts offer such delights as 'the haughtie deedes of warlike ladies',[41] and 'the high chevalrie of the gallant ladies'.[42] These may have been selling points partly aimed at female readers: it is also in the seventh and eighth books that the English translator follows his Spanish author in including complimentary asides to ladies. However, the presence of Amazons can also be accounted for by masculine interests. O'Connor surmises that the primary function of Amazons in *Amadis* is to add exoticism and variety to the range of possible combats in which the knights can engage.[43] When Amazons feature primarily as warriors and separatist gynocrats, they are represented as fierce and unnatural, as in Book v of *Amadis* where they are savage enemies who ally with the Turks to besiege the Christian defenders of Constantinople. In order to be sympathetic figures, Amazons must be softened by love, and thereby become good breeding stock for future heroes: Claridiana in the *Mirror* becomes the mother of the heir to the Knight of the Sun, Claridiano,[44] while in Book viii of the French *Amadis* an Amazon queen named Zahara becomes the mother of the twin children of Amadis of Greece.[45] Women who are not Amazons do sometimes adopt armour, but again only for reasons of extreme love: Gradafilée, again in Book viii of the French *Amadis*, expresses her unrequited devotion to Lisuart of Greece by donning armour to fight in his cause.[46]

Gender-fluidity also operates in the opposite direction. Knights are often admired for their effeminate beauty, which in the *Amadis* cycle enables them to adopt Amazon costumes in order to gain access to their mistresses, as imitated by Sidney: there are examples of this in Books viii and xi.[47] In Tyler's *Mirror of Knighthood*, Rosicleer disguises himself as a maiden, Lyverba, who has been claimed under *droit de seigneur* by her feudal lord, Argion. Rosicleer's unsurpassable heroism requires that as a maiden he must excel in *feminine* charms: 'he was so beautifull as no gentlewoman thereabouts might parage [equal] him' (fo. 71v). However, in the privacy of the bedchamber he leaves no doubt as to his masculinity: having persuaded Argion to undress and get into bed first, he turns on him, and 'smote the necke from the shoulders, the heade beating agaynst the wall, and the body falling headlesse to the grounde' (fo. 73r). The decapitation is figured as a castration of the aroused Argion and affirms the phallic supremacy of Rosicleer's sword.

Such episodes seem to be chiefly concerned with exploration of the gender roles available to men and of the boundaries of masculinity. Just as the introduction of an Amazon defines masculinity by pitting the masculine subject directly against the feminine other in combat, so the male adoption of feminine disguise has a complementary function of allowing a masculine subject temporarily to occupy the position of the feminine other before returning emphatically to the masculine norm. Moreover, the feminine position is usually adopted in the service of virility, in order to penetrate the paternal defences around a desirable woman.

ATTRACTIONS FOR FEMALE READERS

All of these motifs can be regarded as catering to masculine reading pleasures. However, if we accept that the gradual representation of the Iberian romances as women's reading reflects a gradual appropriation of them by women, then we need to consider what kinds of things in them might have appealed to female readers. To do so runs the risk of exercising rather simplistic distinctions between how men read and how women read. We must recognise that, for instance, Margaret Tyler may not be simply disingenuously deflecting attention from its erotic content when she suggests that the main thing she enjoys in *The Mirror of Knighthood* is the vicarious experience of martial deeds. But perhaps we can also assume that the social and cultural positioning of women must have made some generalised differences to their reading pleasures, just as today we often think in general terms of some genres as men's and others as women's.

What kinds of things, then, might women readers have enjoyed in the Iberian romances? First, while we can explain the concern with love primarily in terms of the progeneration of dynasties of heroes, the effect is nevertheless to give prominence, if not indeed sometimes dominance, to women as objects of desire. Martial deeds generally have the motivation of saving or winning a lady: a hero fights better when inspired by the sight of his mistress.[48] Love even gives women supposed power over mighty heroes. Rosicleer writes to Olivia that 'neither the wisest nor the myghtiest were able to resist' the force of love, mentioning its subjugation of Caesar, Mars and Jupiter, and how love 'as it were by sodayne inchantment framed the armestrong *Hercules* to the distaffe and spyndle: [and] *Aristotle* to be bridled and saddled'.[49] When Trebatio and Briana are reunited at the end of Tyler's *Mirror* and decide to run away together, the narrator comments, 'for thys loves sake could the Emperor *Trebatio* willingly have forborne both kiffe and kinred, and acquaintance in his owne countrey, and for hys love durst the Princesse adventure to flye hir Fathers Realme, and to abandon hir selfe to unknowne passages, and to travayle with *Trebatio* into *Greece*' (fo. 178v). Love is supreme, such that, not unlike the feminocentric value structure of modern romantic fiction or soap opera, 'feminine' concerns of courtship take precedence over 'masculine' concerns of the public and official world.

This is corroborated by the topographical significance which is given to private, feminine spaces. Women's chambers or private gardens are the locations where future heroes are conceived. The heroine acts as the guardian of the boundaries of each hero's private world; her role is as the fixed point to which he returns. Indeed, her confinement to private space and a fixed location reveals her supposed power over her questing heroic lover to be merely rhetorical. When Elisena finds herself pregnant, she is unable to get a message to Perion because 'she knew the promptitude of this yong king, that tooke no rest in any place where he came, nor was his hart satisfied, except in this, with following armes, as also seeking strange and hazardous adventures'.[50]

The privacy of the spaces occupied by the heroines is intensified by the emphasis on secrecy as a marker of female perfection; and this privacy and secrecy are key elements in the definition of female heroism in these romances. The relationship of female heroism to a female readership is far more complex than the personification of escapist fantasies in Amazons and in daughters who disobediently pursue their own desires. Heroinism is not such a clear matter of rebelling against prescribed feminine roles, but is more of a negotiation with them. It is true that bodily continence in the form of virginal intactness seems to be set aside as the primary marker of female virtue, but it is replaced as a defining virtue by related qualities of continence of emotional display and of information. It is not really clear why Oriana and Amadis's love has to be kept secret, since from an early stage he is known to be the son of King Perion of Gaul and therefore an eminently fitting suitor for Oriana. Even so,

Oriana repeatedly urges him to conceal his passion in public,[51] and when they meet at court they employ elaborate subterfuges to hold hands secretly under Oriana's mantle[52] or to exchange private signals. It is not until Book 4, when their son is already showing his own heroic promise, that their love is publicly announced and confirmed by marriage.[53] In *The Mirror of Knighthood* when Briana realises that she is pregnant she confides only in her servant Clandestria, who tries to persuade her to tell her parents – the father of the child is after all her lawful husband, and the child will be heir to Great Britain (they still believe Trebatio to be Prince Edward). Briana, however, insists on secrecy, seemingly for its own sake: 'though the chylde which shall bee borne of mee should be Lorde of the whole world, I would not tell this secrete to any bodie, but to thee'.[54] Olivia too practises a seemingly excessive secrecy about her feelings of love which serves to denote her 'honesty' and 'modestie'.[55]

The supreme test of female secrecy is the concealment of pregnancy and childbirth. Again this can be seen as a by-product of a primary concern with heroic masculinity: the new hero must grow up in obscurity so that he can prove his chivalric virtues by his deeds, and so that the quest for his identity can become a dynamic of the narrative. However, at the same time heroines who succeed in concealing their conditions and giving birth to healthy babies, with the assistance only of their female confidantes, afford striking examples of female resourcefulness and self-sufficiency. The safe delivery and nurture of the new hero is shown as dependent upon female skill and strength.

The confinement of heroines to private and secret spaces may appear to be restrictive of women and unlikely to have appealed to women readers. However, the emphasis on withdrawal enables the development of female subjectivity, something which is taken further in Sidney's *New Arcadia* and in Mary Wroth's *Urania*, as we shall see. As the heroines wrestle with concealed erotic dilemmas, we retreat with them into their chambers and into their thoughts, to which the narrative allows lengthy expression. After Olivia has banished Rosicleer,

> in steede of the daylye viewe of his personage, in his absence shee gazed at will uppon the counterfayte and portrature which he had emprinted in hir fancie. This did she the oftener bicause she founde not in hir solitarye contemplation anye other thinge to present it selfe. For amourous thoughtes

are ever enemyes to company, and beeing alone, as commonly shee was by reason of sickenesse, what was there to remove this solytary thought and conversant companion from hir.[56]

Compare Pamphilia in Wroth's *Urania*, whose image of her absent beloved, Amphilanthus, in her mind, seems almost preferable to the real, faithless man, and inspires her to literary creation: 'though the sight which she desired, was hid from her, she might yet by the light of her imaginations (as in a picture) behold, and make those lights serve in his absence'.[57]

The melancholy, sickness and loneliness which Olivia experiences may not seem to us to offer an attractive model of female heroism. However, within the Renaissance code of feminine silence, chastity and obedience, the relatively emancipated, and therefore morally dubious, sexual behaviour of romance heroines has to be offset and mitigated by their suffering. Indeed, the ability to suffer could be said to be the chief determining characteristic of a heroine. Just after Perion and Elisena have consummated their love, he tells her not to be afraid of his inevitable departure, 'for although my body be seperated from your presence, my hart for ever shall remaine with ye, which shall give strength to us bothe, to you to suffer, and to me by my speedye returne'.[58] Elisena, Oriana and Briana all suffer for their submission to true love by the enforced concealment of their unions and by separation from their lovers and infants.

Love serves as a lofty cause which justifies the otherwise potentially morally dubious behaviour of sexually compliant heroines. A notion of chastity is not discarded as the paramount female virtue; rather, it is redefined as constancy in love. The unions between Perion and Elisena or Amadis and Oriana are sacred and equivalent to marriage, even though not publicly or legally recognised, because they are founded on the binding promises of true lovers. The elevation of love as the supreme virtue offers a compromise between propriety and female sexual independence of paternal control.

In the process, sacred iconography comes to the fore, further diminishing any suspicion of the heroine's moral impropriety: love is elevated to the level of a religion of which suffering heroines are the saints and martyrs. After the disappearance of Trebatio, Briana dresses as a widow and retires to a secret chamber, where she 'demeaned rather the life of an Anchresse, or religious woman, then of a Princesse'.[59] When she believes Rosicleer to be of low birth,

Olivia writes to him to banish him from her presence, lamenting as she does so,

> Now dare I compare with the *Romaine* Matrones which for the preservation of their honesty sacrifised themselves, unto their Gods, for what have I done els, but in a manner sacrificed my selfe to God, when for my honour sake I have bounde and lynked my selfe to suche a continuall martyrdome and perpetuall imprisonment, as the absence of *Rosicleer* wyll breede in me, and never more will lyve as a Princesse, but rather lyke a vowesse.[60]

The iconography of erotic sainthood which I discussed in chapter 2 above comes into force here.

The fact that strength of character in itself is not sufficient to denote female heroism is shown by the presentation of Madasima, an enemy of Amadis and his promiscuous younger brother Galaor, who holds them prisoner and only releases them after Galaor has strategically feigned love for her. She comes to Galaor's chamber at night,

> she beeing young, beautifull, and adventerously given: *Galaor* likewise, a man forward to such fortunes, when Love had erected his scaling ladders to the walles, quicklye got possession of the Forte. And so well liked she these amorous skirmiges, as afterward she reported in many places, how she never tasted a more pleasant night . . . Thus was she enclined to voluptuous desire, as without care of her honor, she often fell in this sort. By these meanes escaped *Amadis* and *Galaor.*[61]

Madasima's faults, compared with other women who engage in extramarital sex, are that she assumes political dominance over men; she attempts to constrain the movements of questing knights; she acts out of vanity and pleasure in sex for its own sake rather than overpowering love; and, perhaps worst of all, she lacks discretion and secrecy.

Female heroism in the Iberian romances can thus be seen to consist in sexual willingness combined with fidelity, immobility, secrecy and the ability to suffer. This combination of qualities can be understood as originally generated by the patriarchal concerns of male writers and their imagined male readers. However, what they produce is a compromise between relative female sexual freedom and conventional iconographies of female virtue, which exonerated the sexual woman from blame. This may have been precisely what came to make these fictions appealing for female readers. At the same time the recognition that this was potentially subversive may lie behind the mockery of female readers: the importation of the female *mores* of Iberian romance into real life held manifest dangers and was therefore ridiculed and diminished as mere gullible over-literality. The line from Overbury's *Characters* about the maidservant is a warning to her kind that if they do 'run out of themselves' and emulate the behaviour of 'ladies errant' in real life, they will both look foolish and lose their reputations; but perhaps there would not be such a pressing need to mock them out of the imitation of chivalric romance heroines if those errant ladies did not simultaneously appear so very saintly.

CHAPTER 5

Fictions addressed to women by Lyly, Rich and Greene

I have already briefly discussed in chapters 1 and 2 above the prefaces to John Lyly's *Euphues and his England* (1580), Barnaby Rich's *Farewell to Military Profession* and Robert Greene's *Penelope's Web* (1587). In this chapter I will expand on this discussion, and look at the content of the three authors' fictions, to explore how the idea of fictional prose as an effeminised space became especially prevalent in the 1580s.

LYLY'S *EUPHUES* ROMANCES

The prefaces to *Euphues: The Anatomy of Wit* (1578), the work to which *Euphues and his England* was the sequel, are addressed to male readers. The title page describes the volume as 'Very pleasant for all Gentlemen to read, and most necessary to remember'.[1] The dedication is to Sir William West, followed by an epistle to gentlemen readers. However, Lyly introduces two key ideas: his readership's foolish preoccupation with fashion; and, catering to this, the inconsequentiality and disposability of his writing. He complains that 'Englishmen desire to hear finer speech than the language will allow', and 'to wear finer cloth than is wrought of wool' (*Euphues*, p. 6). For these reasons 'I am content this winter to have my doings read for a toy that in the summer they may be ready for trash' (p. 8). The primary meaning of the word 'trash' at this time was specifically broken and discarded pieces, like twigs and straw fit only for kindling, but it was already developing the wider figurative sense of simply 'rubbish' or 'nonsense'.[2]

It was a short step from characterising his writing as idle and fashionable to associating it with women readers. Thus Lyly's sequel, *Euphues and his England* (1580), carries three prefaces, one a dedication to the Earl of Oxford, the second an epistle to ladies and gentlewomen and the third an epistle 'To the gentlemen readers'.[3] In juxtaposing alternative prefaces addressed to women and men Lyly follows the precedent set by Pettie, and he also imitates Pettie's simultaneously flirtatious and disparaging tone towards his imagined female readers, such as in the very title of his epistle: 'To the ladies and gentlewomen of England John Lyly wisheth what they would' (*Euphues and his England*, p. 199). The linked concepts of idleness, fashion, folly and flightiness are now conveniently personified as female:

> You choose cloth that will wear whitest, not that will last longest, colours that look freshest, not that endure soundest, and I would you would read books that have more show of pleasure, than ground of profit. Then should Euphues be as often in your hands, being but a toy, as lawn on your heads, being but trash; the one will be scarce liked after once reading, and the other is worn out after the first washing.
>
> There is nothing lighter than a feather, yet is it set aloft in a woman's hat, nothing slighter than hair, yet is it most frizzled in a lady's head; so that I am in good hope, though there be nothing of less account than Euphues, yet he shall be marked with ladies' eyes and liked sometimes in their ears. (p. 201)

Why should Lyly have wished to present his work as merely a 'toy' and 'trash' which will be 'scarce liked after once reading'? For Arthur Kinney, such apparent disparagements of their own works by 1580s authors, which, as we shall see, were to become commonplace, are to be understood as self-consciously 'Erasmian', emulating *The Praise of Folly* and other early humanist texts in using playfulness to mask a serious didactic purpose.[4] Richard Helgerson, on the other hand, sees Lyly and his contemporaries as a generation of prodigals who foregrounded the worthlessness of their fictions as correspondent with the waste of their own talents in a society glutted with university-educated sons of the gentry. Unable to find the public employment for which they had been trained, they made a precarious living from writing fictions in which they simultaneously sought to catch the attention of potential patrons and flaunted their own marginalisation. Their writings therefore combine displays of wit and rhetorical prowess with defiant assertions of the pleasures of purposelessness, and with degrees of self-disgust at being reduced to redundancy.[5]

Indulging in idleness inevitably meant subsiding into the world of women and courtship, as made clear in *The Anatomy of Wit*, where

Euphues squanders his talents on the seduction of the worthless Lucilla. Although in the sequel Euphues himself is a reformed character who immerses himself in scholarship and somewhat arid moralising, the volume as a whole takes us further into the realm of the feminine, as Helgerson describes: 'One is addressed to gentlemen scholars, the other to ladies and gentlewomen; one claims to be a moral treatise, the other a plaything; one satirises women and love, the other praises both.'[6] Lyly even appropriates to himself a graphic and physical form of femaleness in the epistle to the Earl of Oxford which precedes the second work:

> I have brought into the world two children. Of the first I was delivered before my friends thought me conceived; of the second I went a whole year big, and yet when everyone thought me ready to lie down I did then quicken . . . My first burden coming before his time must needs be a blind whelp; the second brought forth after his time must needs be a monster . . . He is my youngest and my last, and the pain that I sustained for him in travail hath made me past teeming; yet do I think myself very fertile in that I was not altogether barren. (*Euphues and his England*, p. 193)

Lyly follows Gascoigne in choosing a courtly setting presided over by ladies where the principal occupation is the game of *questioni d'amore*, an ideal medium for exercising wit while achieving nothing; the most that it can lead to is seduction of a mistress, and even in this Euphues's success is fleeting and illusory. *The Anatomy of Wit* shows Euphues first befriending Philautus, then promptly breaching his friendship to woo Philautus's lady, Lucilla. Lyly shows how wit in the service of lust can argue deftly but departs from morality: Euphues, debating inwardly whether to pursue Lucilla, reasons that Lucrece would have yielded if Tarquin had approached her less forcefully, and, echoing Pettie on Camma (see chapter 3 above), criticises her 'rigour, to punish his folly in her own flesh; a fact (in mine opinion) more worthy the name of cruelty than chastity, and fitter for a monster in the deserts than a matron of Rome' (p. 48). Lucilla reciprocates Euphues's treacherous passion, and, a match for him in wit, is equally capable of sophistry to justify the unrestrained pursuit of her desires:

> [L]ove gives no reason of choice, neither will it suffer any repulse. Myrrha was enamoured of her natural father, Biblis of her brother, Phaedra of her son-in-law [i.e. her stepson]. If nature can no way resist the fury of affection, how should it be stayed by wisdom? (p. 73)

Her citation of blatantly transgressive loves alerts us to the impropriety of her position, and this is made even clearer when Euphues, having been spurned by her in favour of yet another lover, turns her examples back against her:

> Why dost thou not love a bull seeing Pasiphaë loved one? Why art thou not enamoured of thy father knowing that Myrrha was so incensed? These are set down that we, viewing their incontinency, should fly the like impudency, not follow the like excess; neither can they excuse thee of any inconstancy. (p. 83)

Iconic female figures become objects of reinterpretations in which wit is showily displayed, but the contradictions between different interpretations at different points alert us to the facts that wit is motivated by personal interest and its reinterpretations can become misinterpretations.

Wit, we learn, is pliant and can be turned to any end, as Feste notes in *Twelfth Night*: 'To see this age! A sentence is but a chev'ril [kidskin] glove to a good wit. How quickly the wrong side may be turn'd outward!' Viola concurs that 'They that dally nicely with words may quickly make them wanton', and Feste fills out her sexual metaphor to suggest that pliant wit slides easily into pliant morals which hold particular hazards for women: 'I would therefore my sister had had no name . . . her name's a word, and to dally with that word might make my sister wanton' (III.i.11–20). In *Euphues*, the combination of pliable wit with pliable sexual morality is implied to be fatal for women in a way that it is not for men. For R.W. Maslen, Lucilla's duplicitous rhetoric 'beat[s] Euphues at his own game', and shows that women's stereotypical association with unreliability, strategic ambiguity and inscrutability to male interpretation renders them natural Euphuists.[7] However, the consequences of Euphuistic rhetorical and moral conduct for each sex are directly opposed. Euphues's unfortunate dalliance with Lucilla prompts him to reform himself and to take up serious study and didactic rectitude. In Lucilla's case, however, her turning from Philautus to Euphues apparently renders it inevitable that she will turn again to another. One change of affection converts her into a personification of inconstancy, prefiguring Beatrice-Joanna in *The Changeling*, whose attraction to a man other than her betrothed prompts De Flores to observe 'Then I'll put in for one', since she has become in effect available to all.[8] Lucilla is punished for her mutability first by her new choice of suitor, Curio, who we are told is unworthy of her in both character and class; and finally by sinking into debt and dying an ignominious death in the gutter, of which we learn only in passing in a somewhat cold-hearted letter from Euphues to Philautus (*Euphues*, p. 170).

All of this is despite the fact that Lucilla is a character who has been given depth, interest and an engaging degree of self-consciousness as we witness at length her internal debates and quandaries. It is she who prophetically voices the fear that 'she that hath been faithless to one will never be faithful to any' (p. 40). Sometimes she voices a sympathetic and apparently justifiable wish to make her own choice in love regardless of her father's views or the rank of her beloved, opining that 'it is . . . the love of the woman that maketh the man' (pp. 88–9). This seems to be an acceptable position when Euphues is the lover concerned, but not when he is displaced by Curio. She is capable of contrition and self-loathing, veering even into misogyny: 'I would it were in Naples a law, which was a custom in Egypt, that women should always go barefoot, to the intent they might keep themselves always at home . . . I mean so to mortify myself that . . . I will . . . for the lute use the distaff, for the pen the needle, for lovers' sonnets David's psalms' (pp. 64–5). The extremity of this sentiment, however, is of a piece with her emerging traits of instability and lack of restraint.

Her sin is not merely the possession of more wit than propriety, but the fracturing of the friendship between Euphues and Philautus. Their homosocial bond is the primary relationship which runs through both volumes of *Euphues*, and all their encounters with women may be seen as significant only in so far as they have bearing upon that bond. What they love about each other is their sameness: Euphues rejoices that 'a friend is . . . at all times an other I, in all places the express image of mine own person' (p. 28), and they share 'not only one board, but one bed, one book' (p. 31). The breach between them is blamed upon digressive dalliance with women: after Lucilla's desertion Euphues complains, 'O inconstant sex! I have lost Philautus, I have lost Lucilla, I have lost that which I shall hardly find again, a faithful friend' (p. 84). The two men then 'after much talk renewed their old friendship, both abandoning Lucilla as most abominable' (pp. 89–90). The deletion of Lucilla enables the even firmer establishment of homosocial allegiance. In the second volume, after another estrangement, Euphues again sets out to renew the friendship, 'weighing with himself that often in marriages there have fallen out brawls, where the chiefest love should be, and yet again reconciliations' (p. 373). They meet again like lovers:

'Many embracings there were, much strange courtesy, many pretty glances' (p. 375).

Thus Euphues learns by experience the full truth of some maxims which he sententiously intoned to Philautus soon after falling for Lucilla: 'True it is . . . that he that dallieth with women is drawn to his woe . . . beauty allureth the chaste mind to love and the wisest wit to lust' (p. 49). Yet even as blame is put on women, a sense remains of the moral relativism underlining fine rhetoric, combined with a sense that misogyny is the refuge of the unsuccessful lover. Euphues composes 'A Cooling Card for Philautus and All Fond Lovers' (pp. 91–107), which could stand alone as a manifesto of misogyny, but which, in its context in the narrative, reads both as a rhetorical exercise and as the product of a personal grudge. Euphues shrewdly pinpoints the logical absurdity of the courtly lover's position: 'If my lady yield to be my lover is it not likely she will be another's leman [i.e. lover]? And if she be a modest matron my labour is lost. This therefore remaineth, that either I must pine in cares or perish with curses' (p. 95). His logic leads him to the conclusion 'Believe not . . . their alluring looks, their treading on the toe, their unsavoury toys. Let every one loathe his lady, and be ashamed to be her servant' (p. 106).

In the process, however, he descends into a far from rational disgust first at the impurity of women's cosmetics and clothes, then at the even deeper foulness of the bodies behind them:

> I loathe almost to think on their ointments and apothecary drugs, the sleeking of their faces, and all their slibber-sauces which bring queasiness to the stomach and disquiet to the mind. Take from them their periwigs, their paintings, their jewels, their rolls, their bolsterings, and thou shalt soon perceive that a woman is the least part of herself. When they be once robbed of their robes then will they appear so odious, so ugly, so monstrous that thou wilt rather think them serpents than saints, and so like hags that thou wilt fear rather to be enchanted than enamoured. (p. 104)

The disdainful association of women with fashionable commodities – Euphues goes on to list 'their shadows [veils], their spots [beauty-spots], their lawns, their lyfkies [bodices], their ruffs, their rings' (*ibid.*) – looks forward to the women's preface to *Euphues and his England*. The image of a woman stripped of her ornaments to be exposed as a monstrous hag also prefigures the stripping of Duessa in the *Faerie Queene*. Above all, the passage anticipates the misogynistic railing of malcontents in the drama, such as Bosola in

Webster's *The Duchess of Malfi* (1614), who charges women with using as cosmetics 'the fat of serpents, spawn of snakes, Jews' spittle, and their young children's ordures'.[9] Just as Bosola can be seen to be taking out his social marginalisation on the easy target of women, who personify court mores, so Euphues's bitterness may be regarded as both produced by his failure in courtship and animated by his author's frustrations in the pursuit of courtiership.

As Helgerson notes, *Euphues and his England* looks as if it is more sympathetic to the feminine than is its predecessor. There are even more games of *questioni d'amore* presided over by ladies, and there are flirtatious asides to gentlewomen readers (pp. 349, 361, 376, 382–3, 409). Euphues and Philautus travel to England, where they marvel at the beauty and virtue of the ladies (p. 299). Two ladies present opposite cases to Lucilla: first Iffida, who refused her suitor because she was already pledged to another, even though this original lover first went abroad then died; then Camilla, who emulates Petrarch's Laura in resisting Philautus's advances and is rewarded with marriage to the noble Surius.

Even these positive images of women, however, form part of a rhetorical game. Euphues reports back to the ladies of Italy his observations on the ladies of England, in a section titled 'Euphues' Glass for Europe'. Italian ladies are found

> reading the epistle of a lover when they should peruse the Gospel of our Lord, drawing wanton lines when death is before their face . . . Imitate the English damosels, who have their books tied to their girdles, not feathers [i.e. fans], who are as cunning in the Scriptures as you are in Ariosto or Petrarch or any book that liketh you best and becometh you worst. (pp. 426–7)

Yet we have already been told in the preface to gentlewomen that the ladies of England have a predilection for fashionable trifles and idle, amorous books. When Euphues apologises to the gentlewomen of Italy for presenting them with a glass from England when they would have preferred 'little dogs from Malta or strange stones from India or fine carpets from Turkey' (p. 415), he sounds strangely like John Lyly addressing his English female readers. It appears, then, that the contrast between virtuous English ladies and foolish Italian ladies is in fact a mask for a contrast between English ladies as they should be and English ladies as they are. The fanciful and hyperbolic assertion that England as a realm of chaste and beautiful ladies is like an enchanted island from *The Mirror of Knighthood* makes it clear that we are being shown a fictional, idealised England (p. 428; see p. 65 above). All the supposed praise of English ladies therefore functions as satire against them, intensified by the acute topicality of Euphues's report: he and Philautus are said to have landed in England on 1 December 1579 (p. 205).

The 'Glass for Europe' climaxes in a lengthy eulogy of Queen Elizabeth, whom Lyly seems to exempt from the criticisms which he levels at women in general (pp. 432–49). A convention in panegyric of the Queen was to praise her as an 'exceptional woman' whose excellence raised her miraculously above the implied general depravity of her sex,[10] and to an extent Lyly can be seen as participating in this. He uses Elizabeth's intact virginal body as an emblem of the unity and impregnability of the nation:

> This is the only miracle that virginity ever wrought: for a little island environed round about with wars to stand in peace, for the walls of France to burn and the houses of England to freeze, for all other nations either with civil sword to be divided or with foreign foes to be invaded and that country neither to be molested with broils in their own bosoms nor threatened with blasts of other borderers. (pp. 439–40)

The cold chastity of the Queen at once stands for the freedom of the nation from civil war (broils of the bosom) and foreign penetrations, and accounts for that security, as a miraculous charm which has invoked the protection of God.

Throughout his eulogy Lyly lays stress on the divine sanction of Elizabeth's Protestant rule, such that we may take his praise to be sincere in so far as he is upholding Elizabeth as the symbolic personification of the Protestant English nation. However, he also repeatedly stresses the unrepresentability of her perfections – 'I leave you gazing [at her back] until she turn her face, imagining her to be such a one as nature framed to that end that no art should imitate' (pp. 441–2). This sets up a neo-Platonic framework: the Elizabeth that he wants to describe exists only in an ideal world of essential truth and beauty beyond the real, mortal world. We may therefore infer that he is eulogising Elizabeth not as a fallible individual, but as an icon of a national and spiritual cause, and as an icon of perfection not only for individual women to emulate, but also, implicitly, for the real Elizabeth to aspire to.[11] Just as he praises the perfection of 'Englishwomen' in order to satirise the shortcomings of actual Englishwomen, so his praise of 'Elizabeth' can be a vehicle for didactic exhortations to the real Elizabeth. We may detect irony when he writes:

What greater marvel hath happened since the beginning of the world than for a young and tender maiden to govern strong and valiant men, than for a virgin to make the whole world, if not to stand in awe of her, yet to honour her; yea, and to live in spite of all those that spite her, with her sword in the sheath, with her armour in the Tower, with her soldiers in their gowns? (p. 439)

This can be read as implying that it is unnatural for a young and tender maiden to rule strong and valiant men, and that the sheathed swords and nightgowns of her soldiers are emblems of the emasculation of the nation. All of these were ideas and motifs upon which Barnaby Rich was to expand.

In the early 1580s the elaborate rhetoric of Lyly's *Euphues* romances was clearly regarded as an impressive literary innovation and set the model for other prose writers to imitate. Robert Greene, for instance, wrote *Euphues his Censure to Philautus* (1587), and gave Euphuistic subtitles to other works such as *A mirror or looking-glass for the ladies of England* (*Mamillia* I, 1583), and *Camilla's alarm to slumbering Euphues* (*Menaphon*, 1589). By the early seventeenth century, though, when they had fallen from fashion, they were lumped together with the Iberian chivalric romances as women's reading, according to John Marston's *The Dutch Courtezan* (1605). Crispinella speaks satirically of constraints which marriage places on women; Tysefew replies, 'Alas for you, sweet soul! By the Lord, you are grown a proud, scurvy, apish, idle, disdainful, scoffing – God's foot! because you have read *Euphues and his England*, *Palmerin de Oliva*, and the *Legend of Lies*!'[12] The *Legend of Lies* appears to be an invention. Tysefew seems to imply here that *Euphues* and chivalric romances are feminocentric books which give women ideas above their station, and that such ideas are as unreal and absurd as the fictions themselves.

RICH'S *FAREWELL TO MILITARY PROFESSION*, 1581

The presentation of Barnaby Rich's collection of romances emulates Lyly in having a prefatory address to gentlewomen which is both insinuating and disdainful, ending 'And thus (gentlewomen) wishyng to you all, what your selves do best like of'.[13] As in *Euphues and his England*, the affectation of compliment to female readers is offset by a juxtaposed alternative preface to male readers; and integral to the claim that the work is women's reading is its characterisation as a trifle, composed 'at a vacant tyme . . . onely to keepe my self from Idelnesse' (*Farewell*, p. 10).

Rich goes somewhat beyond Lyly's courtly *ennui* and playfulness, however, in the degree of bitterness which he expresses at being reduced to such pointless literary activity. He does not bother to claim that he is mingling profit with pleasure; his stories are presented as mere entertainments which elicit contempt from their own author, who wishes that his stories 'might as well please thee in the reading, as thei displease me in puttyng them forthe' (p. 19). This self-disdain is produced by the specific professional frame for Rich's pose of prodigality, as stated in his title: he had served as a soldier in Ireland, and had previously written on military subjects. His preface to male readers is directed 'To the noble Souldiours bothe of Englande and Irelande' (p. 9), and informs his comrades that he had intended to write more on military history and theory, 'But I see the tyme serves not for any suche thyng to be accoumpted of. And therefore to fitte the tyme the better, I have put forthe these lovyng Histories' (p. 10).

Lyly had already implied that his fiction was designed to suit a decadent age, in which women 'pick out those that can court you, not those that love you . . . A plain tale of faith you laugh at, a picked discourse of fancy you marvel at, condemning the simplicity of truth and preferring the singularity of deceit.'[14] As we have seen, this supposed decadence was conveniently personified by imagined gentlewomen readers and their preoccupation with fashion and folly, but underlying this was a deeper concern that *men* had become too easily satisfied with style over substance, with 'finer cloth than is wrought of wool'.[15] Rich similarly uses his projected relationship with a constructed female readership as a means of distilling larger concerns about the effeminisation of men. The implicit satire against female romance-readers in the epistle to women is balanced by the critique in the epistle to soldiers of *men* who

> now adaies goe aboute by as great devise as maie bee, how thei might become women theimselves. How many Gentlemen shall you see at this present daie, that I dare undertake, in the wearyng of their apparell, in the settyng of their Ruffes, and the freselyng of their heire, are more new fangeled and foolishe, then any curtisan of Venice. (*Farewell*, p. 10)

Rich illustrates this at length with an anecdote of an encounter on the Strand with a fop whom he at first mistook for a woman (pp. 10–12). Similarly the *Farewell* ends with a 'Conclusion' which includes a story about a fashion-obsessed woman called Mildred, but opens with a lengthy critique of the extreme and ephemeral fashions 'that many of our yong Gentlemen useth now adaies', such as long frizzled hair which makes them look like water spaniels, ruffs like cartwheels and sleeves which dangle into their food (pp. 204–5).

Both imagined romance-reading gentlewomen and male followers of fashion serve to personify the general emasculation of society. Rich makes courtly profession in the epistle to women that 'I see now it is lesse painfull to followe a Fiddle in a gentlewoman's chamber: th[a]n to marche after a Drumme in the feeld' (pp. 3–4). His apparently genial acceptance of this role-change is swiftly unmasked in the epistle to soldiers, where he asks his comrades, 'to speake a plaine truthe in deede, doe ye not see, Pipers, Parysites, Fidlers, Dauncers, Plaiers, Jesters, and suche others, better esteemed and made of . . . then to any others' (p. 9). His prefatory manoeuvres are revealed as a polemic against the fact that 'the Militarie profession, by meanes whereof menne were advaunced to the greatest renowne, is now become of so slender estimation, that there is no accompt neither made of it, nor any that shall professe it' (pp. 12–13). Rich makes clear that he is concerned not only about the lack of respect accorded to individual soldiers returning from the wars, but about the nation's general lack of vigour in self-defence and overseas military action. He points out that 'the Frenche hath ever been our enemies by Nature. The Scottes by custome. The Spanyardes for Religion . . . then wee come to the Pope, the Turke, and the Devill, and what frendship thei beare us, I thinke every one can imagine' (pp. 16–17). England has survived only because of the amazing grace of God.

God is to be thanked 'moste of all and especially, for our moste gracious and Soveraigne Ladie Queene Elizabeth', whom Rich proceeds to praise for the length of a full page (pp. 17–18). This might look like a surprising turn: surely Elizabeth is the person most to blame for the nation's lack of military aggression, in her pragmatic and abstemious foreign policy, and for the effeminisation of society and culture, as a presiding female monarch? Juliet Fleming reads the anxiety about effeminisation in the framing devices of the *Farewell* as generated by an underlying anxiety about subservience to Elizabeth's female power. On this reading, Rich's praise of the Queen would be entirely ironic: Fleming compares Rich's *Alarm to England*

(1581), where, on the subject of Irish policy, 'pretending to praise Elizabeth for her mercy, for the "wholesome" laws which she tried to instigate in her colony, and for the leniency of her lieutenant Sir Henry Sidney, Rich described the disastrous effects of such gentle policy, and strongly advised its abandonment'.[16] In the *Farewell*, however, Rich praises Elizabeth principally for the true Protestant godliness of her rule: she has liberated the nation from the 'tyrannie' of her sister Mary's reign, 'made open waie and passage, for the worde of God freely to be published', and overcome the 'treasons and privie conspiracies' of 'our peltyng Papistes', all of which proves that she is God's agent. Like his forerunner Lyly, Rich may be seen as sincerely praising Elizabeth in so far as she is the figurehead of nation and Church, while at the same time implying criticism of her as an individual whose femaleness entails deficiency. He describes how Mary Tudor and her government feared that Elizabeth 'should bee that Judith, whiche should cut of proude Holofernes his hedde'; Rich would clearly like Elizabeth to be the warrior-woman who decapitates the beast of Rome, but is purposefully vague as to whether she has yet fulfilled this role. He ends with a prayer for God to preserve Elizabeth and give good direction to her council, at once seeming to detach Elizabeth from blame for inadequate policy, while simultaneously using juxtaposition to implant the idea of her responsibility (*Farewell*, pp. 17–18).

These concerns in the frames of the *Farewell* carry over into the content of the stories. The first tale, 'Sappho Duke of Mantona', opens in a country where soldiers are forgotten in favour of the familiar procession of 'Dauncers, Pipers, Fidlers . . . suche as can devise to please women, with newe fangles [and] straunge fassions' (p. 24). In the fifth story, 'Of two brethren and their wives', Mistress Doritie has three lovers, of whom the most successful is a plain-speaking soldier, who ousts a smooth-tongued doctor and lawyer. This carries through Rich's own supposed courtship of women in his preface to them, where, like Shakespeare's Henry V who woos Princess Katherine by telling her that he can only 'speak to thee plain soldier' (v.ii.132–68), he regrets his inability to 'discourse pleasauntly to drive awaie the tyme, with amourous devises, or . . . to propone pretie questions, or to give readie aunsweres' (*Farewell*, pp. 6–7).

Indeed, where Lyly creates a fictional feminine world of a courtly kind through the use of *questioni d'amore*, Rich's novellas, even while using fantastical romance motifs like shipwrecks in strange lands and miraculous reunions, tend to be more domestic in setting, and foreground the feminine through a persistent emphasis on marriage. Many of the tales concern loving couples who are obstructed from matrimony by disparity in rank and the avarice of parents. Rich appears to be opposed to marriages based on the pursuit of wealth and status and in favour of heroines who defy parents to make their own marriage-choices. In the first story Valeria, a duke's daughter, elopes with the humble Silvanus, 'contented rather to live in the fellowship of an honest lovyng housebande . . . then to live without hym, beautified with the graces and foolishe names of honour and preheminence' (p. 46). She tells him that 'without any regard to the obedience and duetie that I owe to my Parentes I am yours' (p. 45). Her judgement that he is a worthy suitor is vindicated when, in typical romance fashion, he turns out to be a duke's son, and her father's vitriolic abuse of her as a 'filthie strumpet' is swiftly converted to smiling embraces and paternal blessings (pp. 60, 64–5). Not unlike Jane Austen, Rich at once criticises those who marry for money, yet bestows financial rewards upon those who hold out for love. A counter-case is the sixth tale, 'Of Gonsales and his virtuous wife Agatha', in which Agatha's relatives congratulate themselves on having arranged her marriage to wealthy Gonsales even though they know him to be of an unreliable character. The outcome is that he attempts to murder Agatha to please his courtesan, 'a notable example for women to learne how little it is to their commoditie or quiet, to matche them selves to suche, that be rather riche then wise: and how muche it were better for them to bee married to men, then to their goodes' (p. 149).

As in Sharon Stockton's reading of Pettie (see p. 53 above), Rich's commendations of disobedient daughters who marry for merit can be read as primarily promoting the social mobility of deserving and ambitious young men, to which the autonomy of women is merely coincident. Certainly once women become wives it is their unswerving fidelity which is valued. Agatha restores her husband to virtue and herself to his love by remaining utterly constant to him through such trials as the approaches of a more loving suitor and her husband's attempted murder of her; she even saves him from the death-sentence by pleading his cause. In the seventh story, 'Of Aramanthus born a leper', King Rodericke believes false accusations of adultery against his pregnant wife Isabell and sends her into exile, but when he is overthrown and imprisoned by the Turks she leaves her baby and returns in disguise to help him. In a graphic image of female nurturance, she comes to his prison each night, where 'She would leane her self cloase to the grate, and thrustyng in her Teate betwene the Irons, the kyng learned againe to sucke, and thus she dieted him a long season' (p. 175).

Because of Queen Isabell's disguise, 'Neither wiste the kyng what she was, that bestowed on hym so greate grace and goodnesse: yet he blessed her more then a thousande tymes a daie.' While his companions in prison die for lack of sustenance, his gaolers observe him miraculously growing in strength from his unseen nightly 'banquettes'. The episode has much of the resonance of mediaeval iconographies of the Virgin sustaining adult believers with her milk.[17] One means by which satisfactory outcomes are achieved in Rich's narratives is the exercise of outstanding virtue by his heroines which attracts saintly iconography. Thus in the sixth story Agatha's remarkable constancy to her utterly undeserving husband first converts her suitor Alonso from attempting to seduce her, then becomes a neo-Platonic touchstone which converts him to general virtue: her 'chaste and constant minde, caused *Alonso* where before he loved her for her exterior beautie, ever after to reverence her, and in maner to worship her as a divine creature, for the excellencie of her vertue' (p. 165).

In the case of an unmarried woman, however, saintly virtue can be invoked in pursuit of a cause which is secular and even frankly erotic. The third story, 'Of Nicander and Lucilla', inverts the usual courtship problem in that the hero's father opposes his marriage to the heroine on the grounds of *her* poverty: 'the vertues of the women doe not enriche the houses wherein thei came (saied he) but the qualitie of gooddes and wealthe, that thei brought with them' (p. 90). When Lucilla attracts the attentions of the Duke's son, Don Hercules, he considers her only as a potential mistress and not a wife because of her lowliness. Lucilla's virtue is indicated by such detail as her habit of dressing in white (p. 90), and her reaction to Don Hercules's advances of withdrawing from public view except for her outings to church (p. 91). When Don Hercules gains access to her bedchamber and has her at his mercy the images of virgin sanctity reach a crescendo: she tells Don Hercules that if she cannot marry Nicander and offer him her virginity 'as pure and unspotted as I brought it from my mothers wombe', then she will 'vowe me wholie unto almightie GOD, and in his service to spende my daies a virgine, in continual Fastyng and Praier' (pp. 100–1). Yet as with the heroines of the Iberian romances, all this iconography of chaste martyrdom is ironically dedicated to the cause of achieving union with the lover of her own choice. This she does in what is in effect a conversion scene, where the blazing purity of her love convinces Don Hercules not to rape her but instead to give her a dowry to marry Nicander. The scene is echoed in the fourth story, where Fiamma's eloquent profession of her love for Fineo persuades the King of Tunis not only to release her from his harem but to bestow upon the couple a sumptuous wedding feast and 'very riche and costly presentes' to take home with them (p. 119). The infidel King is converted not to Christianity but to belief in true love. Faith in love is attributed with the traditional miraculous powers of religious faith; and the outcome of both stories is that the trials of the heroines earn for the young men marriage to virtuous and well-endowed brides whose proven constancy in love ensures that they will be chaste wives.

One specific form of the adaptation of hagiographic motifs to the service of erotic love is the use of male disguise by women. In the *Golden Legend*, the mediaeval anthology of saints' lives, the saints Marina, Theodora, Eugenia and Margaret (also known as Pelagia) had all adopted male dress in the cause of Christian virtue.[18] Their stories circulated in England in various forms through the Middle Ages, including William Caxton's 1483 translation of the *Golden Legend*. In two of Rich's stories the heroine's determination to be united with her chosen lover extends as far as the adoption of male disguise. The second story, 'Of Apolonius and Silla', is a source for *Twelfth Night*; Silla, the equivalent of Viola, is driven by her unrequited passion for Duke Apolonius to voyage to his court, where she dresses as a boy and serves him as a page. Like Saints Marina, Theodora and Margaret she is charged with paternity by a pregnant woman. In the eighth story Emelia, to evade marriage to the aged Phylotus, escapes from her father's house disguised as a boy and elopes with her lover Flanius, an episode which very probably served as a source for Jessica's elopement in *The Merchant of Venice*. In both cases the male disguise invokes a sense that, just as mediaeval saints would run to extremities in the cause of holiness, so these women will do the same for love, in a particular form of the iconography of erotic sainthood. At the same time, it adds a degree of raciness to the narrative: the counter-case to the female saint disguised as a man was Pope Joan, whose story was told by Boccaccio in *De Claris Mulieribus* (1355–9). Her adventures began when she donned male disguise to follow her lover on his travels but culminated in her election to Pope, impregnation and giving birth in public on the papal throne.[19] A cross-dressed eloping daughter always carried the frisson of potentially ending up in some similarly scandalous state. Moreover, the adoption of male disguise highlighted the alliance of interests between subjected daughters and prodigal young men, both of them socially frustrated and marginalised and the antagonists of father-figures.

In Emelia's story cross-dressing also works the other way, as her brother Philerno, in a spirit of 'disporte' (*Farewell*, p. 188), substitutes himself for her at her betrothal to Phylotus, and goes to live at Phylotus's house as the supposed bride-to-be for the period of wedding preparations. Philerno's adoption of female clothing can be seen as another way in which the gender-concerns of the *Farewell*'s prefaces carry over into its narratives; like Rich as author, Philerno submits to be temporarily effeminised to suit the expediencies of the moment. The purpose to which he puts his feminine disguise, however, is the exercise of virility: as Phylotus's betrothed, but not yet his bride, he is assigned to sleep with Phylotus's daughter, Brisilla, whom he naturally seduces. Rich and Lyly as authors of romances similarly claim to be effeminising themselves in order to gain libidinous opportunity, insinuating themselves into a female genre and into private spaces of female reading where they can woo their audience of women. Indeed, Philerno himself tells stories to win over Brisilla. Still posing as Emelia, he tells Brisilla that 'her' own wedding to Brisilla's father is in fact to be a double ceremony in which Brisilla will be married to Emelia's father. 'Emelia' expresses womanly commiseration and wishes that their joint plight could be solved by one of them being transformed into a fit mate for the other. 'She' alludes to Ovid's *Metamorphoses*, then tells a story of a potentially tragic predicament which was resolved when a goddess transformed a woman into a man, then 'herself' prays to the goddess Venus and – hey presto! – reveals 'herself' to have been conveniently metamorphosed. The two bedfellows, we are told, pass the time very contentedly until the wedding day.

In commiserating with Brisilla about the plight of daughters married off to wealthy old men against their will, Philerno gives voice to protofeminist concerns; yet these are diffused by dramatic irony, since we the readers know that he is really a man attempting seduction. This falls in with a pattern in Renaissance literature of eloquently inviting sympathy for women in positions of social oppression only to disperse that sympathy through comic or sensational situation, thus evading the question of whether society ought to change. Examples include Adriana in Shakespeare's *Comedy of Errors*, whose moving and lengthy exposition of her griefs as the wife of an adulterous husband is reduced to a joke by the fact that she is addressing her husband's unknown and baffled twin who has never seen her before in his life (II.ii.110–51); and Isabella in Thomas Middleton's *Women Beware Women*, who equally movingly complains of being a daughter forced into marriage to a wealthy fool, but falls from this into an incestuous affair with her uncle.[20] As Philerno's story goes forward, he goes through with the wedding to Phylotus, then on the wedding night refuses to sleep with his husband until they have debated who is to have the upper hand in the marriage. Again Philerno gives voice to wives who are constrained to be obedient to old men far removed from them in interests and temperament. However, he wins the debate through sheer physical violence, in a fashion most women were unlikely to be able to achieve: he 'gettes *Phylotus* faste by the graie bearde, and by plaine force pulles hym doune on the flo[o]r, and so bepomels hym aboute the face, that he was like to have been strangled with his owne bloud' (*Farewell*, p. 196). The stunned Phylotus readily grants him 'what superioritie you please' (p. 197). Any sympathy with the plight of young wives is diffused by the slapstick comedy of a 'wife' beating up her husband like this, and by satisfaction at a smug old man getting his come-uppance from a cleverer and stronger younger man. The rights of women are raised only as a by-product of comic purposes and of a narrative of a young man's ingenuity and success.

Similarly, in the story 'Of two brethren and their wives', Doritie's soldier-lover speaks a defence of women in rebuttal of the misogynistic diatribes penned against her by her spurned lovers, the doctor and the lawyer. However, his conventional eulogy of women as 'moste pure and perfecte creatures . . . the storehouse of all grace vertue and goodnesse', and so on (p. 134), is severely undermined by our sense that he is only feeling so kindly disposed towards women because he has been more successful than the other men in securing Doritie's adulterous favours. Just as Euphues's misogyny is produced by his rejection by Lucilla, so here it seems clear that the praise and vilification of women alike are generated by personal experience of success or the lack of it in love; and that each is one side of a debate which is merely rhetorical and conventional. Women are objects of rhetoric whose nature shifts, and can indeed become diametrically opposed, depending on the angle from which they are beheld. This is foregrounded in the letter which the doctor writes to Doritie, 'whiche letter he left unpointed [i.e. unpunctuated] of purpose, because that in the readyng of it, it might bee poincted two waies, and made to seeme either to her praise or dispraise' (p. 130). For instance, one section may be read: 'I have ever taken you to be given in your conditions to practise unseemely, filthie, and detestable thynges: I knowe you have ever abhorred to live chastly, decently, and orderly' (p. 131). Or it may be read: 'consideryng how I have ever taken taken you to be given in your conditions: to practise unseemely, filthie, and detestable thinges, I knowe you have ever abhorred: To live chastlie, decentlie, and orderlie, you have ever bin trained up', and so on (p. 137). Rich is not impressed by such pliable rhetoric; Doritie immediately sees through the doctor's 'knaverie' (p. 138), and she and the soldier devise and execute a revenge which physically discomforts and humiliates both doctor and lawyer. The doctor carries out of town on his back a pack which he believes conceals Doritie but in fact contains the lawyer. The practical ingenuity of the soldier and Doritie triumphs over the professional representatives of rhetorical facility.

The lawyer's splenetic letter to Doritie, condemning all women as '*Cressides* kinde' who would spend all their time on sex 'if thei were not afeard of breedyng of bugges in their beallie', prompts an authorial apology to gentlewomen readers for 'the blasphemie that he had used against your sexe' (pp. 132–3). In the first story, too, the authorial narrator's own invective against an age which favours only 'suche as can devise to please women' is swiftly followed by an apology to gentlewomen for falling into a 'railyng rage' (p. 24). Euphues also ends his 'Cooling card to Philautus' with a mollification of 'grave matrons, and honest maidens'.[21] Such interventions may be read either as devices to sustain the fiction that each author was writing to please women, or as indications that they indeed expected or hoped to find some popularity with women readers. Strikingly, though, at a key point where Rich might have given a portrait of a 'typical' woman reader, he omits to do so. Emelia attempts to conform to her father's insistence that she marry

Phylotus by imagining the benefits of life as a wealthy wife. An extremely vivid and detailed description is given of her imagined day, rising with a cup of malmsey, overseeing the house and spending the afternoon on needlework to make herself fine ruffs, gorgets, sleeves and coifs. She would be a woman of fashion and of leisure: 'she should not neede to beate her braines aboute the practising of housewiferie, but should have servauntes at commaundment to supplie that tourne' (*Farewell*, pp. 184–5). Yet at no point in this day does Emelia imagine passing the time by reading a romance.

At some points in *Euphues* women are positively urged *not* to read romances: in the 'Glass for Europe' they are exhorted to eschew 'Ariosto or Petrarch or any book that liketh you best and becometh you worst' in favour of the Scriptures (*Euphues*, pp. 426–7). This would presumably entail laying down Lyly's own idle book. Indeed, addressing his male audience, Euphues asserts that he has learned 'as the chief argument of my faith: that idleness is the only nurse and nourisher of sensual appetite, the sole maintenance of youthful affection, the first shaft that Cupid shooteth into the hot liver of a heedless lover . . . The man being idle, the mind is apt to all uncleanness' (*Euphues*, p. 98). This may be compared with the grumpy ending of Rich's volume: 'I can no more, but wishe that Gentlemen leavyng suche superficiall follies, would rather indevour themselves in other exercises, that might be much more beneficiall to their Countrey, and a greate deale better to their owne reputation, and thus an ende. FINIS' (*Farewell*, p. 211). Both books instruct us not to waste our time on such books; but the prodigal paradox is that we have to read these books to learn this. In both cases the wittily self-reflexive and self-undermining effect pivots upon the ironic and perspective-shifting depiction of women. There is further irony in the fact that Rich dedicated more of his works to women than any other author – six – though this may be attributed to the fact that he lived for an unusually long time (1542–1617) and was unusually prolific (twenty-six books in forty-three years).[22]

ROBERT GREENE, 'THE HOMER OF WOMEN'

Comments about Robert Greene's works make it appear that he was pre-eminently the writer of the 1580s who wrote for women and found favour with women. Thomas Nashe called him 'the *Homer* of

Women',[23] and an elegy for him lamented that: 'He is dead, that wrote of your delights: / That wrote of Ladies, and of Parramours.'[24] As well as the *Mirror of Knighthood*, the chambermaid in the 1615 edition of Overbury's *Characters* 'reads *Greenes* workes over and over' (sig. ¶4v). In Ben Jonson's *Every Man Out of his Humour* (1599), when Fastidious Brisk praises Sariolina because 'she does observe as pure a phrase and use as choice figures as any be i'the *Arcadia*', Carlo Buffone more sceptically remarks in an aside, 'Or rather in Greene's works, whence she may steal with more security', a reference to Greene's prolific output and his own plagiarising tendencies.[25]

In fact Greene published some fifteen works of fiction between 1580 and 1590, addressing a variety of readerships and in a range of genres, including imitations of *Euphues*, novellas, pastoral romances, cony-catching pamphlets and repentance pamphlets in which he repudiated his fictions as follies.[26] *Pandosto, the Triumph of Time*, his pastoral romance of around 1585, was one work which came to be seen as especially popular with maidservants, perhaps because of its wish-fulfilment plot of a humble maiden who wins the love of a prince and turns out to be a princess after all.[27] As the source for *The Winter's Tale*, this will be given fuller discussion in my chapter on Shakespeare. Other works by Greene which might appear to bear out his reputation as the chief author for women are part II of *Mamillia* (1583?), and *Penelope's Web* (1587).

Mamillia follows the pattern of *Euphues* in having a first part which was dedicated to gentlemen readers as 'a toy to passe away the time',[28] and a second part which appeared to address more feminine concerns. Part II carried prefatory verses by Richard Stapleton directed 'to the Curteous and Courtly Ladies of England', which place Greene in a tradition of debate about women as the refuter of attacks on them by Euripides, Mantuan, Juvenal and Martial (*Mamillia*, pp. 146–8). He:

> plainly proves by reasons rule
>   that everie Authors clause,
> Which rashly railes of womankinde
>   comes more of spight then cause.

Greene is presented as going to battle in the cause of women, one possible source for Nashe's '*Homer* of women' remark:

> champion like he chalenge makes,
>   with Ladie Pallas shield,

To stand in armes against your foes
in open camped field.

Part I contained numerous asides to gentlemen readers, such as 'surely Gentlemen . . . there is no such hinderaunce to a man, as a wife'.[29] However, as these go on they become more critical of men's inconstancy,[30] and in part II the author turns to address women as well as men. At one point he protests 'I cannot passe over without some speech, gentelwomen, the incomparable constancie of *Mamillia*', which, along with the virtues of 'a thousand other ladies' form 'perfect presidentes [precedents] against those unjust pratlers, which seeke like sicophants to discredit womens constancie' (pp. 162–3). Praise of women's constancy – which, on the title page of *Mamillia* II, the book is said to 'canonise' – hardly constitutes a radical advocacy of women's interests, but rather a compromise between a positive portrayal of women which they might enjoy and a conformity to conventional patriarchal standards of feminine virtue. Greene is by no means prepared to argue that it is as acceptable for women to be inconstant in love as men. Indeed, he keeps an eye on a male readership: 'I hope whatsoever the envious crue shall crow against me for defending the loyaltie of women, vertuous and wel disposed gentlemen will neither appeach me of flattery, nor condemne me of folly' (p. 173).

Penelope's Web (1587) provides another reason for Greene to be called 'the *Homer* of women': in his dedication to Margaret and Anne Clifford, he apologises for his lack of Homer's eloquence,[31] highlighting the fact that he is writing of what Penelope and her ladies did while Ulysses was away – the distaff-side of the Trojan war, as it were. However, as discussed at pp. 11–12 above, Greene's claim to tell the women's side of the story is presented in a preface to male readers as offering men the opportunity to eavesdrop on 'womens prattle' and 'pry into *Venus* papers' (*Penelope's Web*, pp. 144–5); that is, to be made privy to what women say about love behind closed doors. Again, he is hardly a radical advocate of women's interests, offering them exemplary stories with such introductions as this:

I cannot thinke (quoth *Penelope*) that there is any husband so bad which the honest government [i.e. behaviour] of his wife may not in time refourme, especially if she keepe those three speciall poynts that are requisite in every woman, Obedience, Chastitie, and Silence . . . because my mayds are young, and may in tyme trye the fortune of mariage, we will this night discourse of this poynt, to discover the effects and efficacie of Obedience

. . . that both we may beguyle the night with prattle, and profite our mynds by some good and vertuous precepts. (p. 162)

As discussed at pp. 30–1 above, it would be anachronistic to assume that Renaissance women found examples of silence, chastity and obedience as unappealing as we tend to find them today. Having, to some degree or another, internalised patriarchal definitions of feminine virtue, it may well be that they found examples of female strength within these terms highly acceptable as models of female heroism. Certainly women writers who entered the fray of the pamphlet debate about the nature and role of women tended to restate the existence of dutiful wives and chaste matrons rather than challenge the terms of the debate.[32] Thus Greene may be seen as both using supposedly entertaining texts for women to indoctrinate them in patriarchal standards, and at the same time providing versions of female heroism which women readers may indeed have enjoyed as satisfactory compromises between the attractions of female strength and the conventions of feminine propriety. Simultaneously, a male audience is consistently addressed in parallel and invited into a supposedly feminine space of fiction to enjoy light entertainment and voyeuristic opportunity. The fact that Greene's supposed championing of women's cause was merely a transitory rhetorical pose is demonstrated by his authorship of *Alcida* in 1588, the year after *Penelope's Web*, which inverted the themes of the prior text to describe women's three chief vices of pride, inconstancy and prattle; and of *Orpharion*, 1590, which balanced praise and satire of women.[33]

CRITIQUES OF IDLE FICTIONS

The claims of 1580s fiction writers to be producing idle toys did not go unnoticed by commentators. Puritans were predictably immune to the pleasures of ironic playfulness. Among the objects of Phillip Stubbes's spleen in *The Anatomy of Abuses* (1583) were leisured gentlewomen who disport themselves in secluded pleasure gardens where they 'plaie the filthie persons' (fo. 48r–v); and stage-plays which 'nourishe Idlenesse . . . and . . . *Idlenesse is the mother of vice*' (fo. 90v). Accordingly he laments the fact that 'good bookes [are] little or nothyng to be reverenced: whilest other toyes, fantasies, and bableries, wherof the world is ful, are suffered to be printed. These prophane Schedules, sacrilegious Libels, and hethnicall Pamphlets of toyes and bableries . . . corrupt mens mindes, pervert good wittes, allure to bawdrie, induce to Whoredome, suppresse Vertue, and erect Vice' (fos.120v–121v). Prodigal authors' own terms could readily be turned against them.

A very different kind of writer, Thomas Nashe, also turned prodigal self-characterisations into an attack, but he speaks not from the position of a Puritan ideologue like Stubbes but from that of a fellow prodigal of superior wit and intellect. The year before describing Greene disparagingly as 'the *Homer* of women', Nashe had made his literary debut in a lengthy prefatory epistle for one of Greene's own works, *Menaphon*, a pastoral romance which appears to have been influenced by Sidney's as yet unpublished *Arcadia* (see p. 145 below). This preface is in effect an essay on the current state of English literature. It is addressed 'To the Gentlemen students of both Universities', and commends Greene as a writer of wit distinct from 'our unexperienst punies' for whom 'a tale of Jhon a Brainfords will, and the unluckie furmentie [a rustic beverage], wilbe as soon interteined into their libraries, as the best poeme that ever *Tasso* eternisht'.[34] By 1590, however, Nashe's division between high and low culture placed Greene on the side of the low, specifically because of his proclaimed affinity with women. The full title of the text in which the '*Homer* of women' remark occurred was *The Anatomie of Absurditie: Contayning a breefe confutation of the slender imputed prayses to feminine perfection, with a short description of the severall practises of youth, and sundry follies of our licentious times* (1590).

In this work Nashe's literary critique begins by attacking 'booke-mungers' who try 'to imitate a fresh . . . those worne out impressions of the feyned no where acts, of Arthur of the rounde table, Arthur of litle Brittaine, sir Tristram, Hewon of Burdeaux, the Squire of low degree, the foure sons of Amon, with infinite others' (sig. A2r). These were the still-popular mediaeval chivalric romances which were increasingly associated with lower-class readers.[35] Nashe swiftly moves from these examples of culturally worthless fictions to complain that many contemporary authors 'to be more amiable with their friends of the Feminine sexe, blot many sheetes of paper in the blazing of Womens slender praises' (*Anatomie*, sig. A2r). It is here that he attacks 'the *Homer* of women' for having mounted a refutation of Mantuan's antifeminist critique.

Nashe strikes a contrary pose of flagrant misogyny, from which it is presumably to be inferred that he is intellectual and *avant garde*.

This extends from his dedication, which personifies Absurdity as feminine and describes women as 'the *Iliads* of evils to all Nations' (sigs. ¶3r–¶4v), through to an extensive exposition of the licentiousness and lustfulness of women (sigs. A3v–B1v). Significantly, women are especially reviled for idleness and pleasure-seeking:

> if the temperature of the wether will not permitte them to pop into the open ayre, a payre of cardes better pleaseth her then [i.e. than] a peece of cloth, her beades then her booke, a bowle of wine then a handful of wooll, delighting more in a daunce then in *Davids* Psalmes, to play with her dogge then to pray to her God: setting more by a love letter, then the lawe of the Lord. (sig. B1v)

Those who praise women are regarded as contaminated with the same idleness: 'Peradventure they thinke . . . by compiling of Pamphlets in their Mistresse praises, to be called the restorers of womankind. But idle heads are usually occupied about such trifling texts, wanton wits are combred with those wonted fittes, such busie braines sowe where they reape small gaines' (sig. B2r). Of course this was to take up, and turn around against them, exactly the terms which those who claimed to write for women had applied to themselves, characterising themselves as consigned to, yet making the most of, the world of idleness, constructed as the world of women. Ironically Nashe himself strikes a similarly prodigal pose at the opening of his text: 'I, having laide aside my graver studies for a season, determined with my selfe beeing idle in the Countrey, to beginne in this vacation, the foundation of a trifling subject, which might shroude in his leaves, the abusive enormities of these our times' (sig. A1r). This differs, though, from the self-characterisations of his prodigal colleagues in implying that his period of idleness is only temporary, a 'vacation' from which he will return refreshed to 'graver studies', and that he is putting even this period of idleness and this playful text to profitable use as a critique of the current state of society and culture. Accordingly Nashe departs from the practice of other authors of supposed trifles in more overtly stating the case against idleness and folly, which entails stating the case against women who now conventionally personify these categories. Yet the paradox remains that he takes this stance in a self-proclaimed 'idle' text, shrouding profit in the leaves of playfulness.

Nashe travels further along this tangent from 1580s fictions in his most well-known work, *The Unfortunate Traveller* (1594), a prose fiction which continues the mode of prodigality and playfulness but does so in a fashion which is distinctively clever, knowing and self-conscious, and resolutely masculine. Women and their virtue are treated throughout with blatant cynicism, and the sole example of a pure woman, Heraclide, is subjected to a rape at once so brutal and so farcical that it constitutes an act of literary iconoclasm against the conventional figure of the chaste and saintly heroine. The work as a whole is related to romance in its historical, martial setting and its picaresque structure, but is clearly an ironical revision of the genre's conventions. Central to this is its refusal of any veneration of heroines, appeal to women readers, or claims by the author or the narrator to have succumbed to feminine standards. Nashe, then, acknowledges the generic femininity of romance even in the vigour of his reaction against it.

CHAPTER 6

The 'Arcadia': readership and authorship

FEMALE READERS OF THE TWO *ARCADIAS*

The self-representations of 1570s and 1580s prose-fiction-writers as delinquents from duty are shared by the prefatory epistle to Sir Philip Sidney's *Arcadia.* This was first printed with the quarto *New Arcadia* in 1590 but composed to accompany the earlier manuscript version known as the *Old Arcadia,* written in 1577–80.[1] It is one of the most striking examples of an Elizabethan fiction-author's self-construction as effeminised by his sojourn in the world of romance. In the first place, the epistle is addressed to Sidney's sister Mary Herbert, whose patronage is even more loudly proclaimed in the work's full title, *The Countess of Pembroke's Arcadia.* Most of the work was probably composed while Sidney was staying at the Countess's seat of Wilton, having incurred disfavour at court by criticising the Queen's proposed marriage to the Duke of Anjou; he was therefore himself enjoying a pastoral retreat from public duties just as were his heroes within the fiction itself. The very first sentence of the epistle declares the romance to be an 'idle work'; later it is described as 'but a trifle, and that triflingly handled', fit only to be read by Mary at 'idle times'.[2] Just as Lyly, Rich, Nashe and others associated idleness with the milieu of women, so does Sidney, but with less satire and more affection. His sister, repeatedly addressed as 'dear', is represented not only as the work's ideal imagined reader, but as its commissioner, inspiration, editor and perhaps even contributing author: 'you desired me to do it . . . it is done only for you, only to you . . . Your dear self can best witness the manner, being done in loose sheets of paper, most of it in your presence, the rest by sheets sent unto you as fast as they were done' (*OA*, p. 3).

Various kinds of feminine imagery are deployed. Lyly's comparison of his own *Euphues and his England* to fashionable but soon-worn-out linen and hat-trimmings is paralleled by Sidney's plea to his sister to look in his fiction 'for no better stuff than, as in a haberdasher's shop, glasses or feathers'. He also characterises his work as a baby fit only to be abandoned, and, while describing himself as its father, adopts a specifically female metaphor of childbirth: his 'young head . . . having many fancies begotten in it, if it had not been in some way delivered, would have grown a monster'.[3] Such imagery may have been given added resonance by the fact that during the period of most intensive work on the *Old Arcadia*, at Wilton in the spring and summer of 1580, Mary Herbert was herself undergoing the final months of pregnancy and the birth of her first child, William, on 8 April.[4] Her brother's 'pregnancy' is courteously implied to be less successful and fruitful than her own.

The Countess of Pembroke is set up in this dedicatory epistle as the ideal reader, and perhaps the only reader ever, of this manuscript text: 'for severer eyes it is not', and she is urged to 'keep it to yourself, or to such friends who will weigh errors in the balance of goodwill' (*OA*, p. 3). However, as with the terms of other authorial prefaces, we may take it that there is a degree of rhetorical exaggeration here. In 1580 Sidney wrote to his brother Robert promising to send a copy of 'My toyful book', the *Old Arcadia*;[5] we may assume that, as with other authors of prose fiction, the choice of a female dedicatee was not unconnected to the idea of 'toyfulness', even as other, male readers were expected. It has become well understood in recent years that manuscript circulation could itself constitute a form of publication, and the *Old Arcadia* certainly did circulate, possibly in dozens of copies: Sidney's close friend, Fulke Greville, in a letter of 1586, the year of Sidney's death, judged the revised or *New Arcadia* to be 'fitter to be printed then that first', presumably the *Old Arcadia*, 'which is so common'.[6] The function of the Countess, then, as addressed not only at the front of the *Old Arcadia* but also at the front of the *New Arcadia* as published in print after Sidney's death, is an emblematic one: to stand for every reader, and to direct every reader in how to read and in what kind of text to expect. We must read in a way which is femininely tolerant, sisterly and intimately complicit in the creation of a private world of imagination and pleasure.[7]

A tone of femininity and privacy is sustained into the text by repeated addresses to 'fair ladies'.[8] Already the supposed lone reader, the Countess of Pembroke, has multiplied into a group of lady readers, presumably a circle of friends and ladies-in-waiting over whom she presides. However, this maintains the enclosed and secluded feel of a feminine coterie, like the élite circle of witty courtiers in Castiglione and his emulators, but even more dominated by women. Indeed the direct address by the author to a group of ladies constructs the text in simulatedly oral form as a Castiglione-style dialogue or game of *questioni d'amore*: he sits in the circle, weaving the narrative for the ladies' entertainment. He offers tempting tastes of later narrative developments 'as you shall after *hear*'; at one point the words of Musidorus are reported as '*it is said* that' he spoke, hinting at an oral traditional source (my emphasis, *OA*, pp. 26, 269). The narrator occasionally interrupts himself to make wry asides directly to the ladies, in which he and they are assumed to have a shared interest in matters of love, and in which he semi-flirtatiously defers to their greater expertise: he is in difficulties in describing the immediate and consuming passion felt by Basilius and Gynecia, 'But you, worthy ladies, that have at any time feelingly known what it means, will easily believe the possibility of it' (*OA*, p. 44).

Thus the foregrounding of a female audience has the simultaneous effect of foregrounding the author. Partly this enables a self-conscious commentary on his own processes of composition: 'I might entertain you, fair ladies, a great while, if I should make as many interruptions in the repeating as [Cleophila] did in the singing' of a melancholy song (*OA*, p. 26; cf. p. 211). Partly it creates a tone of shared knowingness, sophistication and humour, especially in matters of love: as Gynecia expects the arrival of Pyrocles for an adulterous assignation, 'In what case poor Gynecia was when she knew the voice and felt the body of her husband, fair ladies, it is better to know by imagination than experience' (*OA*, p. 199). Overall, the general effect is to render the authorial 'I' almost a character in the fiction himself, close to the front of the text, with frequent use of such phrases as 'I know not whether', 'as I told you', 'I note this to myself, fair ladies', and so on (*OA*, pp. 45, 46, 49).

Yet this is a narrative technique which Sidney does not appear to have found consistently useful. The most frequent addresses to fair ladies are in Book 1; they disappear from Book 2, reappear a few times in Book 3, but remain absent from Books 4 and 5. When he revised his romance to produce the *New Arcadia*, in the years up to 1584,[9] he completely excised the addresses to the ladies, and with them most of the appearances of the self-conscious narrator. One interpretation of this is that the *Arcadia* was progressively developing into a different, in some ways more 'masculine' kind of book. For John Buxton, the *Old Arcadia* was a 'careless romance' written 'to please the ladies', but Sidney then had 'second thoughts'; as the *New Arcadia*, he recreated it as 'a heroic poem . . . in the cause of morality', better appreciated by Sidney's male soulmate Fulke Greville than by his sister and other lady readers.[10] In Book 2 of the revised *Arcadia*, greatly expanded by flashback narratives, we hear a good deal more not only of the epic deeds of the princes but also of their encounters with different systems of rule in different countries. The disappearance of lady readers even from parts of the *Old Arcadia* might then be seen as symptomatic that even at that stage the work was turning into something more serious, moral and political, as Books 4 and 5 begin to concern themselves more with matters of government and justice than with love.

This has been a fairly prevalent critical view: *Old Arcadia* private and feminine, *New Arcadia* more ambitious and public and therefore masculine. However, Blair Worden sees the *Old Arcadia* as not merely beginning to anticipate the political concerns of the *New*, but actually more political, such that the fair ladies are a 'decoy' to distract attention from potentially inflammatory material concerning government and topical concerns: 'Though Sidney's dedication honours his affection for his sister, its picture of a private family audience may be intended less to convey his purpose than to protect it.'[11] H. R. Woudhuysen concurs: 'There was much in what he wrote which was probably best kept out of sight of all except a limited audience.' The fact that he appears to have circulated his manuscripts among his siblings and friends, but not his parents or other older relations, may indicate that he regarded them less as playful and inconsequential than as potentially incriminating in their experimentalism and outspokenness.[12]

Despite the disappearance of the imagined lady readers, real female readers had if anything an increasing part in the publication history of the *New Arcadia*, both in terms of the editorial role of the Countess of Pembroke, and the perceived popularity of the text with women. Sidney does seem to have regarded his sister as one of the chief custodians of his literary works: there is evidence that he shared his working papers of the *Arcadia* with her, and it may be that she was responsible for having scribal transcripts of the *Old Arcadia* made both for her own retention and for her brother to use in making his revisions.[13] After his death she enhanced her role as his prime reader into that of his literary executor. Although the first printed edition of the *Arcadia*, the quarto *New Arcadia* of 1590, was edited by Fulke Greville, it used the title *The Countess of Pembroke's Arcadia* and included the dedicatory epistle, publicising even more widely Sidney's identification of his sister as his ideal interpreter. The Countess capitalised on this in publishing her own preferred version of the text in 1593. The prefatory epistle by Hugh Sanford, whom she employed as editor, criticised the 1590 edition as 'disfigured' and 'blemished', and blatantly appropriated the terms of Sidney's own dedication to enforce the supremacy of the Countess's text: 'it is now by more than one interest The Countess of Pembroke's Arcadia – done, as it was, for her; as it is, by her'. She has passed naturally from being its best reader to being its best editor and virtual co-author: the 1593 volume has been produced 'most by her doing, all by her directing'.[14] At the same time this adaptation of Sidney's own terms to represent the Countess as the saviour of her brother's text from public deformity and shame conceals any imputation that she has actually countermanded his wishes in more widely publicising a text which he had restricted to manuscript circulation.[15]

The Countess's 1593 *New Arcadia* removed Greville's 1590 interventions of chapter divisions and headings and rearrangements of the eclogues. However, the most radical difference between the editions was in their strategies for dealing with the problem that the *New Arcadia* broke off incomplete, and indeed mid-sentence, before the end of its third book. Whereas Greville published only the revised and expanded Books 1 to 3, the Countess added on the ending from the five-book *Old Arcadia*. This was far from a perfect fit, as acknowledged in Sanford's preface – it is 'the conclusion, not the perfection of Arcadia' – but he suggests that it is the nearest to Sidney's intentions that can be achieved in the author's absence (*NA*, pp. 59–60). The closing books of the *Old Arcadia* were themselves also revised for the 1593 edition in details which render the behaviour of the two heroes less morally ambiguous: Pyrocles's seduction of Philoclea at the end of Book 3 is translated into a chaste sleep side-by-side, and Musidorus's interrupted attempt to rape Pamela is omitted. In the past this provoked criticism of the Countess for prudishly bowdlerising her brother's text out of some excessive feminine modesty; the prevailing modern scholarly view, however, is that she was probably following her brother's own intentions as indicated before his death.[16] Whereas for John Buxton the Countess's edition was distorted by a mistaken persistence in seeing the *Arcadia* as a romance for ladies,[17] H. R. Woudhuysen has more recently characterised her as the more secular and sensuously minded of the two editors: Greville's 'rather pious view of Sidney the Protestant knight may not have accorded with his sister's desire to project a more worldly and more literary or aesthetic version of him'.[18]

It was the Countess's version which formed the basis of subsequent editions, of which there were many. The 1598 folio was again overseen by her and augmented by others of Sidney's works; its price of nine shillings was undercut by a pirated edition at six shillings printed in Edinburgh the following year. There followed eleven more editions up to 1739, not to mention translations and redactions like the chap-book versions of the inset narrative of Argalus and Parthenia which appeared between 1672 and 1703.[19] This popularity was often associated with women readers. As early as 1599, in Ben Jonson's *Every Man Out of his Humour*, Fastidious Brisk praises Sariolina because 'she does observe as pure a phrase and use as choice figures as any be i'the *Arcadia*', satirising the use of Sidney's text as a rhetorical source-book by those anxious to impress (II.iii.201–4). In 1609 Thomas Dekker advised gallants to glean *bons mots* from plays for use in courtship, 'upon which your leane wit may most savourly feede for want of other stuffe, when the *Arcadian* and *Euphuized* gentlewomen have their tongues sharpened to set upon you'.[20]

By 1631 Thomas Powell still represents the *Arcadia* as a text with associations of aristocratic refinement, but one which is read by non-aristocratic girls indulging unsuitable and reprehensible fantasies of class aspiration:

> In stead of Song and Musicke, let them learne Cookery and Laundrie. And in stead of reading Sir *Philip Sidneys Arcadia*, let them read the grounds of good huswifery. I like not a female Poetresse at any hand. Let greater personages glory in their skill in musicke, the posture of their bodies, their knowledge in languages, the greatnesse, and freedome of their spirits: and their arts in arreigning of mens affections, at their flattering faces. This is not the way to breed a private Gentlemans Daughter.[21]

Part of the affectation which he fears the *Arcadia* might encourage is literary composition by women themselves eager to be 'Poetresses', and as we shall see, this prediction was not unfounded.

Also from 1631, Wye Saltonstall's 'Poem of a Maid' (i.e. a young virgin) clarifies the dangers of the *Arcadia* as educating girls only in idleness and in the dangerous imaginative and erotic imagination which it entails: 'she reades now loves historyes as *Amadis de Gaule* and the *Arcadia*, and in them courts the shaddow of love till she know the substance'.[22] It is striking that by this date the *Arcadia* is placed in the same aesthetic category as the disreputable *Amadis*. Saltonstall urges that girls should be made to

> shun such pleasure
> As doth pervert the mind by strong temptation.
>
> Nor should they reade books which of some fond Lover,
> The various fortunes and adventures show;
> Nor such as natures secrets do discover,
> Since still desire doth but from knowledge grow. (sig. B1v)

The *Arcadia* appears again as an arousing text enjoyed by women in a poem by Charles Cotton (1630–87), where he comes upon his 'nymph' beside a river:

> The happy object of her eye
> Was Sidney's living *Arcadie*
> Whose amorous tale had so betray'd
> Desire in this all-lovely maid,
> That whilst her cheek a blush did warm,
> I read Love's story in her form.[23]

A 1638 translator of an ancient Greek romance exhorted 'fair ones' to 'A while lay by / blessed Sidney's Arcady' and turn to him instead.[24]

The composite *Arcadia*, then, seems in at least some quarters to have acquired a reputation not as a 'masculine' work of epic heroism, morality and politics, but as the kind of erotically inflammatory escapist fiction read by undisciplined young girls. In 1634 Anthony Stafford felt it necessary to defend it from disparagement as the reading only of ill-educated women: 'Some of them lately have not spared even Apollo's first-born, incomparable and inimitable Sir Philip Sidney, whose *Arcadia* they confine only to the reading of chambermaids – a censure that can proceed from none but the sons of kitchenmaids.'[25]

Aside from this reputation as the reading of maidservants, there is clear evidence that the *Arcadia* was indeed popular among seventeenth-century women of the upper classes. It was read by Mary

Rich, Countess of Warwick in her youth, and Lady Anne Clifford's reading of it is recorded in her diary, her 'Great Picture' and her copy of the 1605 edition (see p. 7 above); moreover, a manuscript of the *Old Arcadia* owned by Lady Anne's father George may have passed to her.[26]

Two female enthusiasts fulfilled Thomas Powell's fears by taking their avid reading of the *New Arcadia* a stage further, as a basis for their own imaginative creations. Sidney's niece, Lady Mary Wroth, must have found in his example of female-friendly romance authorship, and in that of her aunt Mary as patroness of romance, familial sources of empowerment towards writing and publishing her own romance, *The Countess of Montgomery's Urania*, 1621. This unprecedented choice of genre by an English woman author was evidently perceived in at least some quarters as a radical act of authorship, outrageously transgressive of feminine propriety, even by a Sidney with the family history of romance production behind her, as shown by the reaction of the prominent courtier Edward Denny, Baron of Waltham. While the specific ground of Denny's objection to the *Urania* was Wroth's inclusion, in fictionalised but recognisable form, of a recent scandal in his family which reflected particularly badly on his own character, he couched his attack in terms which foregrounded her gender and the unfitness of romance as a genre for women writers: Wroth was a 'Hermophradite' and a 'monster' who should 'repent you of so many ill spent yeares of so vaine a booke'. Instead she should 'redeeme the tym with writing as large a volume of heavenly layes and holy love as you have of lascivious tales and amorous toyes that at last you may followe the rare, and pious example of your vertuous and learned Aunt'.[27] Denny selectively memorialises the Countess of Pembroke as co-translator of the Psalms with her brother Philip, rather than dedicatee and editor of the *Arcadia*, in an effort to impose upon Wroth the common Renaissance injunction that the only suitable literary work for a woman is religious translation.

This was to turn against Wroth her own invocation of her illustrious forebears to authorise her engagement in romance. The title page of the *Urania* proclaims its author to be 'Neece to the ever famous, and renowned Sir Phillips Sidney knight. And to the most exelent Lady Mary Countesse of Pembroke late deceased.' Moreover, numerous details within the text allude knowingly to Wroth's Arcadian heritage, showing her to be a studious reader of her uncle's text and assuming a similar level of affectionate familiarity with his romance in her readers. To list but a few relatively obvious examples: the title *The Countess of Montgomery's Urania* clearly echoes the title *The Countess of Pembroke's Arcadia*; where the *New Arcadia* opens with Claius and Strephon lamenting the loss of the absent character Urania, Wroth's romance opens with Urania herself seeking to discover her own identity and provenance; the published *Urania*, like the *New Arcadia*, breaks off in mid-sentence; and Wroth's incorporation of fictionalised versions of real events and persons, such as the Denny sub-plot or characters like Pamphilia and Lindamira whose histories clearly draw on her own biography, develops Sidney's allusions to topical issues and his inclusion of a version of himself as Philisides. The *Urania* is far more than just an imitation of or sequel to the *Arcadia*, as I shall discuss in a later chapter, but it provides a striking example of one female reader's close and admiring attention to the text, and the growth from this of her own literary aspirations.

Another example is Anna Weamys, whose *Continuation of Sir Philip Sidney's Arcadia* was published in 1651. Little is known of this author beyond the information on her title page that she was a 'young Gentle-woman'. Her youth continued to be stressed in the prefatory matter to the volume, and it appears that she belonged to an educated family, untitled but possibly with aristocratic connections.[28] Whereas Wroth, despite her gestures of homage to the *Arcadia*, used it as a flexible template for her own independent fiction, Weamys took her inspiration from the unfinished nature of the revised *Arcadia*, seeking to tie up the narrative threads left unravelled at Sidney's death. She was not the only author to be spurred by this narrative gap, nor was it only women who found literary inspiration in the *Arcadia*: other continuations were composed by Gervase Markham (*The English Arcadia*, 2 vols., 1607 and 1613) and Richard Beling (*A Sixth Book to the Countess of Pembroke's Arcadia*, 1624); and 'supplements' to smooth the transition from the end of the revised *Arcadia* to the grafted-on *Old Arcadia* ending were written by William Alexander (1613) and James Johnstoun (1638).[29] Indeed, instigations from within the *Arcadia* to the inventiveness of subsequent authors were to be found not only in the cliffhanger of the unfinished new Book 3, but also in the ending of the 1593 composite text. At the end of the *Old Arcadia*, Sidney had listed characters such as Artaxia, Erona and Plangus whose plot-strands remained to be fully resolved, and pointed forwards to the next generation: the fortunes of 'the son of Pyrocles named Pyrophilus, and Melidora the fair daughter of Pamela by Musidorus . . . may awake some other spirit to exercise his pen in that wherewith mine is already dulled' (*OA*, p. 361). The ending of the 1593 text expanded this tantalising invitation to sequel-mongers to include some of the new characters introduced in the revised version and also left hanging in mid-narrative.

This sense of the potentially limitless abundance of narrative is entirely in keeping with the expansiveness of the *New Arcadia*, in which Musidorus and Pyrocles spend long interludes relating their past histories to the princesses and their female companions. The mood of narrative dilation is associated with the femininity of the pastoral romance world: indulgence in leisure, in retreat from public duty, is identified with participation in the private world of women, which in turn is identified with the Arachne- or Penelope-like spinning or weaving of story upon story upon story to pass the time and to delay the moment when action must be taken and decisions must be made. It is also, of course, a form of fertility. Moreover, the pastimes of Arcadia include storytelling and versifying not only by the princes, but also by the princesses (*NA*, pp. 241–2, 301ff., 312ff.). All of these factors might have contributed to the perceptions of women writers as well as men that the narrative generosity of the *Arcadia* was conducive to their own literary compositions.

Weamys does not appear to have known Wroth's *Urania* and shows no influence from the other continuations and supplements except perhaps Beling's.[30] She arguably produces a distinctively 'feminine' response to the *Arcadia* in that her emphasis is very firmly upon the achievement of marriage, an area in which women, at least in fiction, can exercise a degree of agency and can be seen to achieve a kind of triumph. Her climax is the simultaneous marriage of four aristocratic couples (Pamela and Musidorus, Philoclea and Pyrocles, Helen and Amphialus, Plangus and Erona) followed by a fifth, pastoral marriage of Urania and Strephon.[31]

However, while both Weamys and Wroth can be said to respond to the *Arcadia* in ways which are influenced by their gender, the nature of those gendered responses is strikingly different: where Wroth, as we shall see, tends to foreground the autonomous desires of her heroines (even though these might be concealed, as in Pamphilia's case, or adapted to circumstances, as in Urania's case), Weamys develops Urania as a heroine who willingly surrenders all erotic autonomy. She gives up her personal preference for chastity to save the lives of Claius and Strephon, then even submits her choice of suitor to Pyrocles and Musidorus. This contrasts not only with Wroth's heroines but also with Pamela and Philoclea as created by Sidney and continued by Weamys herself, who assert their rights to follow their own desires in love and choose their own marriage-partners. In the view of Weamys's modern editor, Patrick Colborn Cullen, what she may be attempting here is the creation of a heroine whose transcendence of self-definition through romantic desire constitutes an innovative transcendence of the romance genre itself.[32]

A third woman writer to take up Sidney's text was an otherwise unknown Mrs D. Stanley, whose *Sir Philip Sidney's Arcadia, Moderniz'd* appeared in 1725. Rather than expanding upon Sidney's narrative suggestions, Stanley removed not only all additions and supplements but also all the poems including the eclogues, and generally flattened out the imagery and other literary effects, suggesting that 'the *Arcadia* may have remained loved, but not always understood'.[33]

MALE TRANSVESTISM

Clearly, however, Sidney had created in the *Arcadia* a kind of romance which enabled some female readers to feel that they could take on the previously male mantle of romance-authorship; and this was not unrelated to the manner in which he represented the effeminisation of masculine roles in his fiction. As we have seen, his dedicatory epistle and his asides to 'fair ladies' in the *Old Arcadia* characterised him as entering a feminine aesthetic realm; and while previous fiction-writers like Pettie, Lyly and Rich had also represented themselves as surrendering more-or-less grudgingly to a cultural effeminisation, Sidney's tone is far less sardonic than theirs. The effeminacy of his narrative persona, and the fact that this is not necessarily resented or regarded as shameful, is reinforced by the centrality within the narrative of a man dressed as a woman: Pyrocles in his disguise as the Amazon Zelmane (named Cleophila in the *Old Arcadia*). Some degree of identification between Sidney and Pyrocles is implied in both the *Old* and *New Arcadias*. In both, the narrator interrupts himself with an exclamation of his devotion to Philoclea, Pyrocles's beloved: 'alas, sweet Philoclea, how hath my pen forgotten thee, since to thy memory principally all this long matter is intended' (*OA*, p. 95; *NA*, p. 237). In the *Old Arcadia* there is a striking implication of participation in Pyrocles's disguise: 'Such was this Amazon's attire: and thus did Pyrocles become Cleophila – which name for a time hereafter I will use, for I myself feel such compassion of his passion' (p. 25). It may be inferred that the author shares not only in Pyrocles's passion, but also in a literary kind of transvestism as he enters a feminine genre.[34]

The presentation of effeminised masculinity is not without ambivalences. For Mark Rose it is clear from the invocation of the traditional motif of distaff-Hercules that Sidney 'intended his readers to find Pyrocles's disguise offensive' and that it is 'a criticism of Pyrocles's failings'.[35] Musidorus warns Pyrocles that his womanish exterior will inevitably infect his internal nature: 'see how extremely every way you can endanger your mind: for to take this womanish habit, without you frame your behaviour accordingly, is wholly vain' (*NA*, p. 133). Indeed, for Musidorus, who has yet to see Pamela and experience love, Pyrocles's feminine exterior is an emblem of the debilitation of his inner masculine virtue which love has already wrought: 'this effeminate love of a woman doth so womanize a man that, if he yield to it, it will not only make him an Amazon, but a launder, a distaff-spinner or whatsoever other vile occupation their idle heads can imagine and their weak hands perform' (*NA*, p. 134).

As Musidorus himself yields to love, and both he and Pyrocles/Zelmane enjoy the company of the princesses and the pleasures of an idle, pastoral, feminine world, they defer their heroic responsibilities such as the rescue of Erona; their narratives about their past epic deeds indeed highlight the contrast with their present inactivity. In turn both Sidney as romance-author and his audience as romance-readers are implicated in this self-indulgent loitering in the realm of leisurely narrative.[36] Moreover, there are specific implications that there is something foolish and degrading about the feminine spinning of abundant story. Tales are told not only by the princes and princesses, but also by the princesses' pastoral guardians, Miso and her daughter Mopsa, who for a time preside over a storytelling circle of women. Miso proposes, 'I will have first my tale; and then, my Lady Pamela, my Lady Zelmane, and my daughter Mopsa . . . may draw cuts, and the shortest cut speak first' (*NA*, p. 307). Miso's story is a stereotypical old wives' tale, digressive, inconsequential, and embroidered by an oral tradition: 'I will tell you now what a good old woman told me, what an old wise man told her, what a great learned clerk told him' (*NA*, p. 307). Mopsa's tale is an even more vivid reconstruction of the supposedly fantastical and rambling fiction poured out by unrefined women: 'In time past . . . there was a king, the mightiest man in all his country, that had by his wife the fairest daughter that ever did eat pap' (*NA*, p. 311). The heroine runs off with a knight who is bewitched by water-nymphs, he vanishes, she goes to her aunt, who gives her a magic nut, then to another aunt, who gives her another nut . . . then Philoclea courteously interrupts and saves the audience from further pointlessness and tedium.

There is a clear qualitative distinction between the kinds of tales told by Miso and Mopsa and those told not only by Musidorus and Pyrocles but also Pamela and Philoclea: not all women's stories are bad, and Miso and Mopsa's chief failing is to be rustic and ignorant. Indeed, Weamys reiterates Sidney's satire of Mopsa, allowing her to proceed a little further in her narrative.[37] Nevertheless, it is telling that when Sidney wants to show what utterly redundant and senseless storytelling is like, he attributes it to women. He confirms the convention that foolish narrative is feminine; and although Miso and Mopsa are extreme cases, by indulging in stories which are to a degree time-wasting and uncontained, Musidorus and Pyrocles are effeminising themselves in a fashion which is potentially debasing.

However, the disguised princes' stories are of course not entirely purposeless: their narratives of their past adventures serve to communicate to Pamela and Philoclea in encoded form their true heroism and princely identities, and therefore their eligibility as suitors. In this sense their assimilation to feminine practices of storytelling, and Pyrocles's female disguise, can both be seen as strategic uses of voluntary effeminisation in the cause of virility. As we have seen, there were precedents for the adoption of female dress by a hero in *Amadis de Gaule* and *The Mirror of Knighthood*, and in the eighth story of Rich's *Farewell* (pp. 69–70, 91–2 above); in *Amadis* and Rich heroes use their female personae to penetrate the defences around a desirable woman and pursue her seduction, while in the *Mirror* Rosicleer uses his disguise to prove his manhood very vividly in the decapitation of a rapist. When Musidorus charges the disguised Pyrocles with effeminacy, his reply is partly an assertion of such virile purposes of both courage and seduction: 'Neither doubt you because I wear a woman's apparel I will be the more womanish, since I assure you, for all my apparel, there is nothing I desire more than fully to prove myself a man in this enterprise' (*NA*, p. 136).

In fact Pyrocles does not wholly effeminise himself in that his choice of disguise is as an Amazon, a *mannish* woman. As well as the man dressed as a woman, previous fictions afforded precedents for the woman who dresses as a man to pursue her love: examples could be found in the Spanish author Jorge de Montemayor's *Diana* (1559, one of Sidney's chief influences), and in the 1531 Italian comedy *Gl'Ingannati* and its many adaptations, including Rich's 'Apolonius and Silla'.[38] The specific case of a woman who dons armour and fights as a knight in the cause of love was found in Ariosto and the Iberian romances, and appears in the *Arcadia* itself when Parthenia enters combat with Amphialus in revenge for his killing of her husband Argalus. In a layering of disguise conventions, the warrior-woman is the female role which Pyrocles adopts, taking the name of Zelmane from a real, deceased woman who, out of love for him, had dressed as a man in order to serve him as a page on his martial adventures (*NA*, pp. 359–67). As the new Zelmane, Pyrocles specifically alludes to the use of Amazons in the Iberian romances as heroic breeding stock when she tells Anaxius that she was 'begotten by [Pyrocles's] father of an Amazon lady', and Zoilus that she must fight him before she marries him (*NA*, pp. 583, 589). Just as there is a double process of gender-switching in Shakespeare's cross-dressed figures, as boy-actors play girls playing boys, so Zelmane is a man playing a woman playing Amazonian 'mannishness'. In this sense his disguise is less potentially alarming than a full adoption of femininity.

In any case, there is considerable evidence that, in the Renaissance, effeminacy was associated not with homosexuality as it tends to be today, but with excessive attachment to women, including an excess of heterosexual libido.[39] Examples of this convention include Shakespeare's Romeo, who laments that love for Juliet has rendered him effeminate and tempered his valour (III.i.109–10), and Antony, who has worn Cleopatra's tires and mantles (II.v.22); in neither case is there much doubt of their heterosexuality. Fiction-writers like Pettie, Lyly and Rich had insinuated that a purpose of their entry into the feminine world of erotic fiction was a seductive penetration of private female spaces in which the reader was invited to participate; Sidney's princes likewise participate in this current literary convention of the use of narrative entertainment to gain access to the milieu of women and to win over the objects of their desires. Mary Ellen Lamb perceives the reader of the *Arcadia* as implicated in this seductive intent too. It has been pointed out that Philoclea is often represented in metaphors of a book or text: at one point her hand is like the printed hand in the margin of a book, and at another her eyes are like books (*NA*, pp. 175–6, 375). Most notable is the blazon 'What tongue can her perfections tell', where the many 'pens' which may dwell in her each part may be the phallic tools of multiple copyists taking possession of the text for their miscellanies (*OA*, pp. 207–11, *NA*, pp. 287–91). Lamb comments, 'If Pyrocles was feminized by his passion for Philoclea, then readers were similarly feminized by "handling" the sensuous *Arcadia*, as a virgin manuscript or as ravished text, perhaps even begetting copies upon its body.'[40]

What Lamb describes is a Renaissance-style effeminisation, in the sense of submission to *heterosexual* desire, of a reader assumed to be male; or at most a reader of either sex whose scanning of the pleasures of the text aligns either him *or* her with a 'male gaze'.[41] At some points, though, Sidney appears to be giving direct consideration to distinctive reading pleasures of women. Strikingly, Pyrocles's first line of defence against Musidorus's attack on him for effeminacy is a defence of women: 'I am not yet come to that degree of wisdom to think light of the sex of whom I have my life' (*NA*, p. 134). Indeed, the *Old Arcadia* began as if it might partly be a defence of women: Pamela and Philoclea are 'both so excellent in those gifts which are allotted to reasonable creatures as they seemed to be born for a sufficient proof that nature is no stepmother to that sex, how much soever the rugged disposition of some men, sharp-witted only in evil speaking, hath sought to disgrace them' (*OA*, p. 4). Sidney's disdain for self-satisfied railers against women is shown at several points; for instance, in the *New Arcadia* he satirises Anaxius, who boasts that 'I never came yet in company of ladies but that they fell in love with me. And I . . . in my heart scorn them as a peevish paltry sex, not worthy to communicate with my virtues' (*NA*, p. 522). He is consistently depicted as comically boorish and undiscerning. Musidorus's own prejudice against effeminacy and women is completely retracted when he falls in love with Pamela: 'I find, indeed, that all is but lip-wisdom which wants experience' (*NA*, p. 170). His heroism may be seen as enhanced by the broadening of thought and emotional response and the increased self-knowledge which follows upon his encounter with women and love. In such respects the *Arcadia* extends a welcome to women readers.

CHAPTER 7

The 'Arcadia': heroines

FEMALE OBJECTS

As we have seen, Pyrocles's disguise entails both sympathetic identification with women, and also, at the same time, the pursuit of a woman as erotic object. Similarly both *Arcadia*s, while in some ways extending a welcome to women readers, are simultaneously far from immune from the deployment of a 'male gaze' which reduces women to sources of specular pleasure.[1]

The procession of portraits of women behind Artesia, each of which is commented upon and assessed against standards of ideal beauty, establishes the idea of women as to-be-looked-at (*NA*, pp. 157–61). Philoclea in particular is repeatedly eulogised in blazons which reduce her to alluring body-parts, not only in the poem already mentioned, 'What tongue can her perfections tell' (*OA*, pp. 207–11, *NA*, pp. 287–91), but also in the second Eclogues (*OA*, pp. 144–5; *NA*, pp. 432–3), and during Pyrocles's defence to Musidorus of his adoption of female dress: 'her body (O sweet body!) covered with a light taffeta garment, so cut as the wrought smock came through it in many places, enough to have made your restrained imagination have thought what was under it . . . the apples methought fell down from the trees to do homage to the apples of her breast' (*NA*, p. 146). When Zelmane saves Philoclea from a lion, his/her deliberate delay in letting Philoclea know that the beast is slain comically sets the narrator's committed use of the female pronoun for the 'Amazon' against the hero's real male lust:

> [Philoclea] kept on her course like Arethusa when she ran from Alpheus; her light apparel being carried up with the wind, that much of those beauties she would at another time have willingly hidden was present to the sight of the twice wounded Zelmane. Which made Zelmane not follow her

over-hastily, lest she should too soon deprive herself of that pleasure. (*NA*, p. 176)

The comparisons with Arethusa and Alpheus at once liken Zelmane to Ovid's divine rapists, and ironically stress her difference: where they were anxious to catch and possess, her pleasure, while in female disguise, must be confined to looking, and it is therefore in her interests to dawdle and prolong the specular, masturbatory moment of distance. The reader is invited to share Zelmane's privileged point of view, gained by assuming femininity, but exercised in the service of a blatantly male-heterosexual erotic viewing pleasure.

'What tongue can her perfections tell' comprises 146 lines cataloguing the beauties of Philoclea's 'each part': the gaze of poet and reader travels lingeringly from her hair and forehead, via her breasts, belly and thighs, right down to her calves and feet, then 'back to her back' and down her arms to her fingers. Sidney stresses the erotic entrancement of the faculty of sight, the way in which the eye is seduced and led by her every tiny physical perfection: 'if ye gaze' in the 'incirclets' of her ears, 'Your eyes may tread a lover's maze'; her neck 'invites the eye / A little downward to espy' to her breasts (*NA*, pp. 287–91, lines 31–2, 51–2). In the *Old Arcadia*, the poem stands at the end of Book 3 where Pyrocles actually seduces Philoclea. Sidney's authorial identification with Pyrocles's point of view is emphasised by his assertion that this is a song which comes into Pyrocles's mind but which 'the shepherd Philisides [Sidney's fictional persona in the *Arcadia*] had in his hearing sung of the beauties of his unkind mistress' (*OA*, p. 207). He also makes a narratorial joke which makes clear that the poem serves as an extended euphemism for sexual action: 'do not think, fair ladies, his thoughts had such leisure as to run over so long a ditty; the only general fancy of it came into his mind, fixed upon the sense of that sweet subject' (*OA*, p. 211). The gazing of the poem stands for palpable sexual action; the yearning for possession which it voices stands for actual physical possession. The Petrarchan poet's conventional frustration – 'I can look but I can't touch' – is utterly undermined here by its ironic context. The eye moving lingeringly down Philoclea's body stands for Pyrocles's hand and other organs travelling ecstatically from encounter to encounter with her 'each part'. One particular Petrarchan formula which is deployed is the fictional inversion which claims that it is Pyrocles's/Sidney's/the reader's eye which is seduced by Philoclea's beauties, rather than

Pyrocles/Sidney/the reader who wants to seduce Philoclea, thereby absolving the male agent from responsibility or blame. This formula becomes even more deflective and disingenuous than usual as Pyrocles actually does achieve seduction behind the textual curtain of the blazon.

In the revised *Arcadia* the blazon was moved to Book 2, where it corresponds more exactly to a moment of purely specular pleasure in which physical union is longed for but not yet to be achieved. Zelmane sings the song aloud while the undressed princesses and their female companions bathe in the river Ladon. Again, however, the responsibility for desire is displaced from male lust on to female beauty: 'one might judge it was Philoclea's beauty which did speedily write [the song] in her eyes, or the sense thereof which did word by word indite it in her mind, whereto she (but as an organ) did only lend utterance' (*NA*, p. 287). Philoclea is claimed to be the 'author' of the song as of desire, setting up a mirroring relationship between male subject and female object. This accords with Nancy Vickers's observations that in the poetic blazon, going back to one of its sources in Petrarch, the breaking down and consequent establishment of control over the female body can be understood as a defensive displacement of the male viewer's own fear of loss of control and disintegration when confronted with the alarming and disturbing spectacle of female physicality, like Actaeon confronted by Diana.[2] The structure and diction of 'What tongue' emphasises not just the response of the eyes, but naming and ordering: to 'tell' Philoclea's perfections, the verb used in the opening line, is both to speak and report them, and to count and list them. The anxiety which underlies this urge to catalogue and control is brought out further by Wendy Wall, who emphasises that the bathing spot is prohibited to men on pain of death; Zelmane's and the reader's gaze are invested with criminality, as becomes even clearer when Zelmane discovers another male voyeur, Amphialus, hiding in the undergrowth.[3] Zelmane chides him for violating female privacy, yet at the same time offers not to tell the princesses, implying a degree of complicity and certainly of similitude between the two desiring men (*NA*, p. 292).

The tone and terms of 'What tongue' often verge upon what a modern taste might find kitschy. We espy:

> The lovely clusters of her breasts,
> Of Venus' babe the wanton nests:

Like pommels round of marble clear,
Where azur'd veins well mix'd appear,
With dearest tops of porphyry. (*NA*, p. 289, lines 53–7)

This almost baroque combination of floridity and sentimentality is developed further in another notable scene of the objectification of the female body, the death of Parthenia in the *New Arcadia*. Disguised as a knight, she enters combat against Amphialus in revenge for the death of her husband Argalus. Amphialus administers a mortal wound to his adversary's neck, then pulls off 'his' helmet in order to decapitate 'him':

> But the headpiece was no sooner off but that there fell about the shoulders of the overcome knight the treasure of fair golden hair . . . her exceeding fair eyes having with continual weeping gotten a little redness about them; her roundy sweetly swelling lips a little trembling, as though they kissed their neighbour death; in her cheeks the whiteness striving by little and little to get upon the rosiness of them; her neck, a neck indeed of alabaster, displaying the wound, which with most dainty blood laboured to drown his own beauties, so as here was a river of purest red, there an island of perfectest white, each giving lustre to the other . . . though these things to a grossly conceiving sense might seem disgraces, yet indeed were they but apparelling beauty in a new fashion which, all-looked-upon through the spectacles of pity, did even increase the lines of her natural fairness. (*NA*, p. 528)

The listing of hair, eyes, lips, cheek and neck; the predominant colours of red and white; the imagery of precious substances (alabaster) and of landscape (red river and white island) – all of these are standard conventions of the blazon of a mistress. What is unsettling about this example is that, while the usual blazon seeks to establish possession and control over a mistress by reducing her to an inanimate object, a display-case of jewels and artefacts, Parthenia actually is in the process of becoming an inanimate object, a corpse; and Sidney's clear declaration is that this renders her beauty even more perfect. Her eyes are enhanced by the redness of weeping, her lips by their trembling, registers of grief, pain and debilitation. Her white and red are not the ivory skin and rosy blush, or even the metaphorical purity and passion, of the conventional mistress, but the pallor of death and the red of fatal blood-loss. We are invited to take sensual pleasure in her pale flesh, the 'island of perfectest white' – her neck, but perhaps also, as the blood flows down, her breast – as it rises above and is prettily set off by the red river of her blood.

The passage invites such adjectives as fetishistic and necrophiliac.

At the same time, the inscribing of suffering upon Parthenia's body is a lexicon of female virtue – she has embraced this death out of a perfect, chaste and devoted love for her husband. Indeed, her story in the *New Arcadia* began with the evil suitor whom she had rejected for Argalus horribly disfiguring her face with corrosive poison, after which she self-abnegatingly forbade her beloved Argalus to bind himself to her in marriage; from the outset, then, she has been established as a heroine whose truth in love and virtue are painfully marked upon her flesh (*NA*, pp. 90–2).[4] Descriptions of the reciprocal unswerving fidelity which she inspires in Argalus, and of their domestic bliss, have established her as an icon of ideal wifehood (*NA*, pp. 105, 501). She dies as a martyr in this cause, invoking the iconography of mediaeval saints whose virtue was measured in suffering and marked upon their bodies. She expires while praying to God for eternal reunion with Argalus; all the onlookers are overwhelmed by grief, and 'The very heavens seemed with a cloudy countenance to lour at the loss', recalling the crucifixion as did the deaths of saints (*NA*, pp. 529–30).

FEMALE SUBJECTS

Viewed in one light, the death of Parthenia may be seen as one of the more distasteful and extreme examples of the objectification of the female body in Renaissance literature. Yet at the same time its hagiographic depiction of female heroism is not unrelated to the development of female subjectivity in the *Arcadia*, especially in Book 3 of the revised version, in terms which offered opportunities for identification to female readers, and for self-articulation to female writers.

Even in the *Old Arcadia*, specular pleasure in the female body runs alongside an interest in the inner mental states of female characters. Indeed, Gynecia's internal turmoils, as she finds herself overwhelmed by a frenzy of unrequited and adulterous desire for Pyrocles and by jealousy of her own daughter, are at least as fully explored in the *Old Arcadia* as in the *New*, where some of her melancholy and vengeful bitterness is displaced and divided on to Amphialus and Cecropia.[5] Even though she is in some sense the enemy of the hero and heroine Pyrocles and Philoclea, there is sympathetic exploration of her point of view as the wife of an older man, and later, as a figure of self-remorse: 'the afflicted Gynecia did crucify her own soul'.[6] Moreover, Gynecia and her daughters all vent their emotions in verses, helping to legitimise the composition of poetry by women and providing potential models for female 'poetresses'.[7]

Philoclea, as well as being an object of erotic specular interest, is also explored as a psychological subject. In the *Old Arcadia* she is disturbed by her 'strange unwonted motions' of attraction towards Cleophila, whom she believes to be another woman (*OA*, p. 85), and this inner debate is extended in the *New Arcadia*. We are told that 'grown bolder, she would wish either herself or Zelmane a man, that there might succeed a blessed marriage betwixt them' (*NA*, p. 239). The exploration of same-sex desire between two characters who are both apparently female draws upon sources like Ovid's story of Iphis and Ianthe (*Metamorphoses* IX) and the eighth story of Rich's *Farewell* (see p. 91 above), and also occurred in Lyly's play *Gallathea*.[8] Partly Sidney may be offering his male readers the titillation of voyeurism upon lesbianism; it is notable that in the *New Arcadia* Philoclea's long internal dialogue about her troubling feelings for her female friend is closely followed by an arousing description of herself and Pamela naked in bed together: 'there, cherishing one another with sweet though cold kisses, it might seem that love was come to play him there without dart, or that, weary of his own fires, he was there to refresh himself between their sweet breathing lips' (*NA*, p. 245). Yet, as terms in this passage like 'cold' and 'without dart' make clear, Sidney seems to have shared Queen Victoria's reputed belief that there wasn't much that one woman could do for another in the way of sexual pleasure. Philoclea has lamented in relation to Zelmane that 'it is the impossibility that doth torment me: for unlawful desires are punished after the effect of enjoying, but unpossible desires are punished in the desire itself' (*NA*, p. 243). The seeming impossibility of union between them builds up an intense atmosphere of pent-up desire, which is released when 'Zelmane' reveals herself as a man, causing the reader to welcome the prospective consummation of their love and confirming Philoclea's longings as completely 'healthy'.

The scenario of supposed same-sex attraction enables the development and expression of Philoclea's sexual feeling within an apparently chaste setting which diminishes the danger of a slur on her moral purity. It is in this context that we encounter her as a poet, rereading her own earlier verses vowing herself to unspotted virginity, and mentally revising them to register her unexpected subjugation to desire (*NA*, pp. 241–2). Her lyric compositions serve to express not only her internal emotion, but her complex fluctuation between different inner states; the very fact that the second set of verses, on female mutability, exist only in her head and not in writing deepens the delving into her interiority.

However, by far the fullest and most sympathetic exploration of both female subjectivity and female virtue is to be found in Book 3 of the *New Arcadia*. Here Pamela, Philoclea and Zelmane are imprisoned in the castle of the evil Cecropia, who seeks to compel either of the princesses to marry her son, Amphialus. In this setting Pamela and Philoclea grow in spiritual stature, surpassing not only their own characterisation in the *Old Arcadia*, but also the increasingly futile and gory attempts at martial heroics by the male knights who besiege their place of incarceration, and the individual reactions of their princely lovers.[9] Musidorus is reduced to self-loathingly brooding on his failure to rescue them, and Pyrocles to a despairing 'thirst of death' in which he clumsily fails to brain himself against a wall (*NA*, pp. 544, 564–7). Amphialus, who has many qualities despite his desire for Philoclea being the cause for which the princesses are imprisoned, disintegrates into increasing self-division and ultimately suicide, with 'self-ruin the only triumph of a battle fought between him and himself' (*NA*, pp. 573–5). Yet while male characters seem to lose their grip on selfhood, the princesses' sense of self becomes ever more resolute. To Philoclea's beauty and sweetness is now added the ability to dispense spiritual advice and solace (*NA*, pp. 566–7); and Pamela, who was commended in the *Old Arcadia* for her 'bashful eyes' and 'mild spirit' (*OA*, p. 172), becomes the moral centre of the text. She delivers an eloquent prayer to God in which she pledges 'O Lord, I yield unto Thy will, and joyfully embrace what sorrow Thou wilt have me suffer' (*NA*, pp. 463–4); and she counters Cecropia's pragmatic atheism with a lengthy philosophical defence of the existence of an omniscient divine Creator, triumphantly delivered with 'so fair a majesty of unconquered virtue that captivity might seem to have authority over tyranny' (*NA*, pp. 488–92).

This spiritual growth in the princesses is directly related to their subjection to martyr-like bodily suffering similar to that endured by Parthenia. From the outset of the episode two kinds of physical suffering are imposed upon them: incarceration, and the threat of enforced marriage to or rape by Amphialus. The first of these is described in terms which are recognisably a source for the later Gothic genre: Cecropia's castle 'stood in the midst of a great lake upon a high rock, where partly by art, but principally by nature, it was by all men esteemed impregnable' (*NA*, p. 443). Enforced withdrawal into enclosed chambers within this enclosed space encourages withdrawal into the mind, as Philoclea becomes an emblematic figure of melancholy (*NA*, p. 457), and Pamela, as seen in her prayer, an exemplary exponent of Christian meditation. The more Cecropia uses the gloomy setting to assail their minds, the stronger their inner strength grows: she withdraws their servants and comforts, 'Then still as she found those not prevail would she go forward with giving them terrors, sometimes with noises of horror, sometimes with sudden frightings in the night, when the solitary darkness thereof might easier astonish the disarmed senses. But to all, Virtue and Love resisted' (*NA*, p. 551). These aspects of the episode anticipate the exploration of female subjectivity under conditions of confinement and fear in the novels of Richardson, who printed an edition of Sidney's works in 1724, and whose homage to Sidney in naming his first heroine Pamela was noticed and remarked upon by contemporaries.[10] Beyond Richardson too the line of descent can be traced further to the vast and murky development of such motifs and themes in the Gothic genre, and its popularity with female readers and writers.

The specific physical threat offered within the walls of the castle, that of enforced sex, provokes responses from the princesses which elevate the soul above the body and invoke a language of secular martyrdom. Philoclea assures Amphialus that 'though his mother had taken away her knives, yet the house of death had so many doors as she would easily fly into it if ever she found her honour endangered' (*NA*, p. 451). Death and physical pain are as nothing in the cause of the preservation of virtue and control over one's own being, qualities which are implicitly grounded in Philoclea's devotion to Pyrocles. True love has become a quasi-religious cause which is a source of resolution and self-definition for the princesses. Its value is intensified as they seek to conceal the truth about the prior engagement of their affections from their persecutors, cherishing it as a precious secret at the kernels of their beings. This leads Philoclea into a deployment of the language of hagiography which is in fact a dissimulation, directly contrary to her true intentions of union with Pyrocles: she tells Cecropia that 'my heart is already set . . . to lead a virgin's life to my death; for such a vow I have in myself devoutly made' (*NA*, p. 460). Here she is acting the role of a mediaeval virgin-martyr from the *Golden Legend* such as the Saints Lucy, Agnes or Agatha, preferring death to defilement and thereby earning miraculous protection.[11] In the *Old Arcadia*, Philoclea was able to sleep with Pyrocles at the end of Book 3 with no imputation in the remaining two books that she was an impure or fallen woman; the truth of their love, a sense that their destiny was to be together, justified her submission to his seduction, even while *his* honour *was* cast in question by the event. This relatively liberal view of female bodily intactness as not essential to virtue recalls the Iberian romances. In the *New Arcadia*, however, the preservation of Philoclea's virginity enables the adaptation to secular erotic uses of the more traditional values of hagiography, in which bodily intactness is both an index of virtue, and a kind of protective charm.

The mediaeval saints' lives had established an iconography of female virtue in which the body was simultaneously separated from the soul, and represented as the place where the perfection of the soul could be read. When St Lucy is threatened with violation in a brothel, she declares defiantly, 'The body is not defiled . . . unless the mind consents . . . You will never be able to force my will. As for my body, here it is, ready for every torture.'[12] When St Agnes is threatened with torture, she replies that 'If you resort to wounds and torments, I have the Holy Spirit, through whom I make naught of all that' (*Golden Legend*, p. 155). Their souls are unsullied by anything inflicted on the body; yet at the same time, the greater the pain inflicted and endured upon the body, the greater their inner virtue is taken to be. Thus Lucy asserts that 'If you have me ravished against my will, my chastity will be doubled and the crown will be mine' (*Golden Legend*, p. 28); and Agatha, stretched on the rack, exclaims, 'These pains are my delight! It's as if I were hearing some good news, or seeing someone I had long wished to see, or had found a great treasure . . . my soul cannot enter paradise unless you make the headsmen give my body harsh treatment' (*Golden Legend*, p. 155). Indeed, the repeated motif with which the stories of Lucy, Agnes and Agatha begin, and those of other saints like Margaret of Antioch (*Golden Legend*, pp. 368–70), their consecration of their virginity to Christ, assumes a direct connection between bodily and spiritual purity; and the miraculous preservation of their virginity in each case, in spite of violent assaults upon it, affirms this body/soul correlation. Their bodies become texts upon which their inner holiness is indelibly marked: Margaret is racked, lacerated with iron rakes, burned with torches, immersed in water and finally beheaded; Lucy is set on fire, stabbed through the throat and in some versions has her eyes put out; Agatha is racked then has her breasts cut off. It is these vivid bodily totems that were reproduced over centuries of mediaeval art as emblems of their virtue, with Lucy and Agatha each traditionally depicted carrying a dish in which the former bore her eyes and the latter her severed breasts. Although of course male saints too bore bodily marks of pain, the body as a site of suffering and virtue does seem to have been especially to the fore in female religious narratives and also practices: mediaeval religious women 'were somewhat more likely than men to inflict injury on themselves systematically with flails or thorns, stones or nettles', and stigmata were much more common among holy women than men, such that they 'rapidly became a female miracle'.[13]

Stories of female saints were extremely well known in pre-Reformation England not only from the widely circulated Latin *Legenda Aurea* or *Golden Legend*, but also from English derivatives, from the invocation of their stories in legal and theological debates about rape and from Caxton's 1483 translation of the *Legend*, which was frequently reprinted in the early sixteenth century.[14] It seems likely that although the cults of the saints were curtailed after the Reformation, some of their legends continued to circulate simply as stories: indeed, Pettie used the *Golden Legend* as a source for the *Petite Palace*.[15] The story of Lucrece, whose popularity through the Elizabethan period we have seen reflected in its inclusion in collections like Painter's and Fenton's, was another *locus* for debate about the role of the body in the definition of female virtue. Livy, one of the chief classical sources for the story, distinguished between Lucrece's violated body and her innocent mind, and St Augustine had asserted that she was mistaken and sinful in committing suicide since she had resisted rape and therefore remained pure;[16] yet many versions of the story shared Painter's admiration of her destruction of her 'polluted' body.[17]

The Protestant martyrs eulogised by John Foxe offered recent examples of the iconography of martyrdom; Mary Ellen Lamb has pointed out that Pamela's wordy sermonising in debate with

Cecropia casts her very much as a Protestant heroine in this mould, able to display her theological erudition and to defeat her persecutors with rhetoric.[18] Even more recent were the Catholic martyrs of Elizabeth's reign. Elizabeth Hanson, in her study of 'Torture and Truth in Renaissance England', and Elaine Scarry in her more general study of discourses of torture, *The Body in Pain*, have both written of the complexities of the body/soul relationship in such martyrdom narratives.[19] The torturer inflicts pain in order to separate the sufferer's selfhood from their body, to reduce them to a mere lump of inarticulate flesh; yet the sufferer often finds a voice in defiance, or, even if reduced to a corpse, bears scars which serve as a text of their inner virtue and of the torturer's cruelty. The sufferer concurs in the separation of selfhood and body in so far as they assert that their selfhood will remain inviolate in spite of bodily pain; yet as this commonly develops into declarations that the greater the pain, the stronger will be the inner resolution, then the outer marks of pain actually become a register of inner virtue and integrity.[20]

The influence of such established iconographies of martyrdom can be clearly traced in the spiritual progress of the princesses in the *New Arcadia*'s Book 3, in which the relation between body and mind alternates between separation and identification. As Pamela speaks her prayer of Christian fortitude, her body becomes an emblem of holiness: she prays 'with such a fervent grace as if devotion had borrowed her body to make of itself a most beautiful representation' (*NA*, p. 464). Cecropia persists in 'perplexing the poor ladies' minds and troubling their bodies' (*NA*, p. 551). Accompanied by a bevy of vicious old women, she beats the princesses, recalling the alternate temptations and torments inflicted upon St Agatha by Aphrodisia and her band of licentious daughters.[21] Just as Agatha responded with the impregnability of rocks or iron, so Philoclea bears it 'with silence and patience . . . almost forgetting the pain of her body through the pain of her mind'; and on Pamela's turn, 'with so heavenly a quietness and so graceful a calmness did she suffer the divers kinds of torments they used to her, that while they vexed her fair body, it seemed that she rather directed than obeyed the vexation' (*NA*, pp. 552–3). Her defiance of Cecropia overtly echoes the virgin saints: 'do what thou wilt and canst upon me, for I know thy power is not unlimited. Thou mayest well wreck this silly body, but me thou canst never overthrow' (*NA*, p. 553).[22] Sidney sums up:

these princesses, second to none and far from any second, only to be matched by themselves, with the use of suffering their minds got the habit of suffering, so as all fears and terrors were to them but summons to a battle whereof they knew beforehand they would be victorious; and which in the suffering was painful, being suffered, was a trophy to itself. (*NA*, p. 555)

It becomes increasingly unclear what cause it is in which Pamela and Philoclea are seeking victory and trophy: is it love, or a classical stoicism, or Christianity? Or, with resonances of all three of these traditions, has it become simply the integrity of the self, as implied in that telling phrase of Pamela's, '*me* thou canst never overthrow'?

Cecropia resolves that since beating has only made the princesses obstinate, and since they seem impervious to threats of their own deaths, the best way to penetrate their minds is to make them witness one another's deaths (*NA*, pp. 555–6). First Philoclea and Zelmane are forced to watch the execution of a lady who appears to be Pamela (*NA*, pp. 557–8); then Zelmane/Pyrocles is confronted with the spectacle of Philoclea's apparently severed head in a golden basin of blood (*NA*, p. 563). The despair into which this plunges him contrasts unfavourably with the heroic fortitude of the princesses, especially when he resists the arguments of spiritual comfort presented by a mysterious gentlewoman who turns out to be none other than the living Philoclea herself (*NA*, pp. 566–7). She explains how the 'executions' were staged: a dispensable henchwoman of Cecropia's called Artesia stood in for Pamela, while Philoclea herself was forced to stand on a scaffold and stick her head through the false bottom of the blood-filled bowl, whereby she 'played the part of death' (*NA*, p. 569). The unreality of the 'executions' increases the resemblance to saints' lives. Already the princesses' predicament has recalled that of the heroines of the *Golden Legend* in that rape always remains a threat; in no saints' life was a virgin actually raped, as exceptional virtue earned miraculous protection.[23] Now, just as the flames into which St Agnes was thrown divided and left her unscathed, and just as St Agatha's severed breasts were miraculously restored by an apparition of St Peter, so the princesses remain miraculously untouched and whole.[24] Unsurprisingly, Pyrocles, having regretted that he was unable to take a 'holy kiss' from the dying mouth of Philoclea, assumes her on her reappearance to be a 'Most blessed angel' (*NA*, pp. 565, 567).

Sidney's scenario in Book 3 of the revised *Arcadia* is fraught with complications which, despite the sympathetic concentration upon the heroism of the princesses, resist any comfortable reduction to protofeminism. In the first place, female virtue is defined in terms of fetishised virginal bodily intactness. Secondly, female subjectivity is enabled by the withdrawal into imposed confinement, an assignation of women to private and enclosed spaces which is far from emancipatory. And thirdly, the inscribing of female heroism upon the female body is troublingly fraught with resonances of sado-masochism: put very simplistically, it offers sadistic pleasures to the male reader and masochistic pleasures to the female reader. It perpetuates the problematic dualism of mediaeval narratives of the torn flesh of female virgin-martyrs, in which the professed rejection of sexuality takes lurid forms which may simultaneously fuel sexual fantasies.[25] The mock-executions of the princesses are overtly referred to as a 'play' or 'tragedy', spectacles designed not only to impress awe upon the minds of the onlookers within the fiction, but also to strike and perhaps even to entertain the readers of the text. The beating of the heroines by the spiteful old women is an opportunity to display their 'fair bodies' and an invitation to the reader to imagine the marks of the rods upon them.[26]

Emanuel Forde wrote a series of derivative and formulaic romances in the late 1590s which were aimed from the outset at a less aristocratic audience than the *Arcadia*, and which remained popular through the seventeenth century; his *Parismus* (1598) went through fifteen editions by 1704.[27] They read in places like compendiums of the more pornographic episodes from the *Arcadia* and the Iberian romances, and within this, it is notable that Forde finds the imprisonment and beating of the princesses especially congenial to recycling. In *Parismus* Laurana is imprisoned in the Island of Rocks by Andramart, an unwanted suitor, who gives her into the custody of his sister Adamasia. When two old hags are sent to torment her, she makes a heroic speech, but they strip her to the waist and scourge her with whips 'untill the pure purple blood began to trickle downe her precious bodie'.[28] In *Ornatus and Artesia*, Lenon, having incarcerated and failed to seduce Artesia, commits her to the care of yet another old hag called Flera, who rips off Artesia's garments and tears her flesh with her nails.[29] Again the ancestry of Richardson's *Pamela* from Sidney via such intermediaries is evident, and the origins can be traced of the paradoxical critical reactions which

Pamela has provoked ever since its publication, as *both* a lubricious work of voyeurism *and* a sympathetic exploration of feminine sensibility.

In the *New Arcadia*'s own third book, there remains much which may be termed feminocentric. Its iconography of erotic sainthood entailing female heroism through suffering produces elevation of the spiritual stature of the princesses to a point where it exceeds that of the heroes. Beyond this, it also produces detailed exploration of their inner states; assertions of love as a noble cause analogous to a secular religion; and, most significantly, implications that the preservation of the integrity of the female self is a noble cause in its own right. Despite their co-existence with elements which we may find troubling and unsettling, it is easy to see why all of these ingredients might have appealed to female readers and writers.

CHAPTER 8

'The Faerie Queene'

IMAGINED READERS

At first *The Faerie Queene*, like the *Arcadia*, looks as if its ideal imagined reader is an individual woman – in this case, Queen Elizabeth I. Each of the six completed books opens with a proem which directly addresses her. Yet the terms of these addresses are very different from those used by Sidney to his sister. Where Sidney's dedication is warmly intimate, Spenser abases himself before the remote splendour of Gloriana: she is a 'Goddesse heavenly bright', 'Great lady of the greatest Isle', whom he implores to 'raise my thoughts too humble and too vile'.[1] Whereas Sidney's dedication invites all readers to imitate the projected reading manner of his sister, responding to the text with tolerance and affectionate complicity, clearly no reader, either female or male, can aspire to the divine judgement of Gloriana.

The obvious difference here is between a sister and a ruler: Spenser's representations of Elizabeth, including the representations of her as his highest and most discerning reader, are shaped by the conventions of panegyric. Bluntly, he praises her, including praise of her reading skills, in hope of reward and preferment. As many critics have noted, however, his praise becomes increasingly ambivalent as the poem proceeds, moderated perhaps by disappointment that he had not received the rewards he hoped for, perhaps by larger disillusionment that she had failed fully to live up to his ideal of the Protestant monarch. Belphoebe, in Book IV, one of Elizabeth's personae within the narrative, is frankly upbraided for unjust rejection of Spenser's friend Timias/Raleigh: 'Ne any but your selfe, O dearest dred, / Hath done this wrong' (IV.viii.17). Mercilla, in Book V, representing Elizabeth as judge of Mary Queen of Scots, is guilty of 'more then needfull naturall remorse' which delays 'just vengeance' (v.x.4, ix.50). Book vi, the Book of Courtesy, begins with an apology for turning away from Elizabeth, the supposed wellspring of courtesy, and places the poet's own mistress, not the Queen, at the summit of the dance of the Graces (vi proem, x). Finally the Mutability Cantos contain no proem and no address to Gloriana as imagined reader. Arguably this is simply because they are a fragment; but they also represent Elizabeth distinctly unfavourably in the roles of the mortal, unsteady Cynthia, and the petulant Diana. The latter reacts bathetically to Faunus's intrusion 'Like . . . an huswife' whose dairy has been broken into, and not merely abandons Ireland but vindictively lays a curse upon it (vii.vi.8–17, vii.50; vi.48, 55). These many negative aspects of the apparent encomium to Elizabeth in turn place in doubt Spenser's elevation of her as his ideal imagined reader.

Most of the positive representations of women and femininity within the narrative of the poem foreground creativity and fertility. The earth is always referred to as female, often as 'mother earth'. Presiding female figures like Venus in the garden of Adonis and in her temple, or like Nature in the Mutability Cantos, derive their power from their abundant procreativity (iii.vi, iv.x, vii.vii). All the heroines of the poem, with the exception of Belphoebe – even the iconically virginal Una and the warrior-woman Britomart – are destined for marriage and motherhood. Venus and Nature are also hermaphroditic, signalling self-sufficiency and a perfect harmonious balance of qualities, and in this they may be seen as forms of compliment to Elizabeth, self-reliant mother of the nation who combines in one person the femininity of a woman with the masculinity of a ruler. More forceful, however, is a feeling that Spenser's constant definition and celebration of the feminine in terms of fertility is fundamentally at odds with his ostensible purpose of the praise of the Virgin Queen.

A Midsummer Night's Dream is Shakespeare's only play in which Elizabeth appears in person, as the visionary 'imperial vot'ress' glimpsed by Oberon; yet she does so only to drift rapidly, ethereally and coldly out of view, leaving the play to its foremost concerns with youth, love, marriage and 'quick, bright things' (ii.i.155–64, i.i.149). Louis Montrose has written of how the action of the play 'depends upon her absence, her exclusion'.[2] This may be compared with Jonathan Goldberg's perception that Elizabeth's role in *The Faerie Queene* is as a symbol of a wholeness and perfection outside the text which is absent, imaginary, unattainable and unnamable, the text being generated by the endless doomed pursuit of this goal.[3] She therefore functions as a kind of vanishing point towards which the text inclines but which it can never reach. The quest for Gloriana sets the lines of the narrative but is never completed and becomes increasingly irrelevant; each persona of Elizabeth within the narrative represents only an aspect of her and leaves her whole nature and her true essence ever more elusive. Her shaping role as imagined reader correspondingly recedes as the narrative progresses. As Maureen Quilligan notes, whereas the proems to Books I to III address Elizabeth in the second person, the proem to Book IV, opening the 1596 portion of the poem, refers to Elizabeth as reader in the third person, indicating a growing 'abyss' between Spenser and his supposed primary reader.[4]

A role far more like that of the Countess of Pembroke in relation to the *Arcadia* is occupied by Spenser's friend Sir Walter Raleigh. The 1590 edition of Books I–III included 'A letter of the Authors' to Raleigh, annexed 'for that it giveth great light to the Reader'.[5] Spenser says he has written this exposition of his allegory 'aswell for avoyding of gealous opinions and misconstructions, as also for your better light in reading therof, (being so by you commanded)'. Raleigh, then, has clearly seen the text before publication, and has been a cheerer-on and adviser as was the Countess of Pembroke for her brother's romance, who Sidney said 'desired me to do it . . . it is done only for you, only to you . . . Your dear self can best witness the manner, being done in loose sheets of paper, most of it in your presence, the rest by sheets sent unto you as fast as they were done' (*OA*, p. 3). Spenser has given the name Belphoebe to Elizabeth 'according to your [Raleigh's] own excellent conceipt of Cynthia, (Phoebe and Cynthia being both names of Diana)'. All of this implies that behind the elaborate compliments to Elizabeth, the 'real' imagined reader is a male fellow poet, a comrade in literary composition. Spenser returns to a framing device of epistolary exchange with a male intimate who is in on his secrets, not unlike the relationship of Gascoigne's 'G.T.' with 'H.W.' in *The Adventures of Master F.J.*, or 'G.P.' with 'R.B.' in Pettie's *Petite Palace*. Indeed, the 'generall end . . . of all the booke' as set out in the letter to Raleigh is not the feminine-oriented one of praising Elizabeth, but a distinctly masculine one: 'to fashion a gentleman or noble person in vertuous and gentle discipline' by means of 'the historye of king Arthure'.

Thus although its title and its proems might make *The Faerie Queene* look like a celebration of female power addressed to a pre-eminent female reader, there is reason to think of it as a less 'feminine' book than the *Arcadia*. It perhaps comes closest to the *Arcadia*'s affinity with the feminine in Book III, the Book of Chastity, which has a female knight as its protagonist. Quilligan finds in the foregrounding of Britomart and other female figures like Venus, and of their points of view, an exhortation to men to read as women, to resist libidinous reflex responses to figures like Florimell or the bathing Diana, and at least temporarily to espouse feminine values of gentleness and nurturance.[6] Certainly this Book contains far more direct addresses to lady readers than any other of the poem. Spenser apologises to 'Faire Ladies, that to love captived arre, / And chaste desires do nourish in your mind' for his characterisation of the promiscuous Malecasta (III.i.40). Again in the ninth Canto he apologises to 'Redoubted knights, and honorable Dames' for writing of a 'wanton Lady' and 'faithlesse knight' (III.ix.1–2). These addresses are clearly different in tone and context from Sidney's teasing banter with his imagined lady readers as experienced sophisticates in matters of love; instead, Spenser is projecting his lady readers as models of chastity. Thus the curiosity of 'Faire Ladies' is deployed as the pretext for an account of the chaste conception and birth of the chaste Belphoebe (III.vi.1). Both Belphoebe and Britomart are held up for their edification in openly didactic terms:

> To youre faire selves a faire ensample frame,
> Of this faire virgin, this *Belphoebe* faire,
> To whom in perfect love, and spotlesse fame
> Of chastitie, none living may compare. (III.v.54)

The encomium of Belphoebe's chastity is significantly different from those of other chaste figures in that she is not destined for marriage. Here deferential fair lady readers are being constructed and co-opted to eulogise the Virgin Queen. There are troubling undertones to this: Belphoebe is an 'ensample dead' (III.v.54.9), possibly meaning simply an utmost example, but also connoting the sterility of her virginity.[7] The anomalousness of this amidst Spenser's general veneration of chaste matrimony is clear when we compare what Britomart exemplifies: 'ye faire Ladies . . . of faire Britomart ensample take, / That was as trew in love, as Turtle to her make' (III.xi.2). Or again, one of the few other places beyond Book III where female readers are directly addressed is in Book VI, where 'Ye gentle Ladies' are admonished not to be disdainful in love like Mirabella, to be 'soft and tender' in mind as in body, and to know their place in love rather than affecting tyranny (VI.viii.1–2).

WARRIOR-WOMEN

An appeal to female readers, and especially to the pre-eminent female reader, Elizabeth, may be detected in the opening of III.ii, in which men are chastised for their insufficient praises of the martial heroism of women; indeed this turns into an explicit panegyric of Elizabeth. However, Spenser is careful to place the praiseworthy exploits of warrior-women in 'antique times', and to uphold Elizabeth as an example not of the 'warlike puissance in ages spent' of her ancestor Britomart, but 'of all wisedome' (III.ii.2–3). The opening of canto iv seems more enthusiastic about the revival of 'warlike feates' by women, but even here Britomart is commended 'Aswell for glory of great valiaunce, / As for pure chastitie and vertue rare' (III.iv.1–3). Clearly, in the allegorical scheme of *The Faerie Queene*, the armed woman is an emblem of chastity rather than a figure for the contemporary woman to emulate literally in bearing arms. This applies even to Elizabeth herself, even after her leadership of the victory over the Armada in 1588 and her appearance at the camp at Tilbury had somewhat reduced anxiety about the unnaturalness of representations of her as an Amazon.[8]

This becomes even more evident in Book V, where Britomart, the heroic warrior-woman, is pitted against Radigund, her evil antithesis. Britomart has taken arms in the cause of love, continuing the romance tradition of the martial maiden whose potential freakishness is excused by her pursuit of a destiny of wifehood and marriage. Her warfaring is also an allegorical representation of a kind of Puritan work ethic, specifically rejecting the idleness with which, as we have seen, femininity was stereotypically associated:

> I loathed have my life to lead,
> As Ladies wont, in pleasures wanton lap,
> To finger the fine needle and nyce thread;
> Me lever were with point of foemans speare be dead. (III.ii.6)

She defeats all her male adversaries because she personifies chastity and truth in love, not because Spenser delights in female supremacy over men, as becomes blatantly obvious in Book v. Here Radigund, 'halfe like a man', debases Artegall and the other knights in her thrall by making them dress as women and perform the effeminate tasks of spinning and carding. 'Such is the crueltie of womenkynd', Spenser tells us, when they go against Nature and disobey 'the heasts of mans well ruling hand'. On the other hand, 'vertuous women wisely understand, / That they were borne to base humilitie'. Finally there comes a placatory nod in the direction of Elizabeth: 'Unlesse the heavens them lift to lawfull soveraintie' (v.v.25). Britomart's feat of heroism is not merely to defeat Radigund and free Artegall and his companions, but that she

> The liberty of women did repeale,
> Which they had long usurpt; and them restoring
> To mens subjection, did true Justice deale. (v.vii.42)

While willing to make an exception for Elizabeth in so far as she iconically personified virtuous Protestant rule and was the best option available, Spenser, it appears, like many of his contemporaries, was no great enthusiast for female government. In turn, we may take it that he was no great enthusiast for the adventuring warrior woman as a figure for emulation by women readers.

FEMININITY AND DUPLICITY

In Book III, Spenser's compliments to ladies in his audience include definitions of evil women as exceptional rather than typical. In exposing the promiscuous Malecasta he denies any intention to 'blot the bounty of all womankind'; she is merely 'one wanton Dame' ''Mongst thousands' (III.i.40). Again, when a licentious lady appears in canto xi, he laments 'What wonder . . . if one of women all did mis?' (III.ix.1–2). However, elsewhere in both *The Faerie Queene* as a whole and Book III in particular, female vice tends to be casually represented as generic to the sex. Among numerous examples, the false Florimell has rolling eyes 'like a womans', Hellenore practises 'womans subtiltyes', and even Glauce, a good character, 'dissembled womanish guyle' (III.viii.7, ix.7, iii.17).

Beyond this, the allegorical personification of vices by female figures almost always dwells upon their genitals, in a way not found in depictions of male figures. Thus Error is a serpent-woman, 'lothsom, filthie, foule', with 'poisonous dugs', who 'poured forth out of her hellish sinke / Her fruitfull cursed spawne of serpents small, / Deformed monsters' (I.i.14, 15, 22). The stripping of Duessa exposes her as 'A loathly, wrinckled hag' with 'misshaped parts', 'secret filth', and unspeakable 'neather parts'; 'Her dried dugs, like bladders lacking wind, / Hong downe, and filthy matter from them weld' (I.viii.46–8). Geryoneo's monster 'of a Mayd . . . had the outward face, / To hide the horrour, which did lurke behinde', and pours 'Most ugly filth, and poyson' 'out of her infernall sinke' (V.vi.23, 31).

All of these examples, and the others like them in the poem, bespeak a fundamental definition of women in terms of the deviation of their sexual organs from the male 'norm', and an anxiety about those sexual organs as potentially monstrous and nightmarish, a source of horror. Another recurring theme is that of deceit: in all these cases, outward female beauty, or at least a female face, is a front for hideousness and loathsomeness. Duplicity is the trait most repeatedly attributed to women in *The Faerie Queene*, on a scale ranging from the guile of a Duessa or an Acrasia to the more innocent attempts of a Pastorella to escape her gaoler by feigning erotic interest in him (VI.xi.6–7), or indeed Britomart's use of male disguise. 'Womanish fine forgery' is a concern that runs throughout the poem (II.xii.28).

Female figures are therefore crucial to the poem's central preoccupation with the relation between art and truth. As a Protestant Spenser is suspicious of artifice as distraction and deception; yet as a poet he is himself an artificer. Images cannot be rejected outright; instead, true images must be distinguished from false ones. In their recurrent association with deceit, women provide convenient allegorical forms for the exploration of this theme. Moreover, women are not merely used to personify false representation. They are associated not only with skill in creating false images, but also, as we have seen, with the virtuous shaping and creative powers of fertility and maternity. Such a chastely fertile woman can personify, for Spenser, a pure relation between image and truth. When a virtuous woman lays aside her outer garments, what she reveals is not the secret filth of a Duessa, but the 'heavenly beautie' of a Una (I.xii.22). Una's sober garments, and the radiant beauty beneath them, are both true representations of her purity, but the inner layer is even more pure and true than the outer one.

Thus female virtue no less than female vice is made known by means of the stripping away of layers, the revelatory removal of an outside surface to expose what lies within. In Spenser this peeling away of externals to reach an inner truth tends not to extend below the bodily surface to attempt to enter the female mind, as it does in Sidney. As in Sidney, though, the body of the virtuous woman can act as a text upon which the story of her virtue is written in the scars of physical torment.

MARTYRS FOR LOVE

The Faerie Queene contains a number of examples of heroines who suffer in the cause of love and have their emotional pain marked upon their bodies. They include Florimell, who after lengthy pursuit by various assailants is incarcerated by Proteus but resists his advances because of her devotion to Marinell. Pastorella is another, who is imprisoned, defies threatened seduction and then rape because of her 'constant mynd', then is wounded and trapped in the arms of her dead tormentor (VI.xi). Serena is gored by the Blatant Beast then narrowly escapes dismemberment by cannibals. Perhaps the most striking example is Amoret, whose pierced heart provides bloody ink for the enchanter Busirane. In all these instances Spenser perpetuates the tradition of representing female heroism in terms of the endurance of suffering.

All these heroines are more passive than Sidney's Arcadian princesses; emphasis is placed on their dependence on their rescuers, rather than their self-sufficiency and stoicism. They are also accorded much less exploration of their interior states than Pamela and Philoclea. However, this must be understood in the context of Spenser's different, far more allegorical narrative method, in which there is little exploration of the interiority of any character, but rather externalisation and personification of moral, emotional and psychological properties.

Thus in the case of Amoret at the house of Busirane, rather than hearing her own words as a medium for her thoughts we see instead a masque of allegorical figures. She is preceded by Fancy, Desire, Doubt, Danger, Fear, Hope, Dissemblance, Suspect, Grief, Fury, Displeasure and Pleasance; led forward by Despite and Cruelty; and followed by Cupid and by Reproach, Shame, Repentance and a 'rude confused rout' of other figures (III.xii.7–26). A reading of these as sequential externalisations of Amoret's interior states as she passes through her narrative of love – and possibly also as embodiments of the interior states of another female lover, her spectating rescuer, Britomart – is strongly invited by the enumeration of the 'maladies' which make up the 'rude confused rout' as 'Soe many moe, as there be phantasies / In wavering wemens wit' (lines 25–6). Accordingly the masque and Busirane's torture have been taken by most critics to represent some kind of psychological problem in Amoret which obstructs her union with Scudamour. Interpretations of what that problem might be, however, have ranged widely and conflictingly from an excessive physicality in her approach to married love, to a fear of surrender to sexual penetration.[9] For Quilligan the episode is a female pornographic fantasy which balances the male pornographic fantasy of the Bower of Bliss which ended Book II, a significant difference being that the female fantasy is a more overtly sado-masochistic one.[10]

Whatever its true meaning – if it has a single one – another point to make about the episode is that it offers a different way of representing female subjectivity, a way which works from the outside rather than going within, and which is iconic more than discursive. As such it is less immediately congenial to female readers – there is no paralleling of their own activity of 'going within' in the engagement of their minds with the text. It is also less encouraging of emulation by female authors, since it does not offer the kind of authorisation of female self-expression in language found in the speeches and writings of the princesses in the *Arcadia*. It thus shows up by contrast some of the reasons why the *Arcadia* found such popularity with women readers and writers. Nevertheless, the allegorical method was not without potential for female authors, as we shall find when we consider Mary Wroth's *Urania*.

The description of the gaping wound in Amoret's naked breast strikingly perpetuates the convention of measuring female heroism in pain:

> a wide wound therein (O ruefull sight)
> Entrenched deepe with knife accursed keene,
> Yet freshly bleeding forth her fainting spright,
> (The worke of cruell hand) was to be seene,
> That dyde in sanguine red her skin all snowy cleene. (III.xii.20)

As in the death of Parthenia and the torments of the Arcadian princesses, and the martyrologies from which they derived, female torture and mutilation are aestheticised and specularised. However,

Amoret is rescued by a woman, Britomart, who shares not only her sex but also the experience of a physical wound which symbolises the wound of desire, inflicted on Britomart first by Gardante and now again by Busirane (III.i.65, xii.33). Britomart forces the enchanter to undo his spells by chanting his verses backwards, thus freeing Amoret from her bondage and miraculously healing the 'wyde wound' to her 'bleeding brest, and riven bowels' (III.xii.36–8). In so far as Busirane may be seen as a 'sadistic sonneteer',[11] Spenser may be seen here as confessing and seeking to undo his own participation in men's making of poetry out of women's subjection and pain. Such countering of the predominantly masculinist ideologies of the poem as a whole may also be seen as continuing into Book IV, as Britomart and Amoret quest together as loving friends. The pair disrupt chivalric conventions whereby fair ladies are won by virile knights, and briefly forge an alliance alternative to, and arguably more equal and harmonious than, the goal of matrimony otherwise so vigorously enforced in the poem.[12]

The opening of Book IV repudiates an unwanted critical reader, thought to be Lord Burghley, who is opposed to 'looser rimes' of love and 'vaine poemes' (IV. proem 1). He is unable to read as a lover, and therefore, by implication, unable to engage with or participate in the feminine. It is the Queen's sex who are the guardians of 'treasures of true love' (IV. proem 4). Yet even the Queen, by this point in the poem, seems to be becoming too masculine a reader: Spenser implores Cupid and his mother Venus,

> From her high spirit chase imperious feare,
> And use of awfull Majesty remove:
> In sted thereof with drops of melting love . . .
> Sprinckle her heart, and haughtie courage soften. (IV.proem 5)

At this point it seems that Spenser has come to feel himself to be more in tune with Venus and the feminine than is his female supposed primary reader. Despite the patriarchal and even misogynistic values to be found in many parts of the *Faerie Queene*, he values the feminine, or at least his conception of the feminine, because he values romance.

CHAPTER 9

Shakespeare's romance sources

The continuing currency and popularity of romances of the 1580s into the late 1590s and early 1600s is shown by Shakespeare's regular recourse to them as sources. His source for *Twelfth Night* (1601) was 'Of Apolonius and Silla' from the *Farewell to Military Profession* (1581) by Barnaby Rich, and his source for *The Winter's Tale* (1609–11) was *Pandosto* (*c*.1585) by Robert Greene, authors we have already encountered in chapter 5 above. *As You Like It* (1598–1600) was based on *Rosalynd* (1590) by Thomas Lodge, another significant author of prose romances who knew and worked with both Greene and Rich. None of these sources would have been by any means obscure to Shakespeare's original audiences: Rich's *Farewell* was reprinted in 1583 and 1594;[1] *Rosalynd* in 1592, 1596 and 1598; and *Pandosto* in 1588, 1592, 1595, and 1607.[2] Many other of Shakespeare's plays, especially towards the end of his career, show the influence of prose romance conventions in more general terms. This chapter will consider two aspects of romance which especially relate to gender as they emerge in Shakespeare: cross-dressing; and the idea of romance as a feminine genre.

CROSS-DRESSING IN 'APOLONIUS AND SILLA' AND *ROSALYND*

In 'Apolonius and Silla', the emphasis falls upon female cross-dressing as a saintly form of sacrifice. I mentioned on p. 90 above how when Silla (the equivalent of Viola) adopts male disguise to pursue Apolonius (the equivalent of Orsino) there are distinct echoes of the lives of saints Marina, Theodora, Eugenia and Margaret (also known as Pelagia) in the *Golden Legend*, all of whom adopted male dress in the cause of Christian virtue.[3] This generic source is especially evident when, like Saints Marina, Theodora and Margaret, Silla is charged with paternity by a pregnant woman. Rich stresses Silla's self-abasement in playing the part of Apolonius's page: she 'plaied the parte of a serving manne, contented to abide any maner of paine only to behold him' (*Farewell*, p. 67). When her true identity is finally revealed, Apolonius takes it as an amazing proof of the strength of her love that having been brought up in a court, 'with traines of many faire and noble ladies living in pleasure, and in the middest of delightes', she 'would so prodigallie adventure your self, neither fearing mishapps, nor misliking to take suche paines, as I knowe you have not been accustomed unto' (*Farewell*, p. 87).

The adoption of male disguise by Shakespeare's comic heroines has often been seen as a liberation for them, enabling them more scope for action and self-expression than was available to them in female dress. For Silla, although it is true that her disguise forms part of an adventure far from her home, and enables her unusual intimacy with the object of her desire, in other ways it is an imprisonment to her. It forces her to remain silent about her identity and feelings while wooing her own rival on behalf of her beloved; and it locks her, Apolonius and Julina (the equivalent of Olivia) into a seemingly irresolvable love-triangle. Indeed Shakespeare plays up these tragic aspects of the situation, when Viola laments her predicament as a 'poor monster' (*Twelfth Night*, II.ii.32); and when she depicts herself as a saintly martyr to love, sitting 'like patience on a monument, / Smiling at grief', apparently doomed to a withering chastity and death (II.iv.113–14).

Another aspect of this story of cross-dressing is played down by Shakespeare, however: namely, Rich's bawdy tone, in keeping with the general jokiness and mockery of women through the *Farewell* as a whole. Both Silla and Julina are more morally dubious figures than Viola and Olivia, provoking much nudging and winking innuendo. Silla's lust drives her almost out of control, as she first attempts to woo the impervious Apolonius at her father's court with 'amourous baites', then pursues him to his own country, 'feelyng herself so muche out raged with the extreamitie of her passion' (*Farewell*, p. 69). Julina is not in mourning for her father and brother, but is a widow, immediately labelling her as sexually knowing. When Silla's brother, the true Silvio (the equivalent of Sebastian), appears and is mistaken for Silla in her disguise as Silvio, Julina loses no time in sleeping with him. She courts Silla/Silvio with many assertions of her right to follow her own inclinations in love and marriage:

'albeeit, I knowe the worlde will wonder, when thei shall understande the fondnesse of my choice, yet . . . I have ment no other thing, then the satisfiyng of myne owne contentation and likyng' (*Farewell*, pp. 78–9). The modern reader may find such claims to self-determination appealing, but when Julina finds herself pregnant, and apparently by one unequipped to impregnate her, Rich represents this as just and comical retribution upon an exemplar of women 'whiche are Subjecte to longyng, and want the reason to use a moderation in their diet' (*Farewell*, p. 78). He inserts a ridiculous moral whose irrelevance satirises the very convention of extracting didactic sentences from such fantastical narratives, echoing Gascoigne and Pettie (see chapter 3 above):

> I praie you Gentilwomen, was not this a foule oversight of *Julina*, that would so precisely sweare so greate an othe, that she was gotten with childe by one, that was altogether unfurnishte with implementes for suche a tourne. For Gods love take heede, and let this bee an example to you, when you be with childe, how you sweare who is the Father, before you have had good proofe and knowledge of the partie, for men be so subtill and full of sleight, that God knoweth a woman may quickly be deceived. (*Farewell*, p. 84)

In short, the pregnant Julina is a figure of fun. Having accused Silla/Silvio of paternity then received proof that her accusation is impossible, she 'departed to her owne house, with suche greefe and sorrowe, that she purposed never to come out of her owne doores againe alive, to be a wonder and mocking stocke to the worlde' (*Farewell*, p. 87). Shakespeare adopts the idea of Julina/Olivia's self-immuration, but transposes it to the beginning of the story, and gives it the more serious, virtuous cause of mourning for a brother.

Although *Twelfth Night* is a comedy, Shakespeare smooths out many of the more crudely comic elements of Rich's narration. Another of these is Rich's emphasis upon genitalia. We have already seen how Julina brings her paternity suit against 'one, that was altogether unfurnishte with implementes for suche a tourne' (*Farewell*, p. 84). Before this, when Silla realises that Julina is in love with her, she reflects how unaccountable it is that Julina should prefer to a Duke 'suche a one, as Nature it self had denaied to recompence her likyng' (*Farewell*, p. 75). This contrasts with Viola's far more high-minded and poetical reaction at the same moment, moralising on the wickedness of disguise, and exclaiming with eloquent pathos and imaginative metaphor, 'Poor lady, she were better love a dream!'

(*Twelfth Night*, II.ii.24–5). Silla defeats Julina's charge of paternity with a startling gesture: 'here with all loosing his garmentes doune to his stomacke, and shewed *Julina* his breastes and pretie teates, surmountyng farre the whitenesse of Snowe it self, saiyng: Loe Madame, behold here the partie whom you have chalenged to bee the father of your childe, see I am a woman' (*Farewell*, p. 86). Shakespeare could not have his boy actor perform such a gesture, for a very obvious reason. But combined with his other excisions of the more graphic sexual matter in Rich's narrative, this highlights how Shakespeare converts the story from something which, despite its courtly setting and romance motifs, is almost fabliau-like in Rich's hands; and renders it instead a more lyrical, magical and elegiac exploration of apparently impossible desires.

For Silla male disguise is an extremity which denotes both the overmastering power of her passion and the suffering she is willing to endure as a martyr to love. For Lodge's Rosalynd, it is a more emancipatory state. Her reasons for adopting it are not to pursue a lover, but to escape political danger. She dons it with spirit, seeming to take on a phallic spirit of aggression too as she tells Alinda (the equivalent of Celia):

> I, thou seest, am of a tall stature, and would very well become the person and apparel of a page; thou shalt be my mistress, and I will play the man so properly that, trust me, in what company soever I come I will not be discovered; I will buy me a suit and have my rapier very handsomely at my side, and if any knave offer wrong, your page will show him the point of his weapon.[4]

The disguise enables her to test out both the love Rosader (Orlando) professes towards her, and the strength of her own feelings towards him. As such it enables her pursuit of her desires less equivocally than is the case for Silla.

In her disguise as Ganymede, Rosalynd rails against women as wittily as any male Renaissance satirist: ' "You may see," quoth Ganymede, "what mad cattle you women be, whose hearts sometimes are made of adamant that will touch with no impression, and sometime of wax that is fit for every form" .' When Alinda objects, Ganymede explains that she merely 'keep[s] decorum . . . put me but into a petticoat and I will stand in defiance to the uttermost that women are courteous, constant, virtuous, and what not' (*Rosalynd*, p. 49). The implication that controversy about the virtue or vice of women is mere rhetoric, with little essential truth at either extreme, extends an even-handed welcome to Lodge's readers of both sexes.

On the one hand *Rosalynd* looks like a fiction designed to appeal to male readers. Lodge dedicates it to Lord Hunsdon, 'as it is the work of a soldier and a scholar', composed in moments of leisure on an adventurous voyage to the Canaries and the Azores. There is a prefatory epistle to gentlemen readers, but none to women. The source story, the fourteenth-century poem *Gamelyn*, provides a plot of an abused younger brother who achieves his just deserts largely through physical shows of strength; Lodge perpetuates this in his manly characterisation of Rosader, who would gladly die in combat with an enemy or a wild beast but is ashamed to die of hunger (*Rosalynd*, p. 63), and who scorns the tears of his penitent brother Saladyn (Oliver) as 'feminine follies' unbefitting a gentleman (*Rosalynd*, p. 88).

On the other hand, Lodge adds to *Gamelyn* female characters, of which there are none in the mediaeval poem, and moreover places them very much in the foreground. The ruse of Rosalynd's male disguise is itself attributed to female resourcefulness and ingenuity: when Alinda fears for the safety of two women travelling alone, ' "Tush", quoth Rosalynd, "art thou a woman, and hast not a sudden shift to prevent a misfortune?" ' (*Rosalynd*, p. 47). The two friends later devise a successful plan to gain Phoebe's love for Montanus (Silvio), 'as women's heads are full of wiles' (*Rosalynd*, p. 113). Lodge's Rosalynd establishes for Shakespeare's Rosalind a refreshing realism and pragmatism about love: she warns Phoebe to 'love while thou art young, lest thou be disdained when thou art old' (*Rosalynd*, pp. 101–2), and she accuses Rosader of being one who would 'rather pass away the time here in these woods with writing amorets than to be deeply enamoured, as you say, of your Rosalynd' (*Rosalynd*, p. 76). She herself has no intention of being a cold and unyielding Petrarchan mistress: 'I hear Rosalynd praised as I am Ganymede, but were I Rosalynd I could answer the forester [Rosader]: If he mourn for love, there are medicines for love – Rosalynd cannot be fair and unkind' (*Rosalynd*, pp. 71–2).

To an extent her disguise frees Rosalynd to be frank while giving her control over the pace at which the courtship proceeds. However, Alinda, who remains female in her pastoral disguise of Aliena, is just as plain-speaking and spirited. In many scenes she banters vigorously with Ganymede, threatening, when 'he' voices some conventional witty misogyny, to 'pull off your page's apparel and whip you (as Venus does her wantons) with nettles' (*Rosalynd*, p. 50). When she sees the man she is about to marry, Saladyn, looking melancholy, she remarks with arresting bluntness, 'Perhaps thou art sorrowful to think on thy brother's high fortunes, and thine own base desires to choose so mean a shepherdess? Cheer up thy heart, man, for this day thou shalt be married to the daughter of a king: for know, Saladyn, I am not Aliena, but Alinda' (*Rosalynd*, p. 123). These heroines do not need disguise, either male or pastoral, to unbind their self-expression. Alinda speaks in similarly straightforward terms to Rosalynd as they embark upon their exile: she is a 'mad lass, to be melancholy when thou hast with thee Alinda, a friend who will be a faithful co-partner of all thy misfortunes . . . Cheerly, woman: as we have been bedfellows in royalty, we will be fellow-mates in poverty' (*Rosalynd*, p. 47).

Lodge paints an attractive picture of female friendship, one which is possibly influenced by the warm intimacy of the two sisters in the *Arcadia*. The publication date of *Rosalynd*, 1590, might make it appear unlikely that Lodge could have been influenced by Sidney's romance, since the first published version of the *Arcadia* appeared in the same year. However, there are discernible echoes of the *Old Arcadia* in the main plot of *Rosalynd* and in some of its details. Two other romances of around the same time show knowledge of the *Old Arcadia*: Robert Greene's *Menaphon*, 1589, and Barnaby Rich's *The Adventures of Brusanus, Prince of Hungaria*, 1592. It seems that all these three authors must have had access to a manuscript of the *Old Arcadia*, and the likely route for transmission of this manuscript is in fact through Lodge to Greene and Rich: there is some evidence that Lodge had connections of some kind with the Sidney circle, and he certainly knew and occasionally worked with both Greene and Rich.[5]

The way in which Lodge depicts the friendship of two female protagonists strongly suggests Sidney's influence, as does his representation of female subjectivity. Alinda's and Rosalynd's pledges to one another become a means of defining and asserting truth to an authentic self: 'I will ever be thy Alinda, and thou shalt ever rest to me Rosalynd; so shall the world canonize our friendship' (*Rosalynd*, p. 47). Selfhood is also explored in the various passages where both female and male characters withdraw from the action to contemplate their opportunities and dilemmas. After her first encounter in the forest with Rosader, we see 'Rosalynd passionate alone'; after Aliena/Alinda meets and falls in love with Saladyn, we are given 'Aliena's Meditation' (*Rosalynd*, pp. 72, 93–4). In such passages the heroines address themselves and explore their interior states, in a fashion very similar to the long internal monologues in the *Arcadia*. Also as in the *Arcadia*, women as well as men use poetry to express their desires (*Rosalynd*, pp. 79–82, 99–100, 110–11).

Lisa Jardine has usefully drawn our attention to the romance sources for Shakespeare's cross-dressing heroines. Before Jardine, some feminist critics had seen these heroines as enterprising and attractive representatives of womanhood, reflecting an actual emancipation of women in Renaissance society.[6] Jardine, on the other hand, argues that these are fictional roles bearing little relation to the lives of real women: they were played by boy-actors, whose homoerotic appeal is often foregrounded; and their romance sources present folk-tale and fantasy figures of women whose exceptional devotion and service to their destined spouse is proved by their endurance of male disguise.[7] The idea of the homoeroticism of the boy-playing-a-girl-playing-a-boy has been examined further by critics like Kate McLuskie, Jean Howard and Michael Shapiro, who stress that we should not treat such figures as real boys either, but must address questions of theatrical transformation; and who also stress the differences among Shakespeare's cross-dressed heroines.[8] In prose romance, too, we can find different 'spins' being put on the figure of the cross-dressed heroine. In 'Apolonius and Silla' the boy-girl is largely an occasion for innuendo and for marvelling at the strange effects of sexual passion. However, in Lodge, probably under the influence of Sidney, she/he is associated with an interest in the exploration and expression of female subjectivity. In Shakespeare's dramatisation of the story, it is true that the boy-actor playing Rosalind provocatively draws attention to his sexual ambiguity in the Epilogue, and that Rosalind playing Ganymede playing Rosalind describes boys and women as cattle of the same colour, alike 'effeminate, changeable, longing and liking' (*As You Like It*, III.ii.364–71). However, more often than an erotic equivalence between boys and women, what is asserted is the difference between the outer guise of Ganymede and the inner being of Rosalind. On arrival in the forest Ganymede/Rosalind confesses 'I could find in my heart to disgrace my man's apparel and to cry like a woman' (II.iv.3–4); in his/her impatience to know of Orlando's presence in the forest he/she scolds Celia, 'Dost thou think, though I am caparisoned like a man, I have a doublet and hose in my disposition?' (III.ii.178–80); and he/she faints at the news of Orlando's wounding when rescuing Oliver (IV.iii.155).[9]

Shakespeare actually takes this opposition between the masculine exterior and female interior further than Lodge, whose Ganymede/Rosalynd is careful to observe decorum when dressed as a boy and rail against women even in private dialogue with Alinda. Shakespeare's Rosalind repeatedly asserts that she has a woman's heart; and he imports the same outside/inside opposition to Viola, who, unlike Rich's Silla, repeatedly speaks her female passion from within her masculine disguise, in encoded but nonetheless eloquent forms like the 'willow cabin' and 'Patience on a monument' speeches (*Twelfth Night*, I.v.237–45, II.iv.106–20). Both Rosalind and Viola could say with Hamlet 'I have that within which passeth show' (*Hamlet*, I.ii.85); the masculine disguise enables contrasts to be drawn with an implied truer, deeper selfhood which in their cases is female. The layering of personae of boy actor, female character and male disguise, and the reverberations and frictions between these layers, convey an impression of depth which Michael Shapiro terms 'theatrical vibrancy'.[10] The consequent indication of female interiority may be seen not only as a product of the staging of cross-dressing, but also as an influence from prose romance; indeed Shapiro sees cross-dressing novella-heroines as also possessing 'narrative vibrancy' whereby the layering of identities creates an illusion of depth (*Gender in Play*, p. 217).

Lodge's characterisation of Rosalynd may not bear any direct or simple relation to the lives and behaviour of actual women of the time. Nor does her temporary adoption of male disguise present any radical challenge to patriarchy: she is a dutiful daughter who will clearly be a devoted wife to Rosader. Even so she personifies a marked departure from the conventional prescription for the ideal bride given by Rosader's father, who urges his sons to seek women who are 'chaste, obedient and silent' (*Rosalynd*, p. 30). She is not this static icon of feminine perfection, but a character in the narrative whose point of view and transition through varying emotional states are shown as fully as those of the male characters. We can perhaps trace in Lodge's Rosalynd some of the reasons why Shakespeare's cross-dressing heroines have had such enduring appeal for female audiences, female actors and female literary critics.

SHAKESPEARE'S LATE PLAYS AND THE FEMININITY OF ROMANCE

Coleridge used the term 'romance' in his *Notes on 'The Tempest'*, and it became firmly attached to Shakespeare's late plays following Edward Dowden's use of it in 1877 to describe their shared motif of lost children recovered, their romantic landscapes, and their 'grave beauty'.[11] Although Shakespeare's contemporaries are not known to have applied the term 'romance' to dramatic works, the influence of prose romance upon Shakespeare's late plays is manifest in their fantastical subject matter, their use of supernatural interventions and astounding reversals of fortune, their rambling narrative structure and their hybridity of content and tone.

Shakespeare's knowledge of the Iberian romances is evident in several places,[12] and the influence of even more venerable romances is even clearer. *Pericles* derived from *Apollonius of Tyre*, a late classical romance so familiar from various mediaeval retellings that it had virtually passed into English folklore – indeed, Ben Jonson disdained it as a 'mouldy tale'.[13] For *The Winter's Tale* Shakespeare turned to a recent romance source, Greene's *Pandosto*, which in turn went back to ancient Greek romances. Principal among these were Heliodorus's *Aethiopica* (also known as *The Aethiopian History*, or *Theagenes and Chariclea*); Longus's *Daphnis and Chloe*; and Achilles Tatius's *Clitophon and Leucippe*. These fictions were composed in the eastern Roman empire in the first three centuries AD, but gained a new currency in several Elizabethan translations. Thomas Underdowne translated Heliodorus in 1569, with several subsequent editions; Angel Day produced an English paraphrase of *Daphnis and Chloe* in 1587; and *Clitophon and Leucippe* appeared in English in 1597.[14] However, all these texts also appeared earlier in the sixteenth century in other languages like Latin and French which English authors are likely to have read; indeed, Book XX of the French *Amadis* was simply a version of Heliodorus.[15]

These works helped to introduce to Elizabethan fiction settings which were pastoral and classical; a trend which was reinforced by the influence of more recent continental pastoral fictions like Jacopo Sannazaro's *Arcadia* in Italian (1504) and Jorge de Montemayor's *Diana* in Spanish (1559). The Greek romances also provided models of intricate plotting, and of narrative governed by fortune and the wondrous fulfilment of oracles. Typical Greek romance motifs included the capture of children by pirates; separation of husband and wife; nobly born maidens sold into slavery then rescued; and the long passage of time which allows children to grow up, have adventures and be finally reunited with their parents.[16]

Underdowne's *Aethiopian History*, for instance, opens dramatically with a sunrise in which bandits survey the sea from a hill, and see an abandoned laden ship and the scattered bodies of men killed while feasting.[17] Shakespeare followed Sidney and Greene in recognising the effectiveness of such shipwreck-type scenes for initiating mysteries of identity, displacements, quests and strange encounters. The ending of the *Aethiopian History* is even more familiar, as a lost daughter is reunited with her father, her husband is revealed, an oracle is fulfilled, and the assembled company wonder at the 'divine miracles' which have brought about this happy denouement (fos.148r–9r). The resolution is attributed to

> the Gods, whose will it was that this shoulde fall out wonderfully, as in a Comedy. Surely they made very contrarye thinges agree, and joined sorrowe and mirthe, teares and laughter togeather, and tourned fearefull, and terrible thinges into a joyfull Banquette in the end, many that wepte beganne to laughe, and such as were sorrowfull to rejoice, when they found that they soughte not for, and loste that they hoped to finde. (fo. 148r–v)

The intervention of the gods, the snatching of a comic ending from the jaws of tragedy, the mingling of joy and tears, the atmosphere of wonder and the theme of restoration all bring vividly to mind *The Winter's Tale* and others of Shakespeare's late plays.

The influence of Greek romance may be traced in many Elizabethan fiction writers. S. L. Wolff, in his exhaustive study of the subject, found the *New Arcadia* unmistakably Heliodoran in its complex narrative structure and its rhetorical style.[18] Moreover, precedents for the feigned executions of Pamela and Philoclea may be found in Achilles Tatius.[19] Greene's *Pandosto*, although an original work of fiction, is almost entirely constructed out of motifs borrowed from Heliodorus, such as the vindication of chastity by public trial, the reading of an oracle during a trial scene and the abandonment of a child.[20] Shakespeare takes all of this on into *The Winter's Tale*, and possibly worked not only from Greene but also directly from the Greek romances themselves.[21]

From the very inception of the genre, the aesthetic status of Greek romance was ambiguous. The original texts seem to have developed 'separately from, or on the fringes of, the mainstream of "high" literature'.[22] Their Elizabethan translators seem to have regarded them as the nearest thing romance could claim to a respectable classical model; but even Underdowne's commendation of his own work, in a preface to the 1587 edition, regards its worth in merely relative terms within the dubious romance genre:

> If I shall commend the reading of it to any, I might find other better to be commended. If I shall compare it with other of like argument, I thinke none commeth neere it. *Mort Darthure*, *Arthur* of little *Britaine*, yea, and *Amadis* of *Gaule* etc. accompt violente murder, or murder for no cause, manhoode: and fornication and all unlawfull luste, friendely love. This booke punisheth the faultes of evill doers, and rewardeth the well livers.

In the ancient world the Greek romances were sometimes disparaged as mere love stories, but there is little evidence that the readership they addressed was regarded as mainly female.[23] Similarly their Elizabethan translators announced them on title pages and in prefaces to be histories of love, but did not specifically address female readers.

Nevertheless, the subject matter of the romances foregrounds the feminine in several ways. The use of the family as a structuring principle of narrative, and the high value placed upon female chastity, give a high profile to the roles and virtues of daughters, wives, and mothers. Again the influence of this may be directly traced in Shakespeare's late plays. Their predominant theme is regeneration, insistently personified by chaste and beautiful daughters who are about to embark upon marriage and motherhood. Women who are already mothers are also significant. In *Pericles*, Thaisa gives birth to Marina only just out of view. The opening acts of *The Winter's Tale* show Hermione first heavily pregnant, then very soon after giving birth, while the later acts of the same play celebrate the matriarchal figure of 'great creating Nature' (IV.iv.88). Even when mothers are not physically present, they are frequently invoked. In *The Tempest*, Miranda's mother is dead and unseen, but her maternal perfection is set against Sycorax, the epitome of maternal vice who haunts the play, and it is the source and guarantee of Miranda's chastity and worth as a future wife and mother: 'Thy mother was a piece of virtue, and / She said thou wast my daughter' (I.ii.56–7).

Motherhood and ideas associated with it are important in the late plays not just as symbols of fertility, but also as emblems of a certain kind of narrative. As we have seen in previous chapters, mothers and mother-figures were identified with fantastical, rambling, antiquated narrative in the idea of the 'old wives' tale'. In fact Madge's rambling story in Peele's *Old Wives' Tale*, which I discussed on pp. 13–14 above, could serve pretty well as a synopsis of one of Shakespeare's late plays: 'Once upon a time there was a king or a lord or a duke that had a fair daughter, the fairest that ever was; as white as snow and as red as blood; and once upon a time his daughter was stolen away, and he sent all his men to seek out his daughter' (lines 113–17). By calling his dramatisation of *Pandosto The Winter's Tale*, Shakespeare conflates Greene's romance and its ancient Greek sources with this kind of idle fireside story. The earliest usage of the phrase in the *OED* links 'olde wives fables and winter tales'.[24]

Within the play, Mamillius declares that 'A sad tale's best for winter. I have one / Of sprites and goblins' (*The Winter's Tale*, II.i.27). He is a child shown as literally still at his mother's knee, living like most small children in an intimate circle of nurturing women. His close bond with his mother is shown not only by the fact that he whispers his tale in her ear and later drops dead when she is abused, but also by his very name, Mamillius, which is a diminutive of the Latin word for breast. When the idea of the winter's tale is picked up again in the latter scenes of the play, it is overtly associated with the female in the form of first the return of Perdita, who personifies the return of the mother in the daughter, then the return of Hermione supervised midwife-like by Paulina. The news of Perdita's restoration is 'so like an old tale that the verity of it is in strong suspicion . . . Like an old tale still, which will have matter to rehearse though credit be asleep and not an ear open' (V.ii.7, 55). Paulina confesses of Hermione, 'That she is living, / Were it but told you, should be hooted at / Like an old tale' (V.iii.116–18).

Maternity was close to romance not only in the role of mother-figures as storytellers, but also in the astounding narrative material which maternity could furnish. Autolycus's pack of ballads reminds us of this: 'Here's one to a very doleful tune, how a usurer's wife was brought to bed of twenty money-bags at a burden, and how she longed to eat adders' heads and toads carbonadoed . . . Here's the midwife's name to it' (IV.iv.253–9). This is clearly an absurd and far-fetched tale, but it draws directly upon a real thriving Elizabethan and Jacobean tradition of ballads about 'monstrous' births. The Huth collection at the British Library contains a number of such broadsides from the 1560s, including accounts of a child born with slanting eyes, pointed ears and a frill around its neck; another born with 'Ruffes' of flesh around the neck; a pair of Siamese twins; a baby boy born with no hands, feet, tongue or penis; and another with 'the left leg growing upward toward the head, and the ryght leg bending toward the left leg, the foote therof growinge into the buttocke of the said left leg'.[25] Each of these asserts itself as a 'true description', supplied with exact details of date, place, parents and sometimes witnesses, and grotesque woodcut illustrations are supplied. The same formulae are used for descriptions of deformed pigs or of 'a marveilous straunge Fishe' caught in the English Channel,[26] filed alongside in the Huth collection; all alike are 'monsters', sententiously interpreted in the accompanying ballads as warnings from God.

These tales of extraordinary births bring something of the romance world of hobgoblins and changelings into contact with here-and-now experience, inviting the reader to gasp over their astonishing contents while claiming to be 'true descriptions'. Their presentation in broadsides, the cheapest and most accessible form of literature, which might be read aloud and which were vividly illustrated, appealed to the illiterate as well as those who could read. By the early seventeenth century the interpretation of them as signs of God's wrath was being superseded in educated circles by a Baconian view of them as interesting cases for scientific analysis, and a taste for such horrors and wonders was coming to be seen as vulgar.[27] They were literally old wives' tales, in which the named witnesses were frequently midwives or other women in attendance at the childbed. The proverbial unreliability of such reporters meant that the very claims to veracity attached to the stories contained grounds for scepticism. The idea that a midwife would say anything to make a better story, or for profit, is implicit in Autolycus's assertion that his ballad of a 'monstrous' birth has 'the midwife's name to it' (*The Winter's Tale*, IV.iv.259). We find it again in *Henry VIII*, in the response of the Old Lady who attended on Anne Boleyn's childbed to her disappointing reward: 'Said I for this the girl was like to him? I'll / Have more, or else unsay't' (V.i.175–6).

The reports of monstrous births also remind us of what a fraught event childbirth is, potentially bringing forth the joy of new life, but also potentially bringing about the death of the child or the mother or both, or producing a malformed child. While many dangers remain today, of course they were far more prevalent and alarming in the sixteenth and seventeenth centuries.[28] In some of the broadside birth-narratives the baby died a few hours after birth; in others, like that of the boy born without hands, feet, penis or tongue, he was reported to be feeding vigorously, 'And at the makynge hereof was living, and like to continue'.[29] Helen Wilcox has shown how Shakespeare's tragicomedies, in which she includes the 'problem plays' and the late plays, not only identify maternity with regeneration, but also show it as a hazardous and obstructed process. She concludes that it is exactly its mingling of regenerative and tragic potential that makes maternity central to Shakespeare's blend of apparently opposing genres:

> motherhood in early modern England consisted of many paradoxes, relating to chastity and fertility, absence and presence, life-threatening and life-giving qualities. Thus it is entirely apt that maternity should epitomize the paradoxical complexity of the tragic/comic mix in these plays, and exemplify a genre which brings both death and new life into its cycle of action.[30]

In short, we might think of tragicomedy as a maternal genre.

Certainly maternity is associated in the late plays not only with positive and life-giving powers, but also with more negative themes. Mothers are often dead or believed dead. In *The Two Noble Kinsmen*, Emilia's anxieties about the combat between Palamon and Arcite are expressed as a fear that she will bereave at least one mother and draw maternal curses upon her (III.vi.245; IV.ii.4–6). Walter Cohen has noted that the final scenes of the play are fraught with images of sexuality and reproduction which are used to express grief and loss:[31] the combat reaches a 'consummation' fulfilling Emilia's fears that 'Palamon would miscarry', and Hippolyta's eye 'conceives a tear / The which it will deliver' (V.V.94, 101, 137–8).

The uncertainty of narrative outcome which is inherent to both tragicomedy and romance is often expressed through maternal metaphors. In *Pericles*, Gower undertakes to show 'Th'unborn event' (XV.45); while in *The Winter's Tale* the truth is 'pregnant by circumstance' (V.ii.28). Wolsey reflects that the 'poor man that hangs on princes' favours' suffers 'More pangs and fears than wars or women have' (*Henry VIII*, III.ii.368–71). Hermione's lady-in-waiting, noting that 'She is spread of late / Into a goodly bulk', wishes 'good time encounter her' (*The Winter's Tale*, II.i.21–2); instead Leontes's tragic intervention causes her to be 'something before her time delivered' (II.ii.28). Even the sea which so persistently appears in these plays either as a place of actual shipwreck or as a metaphor for turbulent fortune can be understood as a kind of amniotic fluid from which characters supposed dead are reborn.

Central to these maternal metaphors for unpredictable narrative outcome is the term 'issue', repeated insistently through all these plays.[32] In one sense it means simply offspring: Antigonus mistakenly designates Perdita 'the issue / Of King Polixenes', and Polixenes laments that his actual 'issue', Florizel, has not proved gracious (*The Winter's Tale*, III.iii.42; IV.ii.22). Cymbeline greets his lost sons with the question 'How, my issue?' (V.vi.332). However, it can also mean a conclusion or consequence. In *The Winter's Tale*, Hermione's waiting-woman Emilia expects 'a thriving issue' of Paulina's goodness (II.i.48); the envoys to the oracle at Delphos head for home with the wish 'gracious be the issue' (III.i.22); and Autolycus solicits the narrative of Perdita's restitution with the words 'I would most gladly know the issue of it' (V.ii.7). In *Henry VIII* the Old Lady who delivered Anne Boleyn's child and seeks more reward for saying that the baby resembles her father asserts 'I'll put it to the issue' (V.i.177).

These two senses of the word 'issue', as both progeny and event, frequently come together. The penitent Leontes believes that 'the heavens, taking angry note, / Have left me issueless' (*The Winter's Tale*, V.i.172–3). Queen Katherine's womb has been a tomb to Henry VIII's 'male issue', and must be replaced by the fruitful womb of Anne (*Henry VIII*, II.iv.188). Arcite and Palamon in prison lament, before they see Emilia, that they will have 'no issue know us' (*The Two Noble Kinsmen*, II.ii.30–2). In all these cases, to be without issue in the sense of children is also to be without issue in the sense of a future, a movement forward in story.

Maternal imagery is also often used at crucial moments to describe intense emotion, poised between grief and hope. Pericles, on recovering the mother, Thaisa, in the daughter, Marina, declares that 'I am great with woe, and shall deliver weeping' (*Pericles*, xxi.94). Cymbeline, at the restoration of his three lost children, asks: 'O, what am I? / A mother to the birth of three? Ne'er mother / Rejoiced deliverance more' (*Cymbeline*, V.vi.369–71). Prospero describes how, when tossed on the sea with the baby Miranda, he wept and 'Under my burden groaned' (*The Tempest*, I.ii.155–6). Henry VIII laments that his 'issue's fail' has given him 'Many a groaning throe' (*Henry VIII*, II.iv.188, 195–6). All of these are climactic moments of wonder, and of the consequent release of pent-up and contradictory emotions, of exactly the kind upon which romance and tragicomedy depend.

In these ways the concept of the maternal is central to the

narrative principles of Shakespeare's late plays. Yet in all the examples given in the last paragraph the maternal is being used to express heightened emotions felt by the central *male* protagonist and authority-figure. This highlights the profoundly ambivalent attitude to the maternal in most of these plays. Not only is maternity associated with death as much as life; but the physical reality of mothers is often excluded, by death or distance, while the associations of maternity with intense emotions and potent forces are appropriated to patriarchal figures. This may be connected with various recent critical readings of the late plays. Janet Adelman has argued that the figuration of mothers throughout Shakespeare's works is punitive, epitomised by *Hamlet*: the problematic maternal body is 'made into a monster or a saint, killed off or banished from the stage', yet 'remains at the center of masculine subjectivity, marking its unstable origin'. Adelman sees the romances in terms of a schematised response to this psychic problem: 'the sanctified mother who can bless is recovered in Thaisa and Hermione, the witch-mother reemerges in Cymbeline's Queen and in Sycorax'.[33] Meanwhile Richard Wilson also sees the attitude of the late plays to maternity as mainly negative: they foreground the dependence of identification of a child's father upon women's unverifiable reports, and coincide with movements to take midwifery out of the realm of women and folklore and into the realm of men and empirical science.[34]

Similarly, although the late plays embrace the fantastical, digressive and time-filling narrative principles of romance, they do not always do so comfortably. The text of *Henry VIII* often invokes the idea of old fantastical story only carefully to distinguish itself from it. The knights at the Field of Cloth of Gold are reported to have jousted so well 'that former fabulous story / Being now seen possible enough, got credit / That *Bevis* was believed' (I.i.36–8). Later, the porter's assistant at the christening of Princess Elizabeth, overwhelmed by the popular crowds forcing their way in, protests that 'I am not Samson, nor Sir Guy, nor Colbrand,[35] / To mow 'em down before me' (V.iii.21). Similarly, the Prologue to *The Two Noble Kinsmen* expresses anxiety that if the play is unsuccessful, Chaucer will complain that its author 'my famed works makes lighter / Than Robin Hood' (lines 21–2). In naming popular romances these late plays invoke them as a frame of reference but at the same time claim their own elevation above them.

However, the idea of idle story and its pleasures does remain very much present. The Prologue to *The Two Noble Kinsmen* proposes that the play will 'keep / A little dull time for us' (line 31); the Epilogue refers to it not as a play but as 'the tale we have told' (line 12). Gower introduces scene xvii of *Pericles* with the words 'Thus time we waste' (line 1). It is notable, though, that Gower is a *male* custodian of old, time-filling story. In fact despite the kinds of configurations I have described, there is no example in the late plays of a woman actually telling a story. It is invariably gentlemen who relate to one another the miraculous reunions and other wondrous off-stage events. In *Cymbeline*, it is Belarius who has told tales of courts and princes, and his warlike adoptive sons, living in all-male seclusion, worry about their own narrative capacities:

What should we speak of
When we are old as you? When we shall hear
The rain and wind beat dark December, how,
In this our pinching cave, shall we discourse
The freezing hours away? (III.iii.14–15, 35–9)

The choric figure of Time in *The Winter's Tale*, which on the face of it could readily be female as the birth-giver or midwife to event, is definitely male, referring to 'himself' (IV.i.31), and drawing on the patriarchal iconographical tradition of Time as the Old Father to his daughter Truth.[36] In *The Tempest* it is Prospero who narrates her origins to Miranda and who is the organiser of narrative event for all the other characters.

In the end, then, just as maternity is often invoked only for its potent associations to be appropriated by patriarchal figures, so authority over narrative is also frequently given to men. An idle and digressive narrative genre is plundered for its pleasures, but placed in the hands of ordering patriarchs, as if to leave it to women like Peele's Madge would be to risk an uncontainable, unstructured and disorderly flow of story. After all, these are plays by a man or men (that is, Shakespeare and Fletcher) whose careful attention to form is apparent beneath the surface digressiveness, just as the Elizabethan romances which announced themselves to be directed by the interests of ladies and gentlewomen were composed by male authors who took them more seriously than they pretended. The idea of Shakespeare's tragicomic romances as maternal in genre is fruitful in so far as maternity is inherently tragicomic, but the tradition which connects maternity with the actual *generation* of romance narrative is present in most of these plays only in repressed form.

An exception to this is *The Winter's Tale*, especially in the role of Paulina. Eleven of Shakespeare's plays have what Dennis Kay has called 'postponed endings' – the postponement of full explanatory narrative beyond what is shown on stage.[37] While, as Kay shows, the effects of this vary, they often include the sense of a romance-like abundance and fertility of narrative spilling over beyond the confines of the five Acts we have seen. In a few cases, it is female characters who lead their companions away for further narrative: these are Paulina in *The Winter's Tale*, along with the Abbess in *The Comedy of Errors* (v.i.395–401), Portia in *The Merchant of Venice* (v.i.294–8), and Mistress Page in *The Merry Wives of Windsor* (v.v.218–19). Among these *The Comedy of Errors*, an early play (1591–2?), especially anticipates many of the concerns of the late plays; indeed its source is the same as that of *Pericles*, Gower's retelling of the ancient romance of Apollonius of Tyre in the eighth book of his *Confessio Amantis*.[38] Among Shakespeare's female presiders over postponed endings it is the Abbess in *The Comedy of Errors* who in her closing words most overtly draws together the themes of maternity and narrative:

> Renownèd Duke, vouchsafe to take the pains
> To go with us into the abbey here,
> And hear at large discoursèd all our fortunes,
> . . .
> Thirty-three years have I but gone in travail
> Of you, my sons, and till this present hour
> My heavy burden ne'er deliverèd.
> The Duke, my husband, and my children both,
> And you the calendars of their nativity,
> Go to a gossips' feast, and joy with me.
> After so long grief, such nativity![39] (v.i.395–7, 402–8)

The burden which she delivers after a thirty-three-year labour is both her 'reborn' sons, and the story of her motherhood and self-concealment.

The combined emphasis on regeneration and romance in the late plays might lead us to expect such direct linking of maternity and narrative to be found again there, yet it is not openly stated. The nearest we get to it is in *The Winter's Tale*, where, as well as Mamillius, his mother's son, as storyteller, we also find Paulina as a sort of midwife of events. When she bursts into the tragic, masculine world of the first half of *The Winter's Tale* with Hermione's baby in her arms, Leontes frantically abuses her with just about every term popular culture offers for a woman who talks too much: she is Dame Partlet, Lady Margery, 'a callat / Of boundless tongue', and a midwife to boot (II.iii.76, 91–2, 160). In a sense his troubles all begin from his doubts as to the validity of old wives' and midwives' testimony: Mamillius is said to be like him, but 'women say so, / That will say anything', and they are as false 'As o'er-dyed blacks, as wind, as waters, false / As dice' (I.ii.129–32). The play ends, however, with the voluble Paulina receiving his gracious submission: 'Good Paulina, / Lead us from hence, where we may leisurely / Each one demand and answer to his part' (V.iii.152–4). It is Paulina who is invited to preside over the narratives which will fill the 'wide gap of time' (line 155) and which spill over abundantly beyond the end of the story as shown.

Paulina, the very epitome of an old wife – she calls herself a 'foolish woman' (III.ii.225) – is not found in *Pandosto*. The ending which she engineers is also radically different from that of *Pandosto*. In Greene's narrative, Pandosto, the Leontes figure, has much stronger incestuous feelings for his daughter than does Shakespeare's king, and ends by killing himself in a 'melancholy fit'.[40] There is no return to life for his long-dead abused wife. Shakepeare instead gives us a *tour de force* ending centred upon the miraculous return of the mother. Indeed, Hermione is not only a mother, but also, by now, an old wife, her wrinkles speaking of the astounding tale she could tell. We have seen that Greene was regarded in Shakespeare's time as a writer popular with women; yet Shakespeare adds more of the feminine and the maternal to the source material he finds in Greene.

All the late plays engage with the set of ideas which link femininity, and especially maternity, with romance narrative, but in the end *The Winter's Tale* seems distinctive in its embrace of these themes. Not only is it the late play in which the female body both before and soon after childbirth is most graphically shown on stage, but it is also the one in which the invocation of 'old tales' is most frequent. It is the late play in which 'great creating nature' is most present, and also the one in which the term 'issue' with its dual sense most often occurs. Maternity and narrative come fruitfully together in its celebration of old wives and their tales.

CHAPTER 10

Lady Mary Wroth's 'Urania'

The first published English romance by a woman was *The Countess of Montgomery's Urania*, 1621, by Lady Mary Wroth. Over the last twenty years this work has justly received an increasing amount of critical attention.[1] Understandably, much of this discussion has explored the relation of the *Urania* to the *Arcadia* of Wroth's uncle, Sir Philip Sidney, as mentioned above at pp. 108–9. Gradually, however, we are beginning to appreciate more fully Wroth's deep immersion in, and creative use of, a wide range of romance sources, an appreciation significantly fostered by the late Josephine Roberts's illuminating introduction to her magnificent edition of the 1621 *Urania*.[2] This chapter aims to use the romances I have already discussed as contexts for an exploration of how the relations between women and romance are developed by the *Urania*; and to convey something of the work's distinctive qualities.

WROTH AND THE TRADITION OF ROMANCE

As is by now widely known, the *Urania* is a *roman à clef* in which many of the characters shadow Wroth herself and members of her circle.[3] In particular, the central love story, between Pamphilia and Amphilanthus, reflects upon Wroth's own adulterous relationship with her cousin, William Herbert, Earl of Pembroke. One inset narrative provoked the ire of Edward Denny, Baron of Waltham, by exposing a scandal in his family.[4] Wroth disowned 'the strang constructions which are made of my booke',[5] but they provide detective puzzles for the modern scholar which are intriguing but by no means unsolvable, and must have been readily discernible by many of her contemporaries.[6] John Chamberlain commented that Wroth 'takes great libertie or rather licence to traduce whom she please, and thincks she daunces in a net'.[7]

Wroth was by no means the first to make fictional use of real-life material. As we have noted, as far back as the 1570s authors like Gascoigne and Pettie were tantalisingly implying real-life referents for their racy plots and characters, and allying the voyeuristic appeal of this with the power of romance to offer glimpses into women's bedchambers (chapter 3 above). There is a manifest difference, however, when this mingling of fact and fiction is engaged in by a woman, and her disclosure of true-life-secrets becomes mixed up with the idea that she is improperly exposing herself, an implication present in Chamberlain's application to her of the proverbial phrase 'dancing in a net'.[8] Wroth may have regarded herself as attempting something more like her uncle Philip's address to an élite audience of knowing intimates in the *Arcadia*, where Philisides is a version of himself, Queen Helen is a version of Queen Elizabeth and Argalus and Parthenia are versions of his own parents; and in *Astrophil and Stella*, where the eponymous couple both are and are not Philip Sidney and Penelope Rich. Jorge de Montemayor's pastoral romance *Diana* was a respectable precedent for both the *Arcadia* and the *Urania*; the author of that work explained in his preface that readers 'shall finde divers histories of accidents, that have truly happened, though they goe muffled under pastorall names and style'.[9] More recently, John Barclay's *Argenis*, published in 1621, the same year as the *Urania*, was a political romance with an explicit one-for-one key. Even though it touched upon sensitive matters such as the Overbury murder and the fall of Somerset, King James had been delighted with it.[10] All of these precedents might have encouraged Wroth to think that the *roman à clef* was an accepted and sanctioned romance form.

For Gascoigne and Pettie the purpose of their *romans à clef* seems to have been at least partly commercial, setting into a tremble the delicate membrane between fact and fiction to create a *frisson* for the potential reader and purchaser. For Sidney, who did not engage in print publication in his lifetime, this was evidently not so; instead he was creating an entertaining *frisson* of recognition for the select circle among whom his works circulated in manuscript. The difference is between the offer of partial revelation of an unfamiliar but enticing world, and displaced representation of a known world. Wroth may have fallen foul of a confusion between these two positions. The level of her involvement in the 1621 publication of the *Urania* remains unclear. She may have written mainly for her own pleasure and to entertain her immediate circle; this is suggested by the existence of a two-book unpublished manuscript sequel, now in the Newberry Library in Chicago.[11] After the Denny row erupted, Wroth wrote to the Duke of Buckingham protesting that the books 'from the first were solde against my minde I never purposing to have had them published'. However, she said this in a letter asking him to return a presentation copy which she had herself sent to the Duke.[12] Denny complained that he had been made 'the onely chosen foole for a May-game, before all the World and especially before a Wise King and Prince, with all the nobility', suggesting not only the sensational notoriety which the *Urania* had swiftly attracted but that Wroth may herself have attempted to use it for self-promotion at court.[13]

Just as Sidney constructed his imagined ideal reader as a tolerant sister, so by assigning the *Urania* to the Countess of Montgomery, Susan Herbert, the wife of her cousin Philip, Wroth was constructing her imagined ideal reader as an affectionate, female, romance-loving relative and friend. The text of the *Urania* is full of examples of characters who express their passions and griefs in fictional, symbolic, or otherwise encoded forms, and of other characters who interpret their meaning but courteously refrain from announcing it, or even refrain from pursuing explicit decodings. Some knights whom Amphilanthus has defeated wish to know the identity of their victor: 'Hee answered, the Lost Man; they found some thing was in that name, wherefore they would not presse, but left him.'[14] Dorolina recognises that Pamphilia's story of Lindamira, a version of both Pamphilia's and Mary Wroth's autobiography, is 'some thing more exactly related then a fixion, yet her discretion taught her to be no Inquisitor' (*U1*, p. 429). Perissus, Limena and the Queens of Naples and Sicily walk in a grove where 'Going along the Spring they found many knots, and names ingraven upon the trees, which they understood not perfectly, because when they had decipher'd some of them, they then found they were names fained and so knew them not. But *Perissus* remembred one of the Ciphers, yet because it was *Pamphilias* hee would not knowe it' (*U1*, p. 416). Wroth may have expected her audience to engage in this discreet, very Sidneian game with her. However, this was countermanded by several factors which provoked strong reactions. For one thing, print publication carried connotations of exposure working in two social directions: downwards, exposing Denny and other aristocrats to any vulgar reader into whose hands the book might fall, and upwards, embarrassing him before King and court. Wroth's anomalous gender as an author of romance was also clearly an issue; Denny told her to 'Work oth[er] Workes leave idle bookes alone / For wise and worthyer women have writte none'.[15] We should not disregard, either, the frequently vitriolic nature of her own wit, going beyond the kind of material previously encountered in romances: Sirelius, the fictional version of Denny, was depicted as 'a phantastical thing, vaine as Courtiers, rash as mad-men, and ignorant as women' who attempted to kill his daughter to excise her stain of adultery (*U1*, p. 439). Other evidence indicates that Wroth may not have been exaggerating Denny's violent temperament,[16] but in publicly representing him in such terms, and in publicising the scandal concerning his daughter who had died in 1615,[17] Wroth was in effect picking a fight.

Like her uncle, Wroth not only drew upon personal material for her plots and characters, but also depicted and commented upon topical political controversies. Like the *Arcadia*, the *Urania* was among other things a pastoral romance, and George Puttenham had explained in his *Art of English Poesy in* 1589 that pastoral was a veiled means 'to insinuate and glaunce at greater matters, and such as perchance had not been safe to have been disclosed in any other sort'.[18] Josephine Roberts has shown something of the extent of the *Urania*'s engagement with contemporary politics.[19] Its topicality also included the same technique used by Lyly in *Euphues and his England* of doubling back on itself to bring fictional characters to England; this occurs in Book IV of the 1621 *Urania*. Although the beauty and virtue of some of the women Wroth's knights encounter impress them, in other respects they are less pleased. Parts of the country are 'stony, wooddy, rocky, and as odde as could bee, lamentable travelling in it, the people rude and churlish' (*U1*, p. 532). The Prince of Venice asks an English lady, 'Have you no Knights Adventures in this Countrie . . .? Knights we have (said the Lady) good store, and adventures; but they seldome are put together, our Knights leaving the adventuring part, unlesse out of necessitie' (*U1*, p. 542). As in *Euphues and His England* and Rich's *Farewell* this is couched as eulogy of the peace presided over by the present monarch,[20] but as in those texts this is undermined by a strong residual sense of dismay at the martial decline of the nation. Whereas in the Elizabethan texts this was criticism of a female monarch by men seeking action, it is now a critique of a male monarch by an aristocratic woman writer who places herself at a tangent to the court and its policies and is to some degree, even in her choice of genre, nostalgic spokeswoman for a past age and its heroes.

If the published *Urania* performs acts of exposure regarded by some as excessive, nevertheless a dominant theme within the narrative is the need for secrecy. As has been widely discussed, Pamphilia does not reveal her love to anyone, including Amphilanthus, until a good way into the narrative, and the tenacious way in which she sustains, cherishes and conceals this secret passion gives her inner strength and self-conviction. This characterisation is reinforced by the sonnet sequence which was published at the end of the 1621 volume, *Pamphilia to Amphilanthus*, in which the female speaker plumbs ever more profound depths of interiority and melancholy while addressing abstract entities such as Love, Grief, Time, Sorrow and Night, but hardly ever her beloved.[21] The prizing of secrecy as a mark of female virtue is one of the many features which the *Urania* shares with the Iberian romances, where, as we saw at pp. 71–3 above, heroines like Oriana, Briana and Olivia conceal their passions, often at great personal cost, for no readily apparent reason except to prove their constancy, discretion and resourcefulness. As we noted there, although a high value is placed on the containing of information and emotion, this to a large extent displaces the prizing of bodily continence; heroines lose their virginity to their destined lovers without impairing their heroic status. Pamphilia never explicitly loses her virginity, but she does engage in numerous private and passionate encounters with Amphilanthus, and when alone is even more obviously consumed by desire. Several critics have drawn attention to Mary Wroth's redefinition of chastity as constancy in love rather than resistance of sexuality. Kim Walker comments that this 'suggests that the *Urania* provides a space within an apparently orthodox virtue for woman as a desiring subject'.[22] Reading previous fictions, including not only the Iberian romances but also texts like Rich's *Farewell* and the *Arcadia*, tells us that the desiring woman as saintly heroine was by no means unprecedented in the romance tradition. What is radical about Wroth's intervention, however, is the close identification of heroine and female author, indicating Wroth's empowering self-identification as just such a desiring yet praiseworthy and virtuously suffering figure.

Aside from the general supposed popularity of the Iberian romances with women readers which was culturally assumed by the

1620s, Wroth would certainly have been familiar with them through her friend Susan Herbert, the Countess of Montgomery. Susan Herbert was William Herbert's sister-in-law and was shadowed in the *Urania* by both Urania herself (Amphilanthus's sister), and Veralinda (Amphilanthus's sister-in-law). The four-volume English translation of *Amadis de Gaule* by Anthony Munday which appeared in 1618–19, around the time Wroth started writing the 1621 *Urania*, was dedicated to Susan's husband Philip. Munday mentioned in the prefaces to the first and third volumes that he had borrowed his sources from the Countess of Montgomery, and that he had completed the work at 'the urgent importunitie of that worthy Lady'.[23] Wroth could read French and so could have read *Amadis* in de Herberay's version as well as Munday's, but her friend's close connection with the text as owner and patron would certainly have assisted her knowledge of it.

Much of the detail of the *Urania* points to Wroth's close acquaintance with the Iberian narratives. In their intimacy since childhood Pamphilia and Amphilanthus resemble not only Mary Wroth and William Herbert, but also Amadis and Oriana, who owe their love to 'the nourishment they received together in their younger yeares, and their first amitie'.[24] The important episode in the 1621 *Urania* of the Throne of Love is drawn from *Amadis*; and the enchantress, Melissea, who makes periodic entrances to prophesy or to break enchantments is related to Urganda the Unknown in *Amadis de Gaule* and Orbiconte in *Palladine of England* as well as Felicia in Montemayor's *Diana* and Melyssa in *Orlando Furioso*.[25] The structure of the *Urania*, which is interlaced but sequential and episodic, owes less to the *New Arcadia* than to the Iberian romances and Ariosto, with the extensive travels of the heroes taking place in the present time of the narrative rather than in voluminous flashbacks. The Newberry manuscript also includes a detailed description of the monastery of the river near Buda, Briana's abode in *The Mirror of Knighthood* where she is seduced by Trebatio, which shows Wroth's knowledge of that text, presumably in Margaret Tyler's translation (*U2*, Book II, fo. 56v). It is very tempting to surmise, as Josephine Roberts does, that Wroth read and was inspired by Tyler's preface asserting the propriety of romance-writing by women.[26]

Many scholars have noticed how forcefully Wroth's dynastic credentials are asserted on the title page of the 1621 *Urania*: 'Written by the right honorable the Lady MARY WROATH. Daughter to the right Noble Robert, Earle of Leicester. And Neece to the ever famous, and renowned Sir Phillips Sidney knight. And to the most exelent Lady Mary Countesse of Pembroke late deceased.' This effects more than just the obvious foregrounding of the Sidney name and titles; it also echoes the dynastic structures of Iberian romances, as often announced on the title pages. Thus the full title of *Palmendos* was given as, 'The Honorable, pleasant and rare conceited Historie of Palmendos. Sonne to the famous and fortunate Prince Palmerin d'Oliva, Emperour of Constantinople and the Queene of Tharsus'.[27] Just as Palmendos is the latest bearer of the flame of Palmerin, so Wroth is the latest paragon in literary exploits of the illustrious Sidney line.[28]

Just as the Iberian romances generated sequels through dynastic progeneration, so the Newberry manuscript passes much of the action on to the second generation, as the children of Pamphilia and Amphilanthus's siblings and friends reach adulthood and embark upon their own quests and adventures. In particular, the Iberian romances were pleased to embrace illegitimate offspring for the extra narrative they could provide, such as Amadis's half-brother Florestan; likewise the Newberry manuscript features several 'natural' sons. These include a mysterious young knight named Fair Design, who is strongly implied to be Amphilanthus's natural son and thus a representation of the son Wroth bore to her cousin. Fair Design, like the 'fair unknown' heroes of the Iberian romances, is on a quest for his own identity and for love. Unlike his best friend Andromarcko, natural son of Polarchos, who is lovingly acknowledged by his father, Fair Design's quest remains unfinished. His first appearance is an encounter with Amphilanthus at which he explains: 'I knowe noe parents, nor have I a name more then the unknowne, I have a sipher on my hart which is sayd to bee her name whom I must by many hard adventures att last gaine, and knowe her by having a sipher likewise which shall discover my name, and then I shalbe knowne.' Amphilanthus knights him as armour and other trappings for him appear on a cloud, the shield bearing the same cipher as his breast, leading him to be called 'the knight of the faire designe' (*U2*, Book II, fo. 29r). Later, the Newberry manuscript ends with Andromarcko telling Amphilanthus that the mysterious young hero's adventure, to break an enchantment, 'will not bee concluded thes many yeeres, nay never if you live nott to assiste in the concluding, soe his search is for you . . . the best, and hapiest [Fair

Design] I assure myself wilbee in finding you; Amphilanthus was extreamly' (*U2*, Book II, fo. 62r). Here the text breaks off, in a much more profoundly unresolved way than the open-ended last sentence of the 1621 *Urania.* Such convenient correspondence between romance conventions and circumstances of her life – on top of all her Sidney baggage – almost leads one to think: how could Wroth *not* have written a romance?

Some of the instances of cross-dressing in the *Urania* imitate conventions of the Iberian romances. In the Newberry manuscript, Clavarindo adopts women's apparel to liberate the young princes and princesses, the children of the principal characters of the 1621 *Urania*, from an island where they are being held captive by a giant. As when Rosicleer disguises himself as Lyverba in *The Mirror of Knighthood*, he surpasses women in beauty: 'ever itt is seene that wher a man is faire, hee excells all woemen' (*U2*, Book I, fo. 23r).[29] Also like Rosicleer, he leaves no doubt as to his manhood, defeating first the giant, then the treacherous King of Natolia: 'hee made noe ende of his speech, for Clavarindo . . . cleft his head and toungue asunder, and soe concluded his speech, and his lyfe together' (*U2*, Book I, fo. 23v). Numurandro also adopts female disguise for martial purposes, to penetrate enemy troops, accompanied by Lusandrino in the guise of a 'pesant clowne', recalling the female and rustic disguises of Pyrocles and Musidorus (*U2*, Book I, fo. 30r).

There is even fuller reminiscence of Pyrocles's cross-dressing in the 1621 *Urania*, in which Leonius becomes Leonia to woo the shepherdess Veralinda. However, whereas Philoclea suffers from doubts and fears concerning the propriety of her growing affection for one of her own sex,[30] the apparent same-sex intimacy between Veralinda and the nymph Leonia is far more harmonious and untroubled, even before Leonia's true sex is revealed. Veralinda liked Leonia's kiss

> better then any of her fellows kisses, for this seemd more passionately kind . . . they beheld each other, the Shepheard[es]s passionately beholding *Leonia* in memory of her love, and the Nimph amorously gazing on her in her owne passions . . . never weary of any time but night, which they accused of too great cruelty in holding them asunder, which faire *Veralinda* oft would have helped in her wish, but her Father would not permit it. (*U1*, pp. 371–2, 387)

Moreover, Leonius's motives for his deceit are not the usual ones of penetration of patriarchal defences so much as a desire to infiltrate

Veralinda's own mind and heart: as he reveals himself he confesses, 'I am the man, who for feare you lov'd me not, to move your love madc my selfe a woman' (*U1*, p. 389). There is a striking assertion here that the best way to win a woman may be not with virile force, but by entering into femininity.

On the whole, though, cross-dressing is not a major interest for Wroth. Her allusions to boy-actors who act the part of women are pejorative, foregrounding their falsehood. A traveller is wooed by the libidinous Queen of Romania, 'yet he unmoveable, was no further wrought, then if hee had seene a delicate play-boy acte a loving womans part, and knowing him a Boy, lik'd onely his action' (*U1*, p. 60). Another lady is 'as full of faulshood as of vaine and endles expressions, being for her over acting fashion, more like a play boy dressed gaudely up to shew a fond loving woemans part, then a great Lady' (*U2*, Book 1, fo. 58v). None of Wroth's leading female characters cross-dress. Pamphilia is a ruling queen, and is sometimes praised for having 'a brave and manlike spirit' (*U1*, p. 483), but Wroth is ill-disposed towards women who are *too* masculine,[31] and the role of warrior-woman does not seem to have interested her very much.

Incidental female characters who cross-dress are treated in divergent ways. In the 1621 *Urania* Lisia is affronted by false accusations by the capricious princess whom she serves that she visited the princess's brother's bedchamber by night dressed in man's apparel, recalling the gossip circulating in around 1600–1 that Mary Fitton, William Herbert's mistress, was using male disguise to make clandestine visits to his chambers at court.[32] Also in the 1621 volume we find an incidental story of a spurned mistress who follows romance conventions more closely by disguising herself as a youth to rescue and serve her faithless beloved, then dies pathetically:

> farewell my Lord, and I beseech you mourne not for mee, whom you thought so little worthy of your love . . . with many prayers for my safety, wishing all the blessing that heaven granted to any, to bee powred on me, shee dyed in mine armes, breathing her last into my breast; for I kiss'd her when her breath left her. (*U1*, p. 381)

Wroth is at pains to emphasise that the lady's transvestism is 'not out of any wantonnesse', but a mark of the purity of her love: 'Love (my Lord) hath brought me to this, and all other miseries . . . censure me then a lover and not immodest' (*U1*, pp. 380–1). The lady is a literary descendant of the original Zelmane, of Silla and of the cross-dressing saints who came before them, adopting male disguise not as a means to liberation and adventure but as a willing humiliation and degradation in the holy cause of love.

The fates of other heroines build upon the models of female heroism derived by romances from sacred sources like the *Golden Legend.* Meriana is subjected to incarceration by an unwanted suitor and a faked execution in the sight of her beloved, Rosindy: she appears to have been beheaded on the battlements of her persecutor's castle, but has in fact been made to stand inside a hollow pillar upon which sits her supposedly disembodied head (*U1*, pp. 132–4). The episode not only recalls the staged deaths of Pamela and Philoclea, but appears to carry through a threat made prior to that by Cecropia:

> she sent a messenger to the camp to denounce unto Basilius that if he did not presently raise his siege, she would cause the heads of the three ladies, prisoner, to be cut off before his eyes. And to make him the more fear a present performance, she caused his two daughters and Zelmane to be led unto the walls where she had made a scaffold, easy to be seen by Basilius. (*NA*, p. 546)

Behind this again lie the incarcerations, decapitations and mutilations of mediaeval saints. Like the Arcadian princesses and numerous other romance heroines, Meriana has become a martyr to the cause of true love, remaining devoted to Rosindy through all her tribulations and preferring death to inconstancy to him.

Another striking case of erotic sainthood is Limena, whose husband Philargus subjects her to numerous torments including daily stripping and scourging while tied by her hair to a pillar and 'from the girdle upwards al naked, her soft, daintie white hands . . . fastened behind her, with a cord about both wrists, in manner of a crosse, as testimony of her cruellest Martyrdome' (*U1*, p. 68). Philargus's purpose is to extract a confession of Limena's adultery with the man she loves, Perissus. Perissus and Limena were in love before her marriage to the boorish, hunt-loving Philargus, which she entered into in obedience to her father and without affection. This is one of the many inset narratives in the *Urania* which seem to bear relation to Wroth's marriage to Sir Robert Wroth and adulterous relationship with William Herbert, and one of the many in which a husband is cast as a villain and extramarital love is highly prized. The iconography of female virtue is thus taken a step further into the secular and erotic dimension: chastity consists not in denial of sexuality, not even in mere sexual fidelity, but in fidelity to a lover above an imposed husband.

Yet throughout this process the hagiographic conventions persist of the definition of female virtue through suffering and the scarring of the female body. As Philargus threatens ever more violence against Limena, she protests ever more clearly her inner spotlessness. At the same time, the marks upon her body become a text recording his cruelty and her virtue, especially at the culmination of the episode when she displays her injuries while narrating her own story: 'When I had put off all my apparell but one little Petticote, he opened my breast, and gave me many wounds, the markes you may here yet discerne, (letting the Mantle fall againe a little lower, to shew the cruell remembrance of his crueltie)' (*U1*, p. 71). The frequent undressing of Limena and display of her breasts, as here, give the episode an erotic charge which might seem unsettling and unexpected in a text by a woman author; but the fact that Limena's physical display is self-willed, and illustrative of her narrative of endurance, suggests that far more is going on than just the objectification of the victimised female body. Like mediaeval saints whose protestations of devotion to Christ became more fervent the more they were tormented, Limena is inspired by her sufferings not only to affirm her unswerving dedication to her beloved, but also to find an eloquent voice; and in that voice to assert her ardent self-certainty: '*Philargus*, saide shee, I knowe in mine owne heart I have not wrong'd you, and God knowes I have not wrong'd my selfe' (*U1*, p. 10). Her displays of her naked body – she also displays her snow-white breast in her first confrontation with Philargus, inviting him to stab it (*U1*, p. 11) – are less erotic spectacles than declarations of an inner purity, beneath clothing and outward shows, which in turn point towards a deeper purity within the body, in the mind, heart and soul.[33]

Pamphilia is not subjected to physical torments like those of Limena and Meriana. However, her willing embrace of the mental and emotional torments of unfulfilled love perpetuates the iconography of suffering as the measure of female heroism.[34] When she finds that a friend of hers, the nymph Silviana, has broken her vow to Diana and married, reverting to her original name of Alarina, she tells herself, 'yet *Pamphilia* be thou still just, and though but thy selfe, and so alone to suffer glory in such martyrdome' (*U1*, p. 410). Moreover, in the later parts of the *Urania* her enduring constancy is outwardly marked by another kind of physical scar, the marks of ageing. When Amphilanthus makes one of his periodic returns to Pamphilia in Book IV of the 1621 *Urania*, she asks herself, 'Can he smile on these wrincles, and be loving in my decay?' (*U1*, p. 482). Many other ladies whom she encounters or hears of on her travels have lost their beauty in the cause of love, and, piling cruelty upon cruelty, have thereby lost their love as well. Emilina was courted then deserted by an impostor travelling under Amphilanthus's name, who 'slighted her, and told her she was growne old, and her beauty alter'd, willed her to recover that, and when he return'd from a journey that he had in hand, he would be as he was' (*U1*, p. 248). Bellamira, another persona for Mary Wroth, relates how, although her lover 'oft protested to bee fixed on my worth, and love for him', yet her 'face's alteration' gave him 'liberty from former bands, to looke else where . . . what can this wrinckled face, and decayed beauty hope for?' (*U1*, pp. 335–6). Lady Fancy, though reluctant to marry, eventually decides to do so for pragmatic reasons:

> yett this againe comes in my minde, beauty dayly decays, age must inheritt that treasure beauty, and youthe possest, live then, a husband will cherish age as in him self hee must have itt, a fine house a good fire, a soft bed in winter, noe wants, good clothes for all seasons, hansome discourse with a reasonable husband children to pass away the time with all thes are speciall good, and all thes a happy wife hath to comfort her in her yeers. (*U2*, Bk. I, fo. 12v)

However, her erstwhile lover 'scornfully told mee, I needed nott to bee coye since the wringles incircling the corners of my eyes, and forhead might suffer yeers, and decaying to bee written in them, this makes mee doubt my fortunes' (*ibid.*).

Wroth's frank recognition of the ageing process has been seen by some readers as a radical and realistic departure from the timeless world of romance. In fact it is not wholly unprecedented: the Iberian romances, with their long dynastic sequences, perforce deal in the passage of time. In *The Mirror of Knighthood*, Trebatio returns from his twenty-year detention by Lindaraza's enchantment the same age as when he left, thirty-five, but Briana has aged from fourteen to thirty-four. She has had to 'endure a farre greater penaunce then *Penelope* did by *Ulysses* absence'. We are told that 'they both satte downe together kissinge and collinge each other lyke two younge lovers', with a clear implication that this is incongruous behaviour and unusual passion in two so old.[35] However, we do not find the same precise attention to the physical signs of female ageing as we do in Wroth. Her use of the motif of the waiting, ageing woman builds upon a romance tradition, traceable back to the classical precedent of Penelope, but does indeed take it towards realism in her observations of wrinkled faces, and of loss of love, rather than happy reunion, as the most likely end of the story.

Pamphilia's wrinkles, like Limena's scars, are a mark of the virtue and devotion which lie within her being. Her endurance of suffering develops into a profound exploration of female subjectivity and interiority. She is characteristically to be found in her closet or in secluded woods and landscapes: 'the saddest places were the most pleasing to her, the solitariest Caves or Rockes her chiefe abiding places' (*U1*, p. 411). In these spaces she meditates on her emotions, reads and writes, following and exceeding the example of the Arcadian princesses. Shortly after her first entry into the narrative,

> *Pamphilia* alone began to breath out her passions, which to none shee would discover, resolving rather to perish . . . Alas, would she say (weeping to her selfe) what have I deserved to bee thus tyrannically tortured by love? . . . Being heavie, she went into her bed, but not with hope of rest, but to get more libertie to expresse her woe . . . taking a little Cabinet with her, wherein she had many papers, and setting a light by her, [she] began to reade them, but few of them pleasing her, she took pen and paper, and being excellent in writing, writ these verses following. (*U1*, p. 51)

In the Newberry manuscript, Pamphilia's suitor Rodomandro, King of Tartaria, finds her characteristically 'alone, onely boockes about her, which she ever extreamly loved, and she writing, butt when she parceaved him, she clapt her papers into her deske'. He proposes marriage, to which she replies that 'such is my sad, and soe determined to bee sad lyfe, as makes mee farr undeserving of such a fortune, a booke, and solitarines, beeing the onely companions I desire in thes my unfortunate days'. Rodomandro answers with a rather touching sensitivity and appreciation of her character: 'love your booke, butt love mee soe farr as that I may hold itt to you, that while you peruse that, I may joye in beeholding you . . . bee solitarie, yett favour mee soe much as that I may butt attend you, when you waulke in deserts, and woods', where he will guard her from 'serpents, and veminous [*sic*] beasts' (*U2*, Book II, fo. 21V). It is not surprising that of all her many suitors Pamphilia accepts this one, even while persisting in her love for Amphilanthus.

Pamphilia's withdrawal into solitude and melancholy is saved from appearing nihilistic or feeble by many factors. Among these are her defiant resistance of seventeenth-century expectations that a woman will marry, and will accept direction in her choice of a spouse; instead, Pamphilia personifies female heroism as something which exists outside wifehood. Moreover, she defines herself not only against the institution of marriage, but even against her beloved: as Amphilanthus repeatedly proves himself unworthy, she persists in loving in defiance of his behaviour, and almost regardless of him, loving not for his sake but for her own satisfaction.[36] Thus the apparent masochism of her situation is transmuted into resolute self-esteem and self-conviction. After one of Amphilanthus's departures, she turns with affection to her own thoughts as good and reliable friends: 'Deere companions in my solitaryness, said she, furnish me with your excellency in constancy, and I will serve you with thankfull loyalty' (*U1*, p. 270). After one of his returns she reflects that she ought not to have forgiven him and welcomed him back, but 'policie was it not that bred this in me, but pure love, and unfortunate subjection, yet I love my selfe for it, and will strive to continue it' (*U1*, p. 482).

Other attractive characteristics include her warm friendships with other women with whom she enjoys sharing both true and fictional stories of love; and the strong connection which Wroth asserts between her ability to conceal and control her feelings – that is, her self-government – and her ability to govern her country: 'she joyed in nothing, nor communed with any but her owne sad selfe . . . yet she lost not her selfe; for her government continued just and brave, like that Lady she was, wherein she shewed her heart was not to be stirr'd, though her private fortunes shooke round about her' (*U1*, p. 411). Unlike the Arcadian princesses or most other romance heroines, she is a ruling queen. Her country which bears her own name, Pamphilia, was indeed a real country identified on contemporary maps, as were almost all the locations in the *Urania*.[37] Her name thus signifies both personal qualities of female heroism – a conflation of Pamela and Philoclea – and ruling power at the level of nations and empires.[38] Wroth represents her as a judicious and respected monarch. Her pleasure in withdrawal into privacy therefore connects with the public and political dimensions of the narrative, rather than unequivocally endorsing the confinement of women to the private sphere.

Wroth also depicts the characters and emotional states of Pamphilia and others by alternative means to the Arcadian exploration of interiority and literary subjectivity. She incorporates alongside this a more Spenserian technique of emblem and allegory. In the adventure of the Throne of Love, Pamphilia and Amphilanthus release a number of knights and ladies from an enchantment by passing through three towers: Desire, which opens to Amphilanthus; Love, which opens to the two of them together; and 'the last Tower, where *Constancy* stood holding the keyes, which *Pamphilia* tooke; at which instant *Constancy* vanished, as metamorphosing her self into her breast' (*U1*, p. 141). Just as Spenser is able to make Britomart both a feeling, acting character in his unfolding narrative and the personification of Chastity, so Pamphilia is both an individual and a symbol. In the next book of the 1621 *Urania* she reaffirms this: 'let me be ordaind, or licensed to be the true patterne of true constancy' (*U1*, p. 203).

Wroth's characters tend not to encounter as many allegorical personifications along the way as do Spenser's, although Wroth briefly plays games with this device in the Newberry manuscript when her heroes meet Lady Fancy and hear about her lover, Love, 'noe fained names butt indeed our true names' (*U2*, Book I, fo. 12v). But the strongest recollection of Spenser is in the episode of the Hell of Deceit, in Book IV of the 1621 *Urania*. In a striking inversion of Amoret's imprisonment by Busirane, Pamphilia has the following vision of Amphilanthus with two of his mistresses:

> a place like a Hell of flames, and fire, and as if many walking and throwing pieces of men and women up and downe the flames, partly burnt, and they still stirring the fire, and more brought in, and the longer she looked, the more she discernd, yet all as in the hell of deceit, at last she saw *Musalina* sitting in a Chaire of Gold, a Crowne on her head, and *Lucenia* holding a sword, which *Musalina* tooke in her hand, and before them *Amphilanthus* was standing, with his heart ript open, and *Pamphilia* written in it, *Musalina* ready with the point of the sword to conclude all, by razing that name out, and so his heart as the wound to perish. (*U1*, p. 494)

Pamphilia desperately flings herself into the flames to rescue him, but is flung back again. Whereas the flames encompassing Busirane's castle can only be traversed by one as pure as Britomart, here only the unchaste can pass: 'Faithfull lovers keepe from hence / None but false ones here can enter.'[39]

Amphilanthus does indeed embark on a long sojourn with these two mistresses, towards the end of which Musalina is responsible 'by divellish art' for his own complementary vision: within a stone he sees

> *Pamphilia* dead, lying within an arch, her breast open and in it his name made, in little flames burning like pretty lamps which made the letters, as if set round with diamonds, and so cleare it was, as hee distinctly saw the letters ingraven at the bottome in Characters of bloud; he ran to take her up, and try how to uncharme her, but he was instantly throwne out of the Cave in a trance. (*U1*, p. 554)

He is distracted by cries for help from Musalina, and Wroth caustically remarks, 'she must be followed, *Pamphilia* is forgotten, and now may lie and burne within the Cave'.

The Hell of Deceit is an extremely graphic and effective means of representing the experience of infidelity. While Wroth's depiction of Pamphilia explores ideas of selfhood and the literary expression of subjectivity which look forward to novelistic models of psychology, and to Romantic ideas of the self realised in solitude, at the same time she makes extremely fruitful use in episodes like this of non-naturalistic and symbolic methods of representing interior states. These at once look back to mediaeval and Spenserian techniques of allegory, and look forward to later non-naturalistic conventions such as the Gothic.

Wroth is extremely self-conscious about her relation to the romance tradition, and other aesthetic forms. Jennifer Lee Carrell and Josephine Roberts have pointed out how, in the wake of the great success of *Don Quixote*, published in English in two parts in 1612 and 1620, it was even less possible than it might already have been at this late stage in development to take the conventions of romance entirely seriously.[40] A knowing sophistication is present from the early stages of the *Urania*, when Parselius, clearly understanding the conventions of the genre he inhabits, hopes that the shepherdess Urania is really a lost princess so that he can marry her without having to worry about class (*U1*, p. 21). A satirical slant is especially evident in Book IV in the episodes in England with their bathetic juxtapositions of romance ideals with quotidian realities. Wroth's band of princes meet two English ladies; the Prince of Florence embarks upon an extravagant encomium of their beauty, but 'The Ladies left him in his speech, and taking handes walked away, as who would say, by that time the Oration is done, wee will come againe, smiling on themselves and their uncivilnesse' (*U1*, p. 533).

Romances are often referred to within the text with a sense of their unreality, inadequacy or inconsequentiality. There is a highly ironic example of this when Pamphilia sits in a wood reading a book which sounds strangely like the *Urania*:

the subject was Love, and the story she then was reading, the affection of a Lady to a brave Gentleman, who equally loved, but being a man, it was necessary for him to exceede a woman in all things, so much as inconstancie was found fit for him to excell her in, hee left her for a new. Poore love said the Queene, how doth all storyes, and every writer use thee at their pleasure. (*U1*, p. 264)

She condemns writers who malign love as traitors, declares her own loyalty to the cause and throws the book away, passing her time instead in laying her hand on her heart to feel its violent beating, and dwelling on love in her imagination. True emotion, and her own thoughts, are preferred over conventional stories. Alarinus laments of his mistress, 'Must . . . she be named as if in a Romancy, that relates of Knights, and distressed Damosells, the sad Adventures?' (*U1*, p. 504). Another lover presents his mistress with 'many severall copies, and small romancies . . . seeing she did delight in thos harmles pretty expressions of witt' (*U2*, Book I, fo. 5r). There is contempt for a lord who made 'blasphemous swearing and curses the greatest part of his discourse, for learning, ore reading above a Romancie hee never troubled himself with all therfor certainly itt must prove a brave state wher such shalbee, and are the governours' (*U2*, Book II, fo. 5v).

In these instances Wroth participates in the disparagement of romance which was commonplace by the 1620s, and seems to distance herself from the genre. Fiction, however, is a term which carries high value, as long as it is grounded in, or as good as, real experience. Pamphilia walks with the rescued Limena, whom she calls her 'second selfe', not without irony since both of them are in some degree versions of Mary Wroth. She beseeches her,

you that so perfectly and so happily have loved, cannot in this delightfull place, but remember those sweete (yet for a while curst) passages in love, which you have overgone: speake then of love, and speake to me, who love that sweete discourse, (next to my love) above all other things, if that you cannot say more of your selfe, then your deare trust hath grac'd me withall, tell of some others, which as truly shall be silently inclosed in my breast, as that of yours; let me but understand the choice varieties of Love, and the mistakings, the changes, the crosses; if none of these you know, yet tell me some such fiction. (*U1*, p. 188)

Much later, near the end of the Newberry manuscript, Pamphilia, Amphilanthus and Melasinda 'past the best part of the night in pleasing discourse of the flowring time of their first lovings, every one, nott nice, butt truly telling their infinitely suffering passions, butt the prize fell to Pamphilias share by their owne confessions' (*U2*, Book II, fo. 57v). She is the best storyteller because she is the most feeling lover. Poetry, too, is valued in so far as it has its basis in true feeling: 'poetry . . . att the best is butt a frency, and yett in Lovers itt is a most commendable, and fine qualitie beeing a way most excellent to express their pretious thoughts, in a rare, and covert way, butt they are meere poetts that I spake of when I condemned poetry' (*U2*, Book I, fo. 13r).

It is worth recalling Philip Sidney's inclusion of prose fiction in his definition of poetry, and his defence of it as a medium 'not labouring to tell you what is or is not, but what should or should not be'.[41] Just as the *Arcadia* could be classified in Sidney's terms as a poem, so Wroth may have conceived of the *Urania* as something with higher pretensions than a mere romance. She certainly seems to have taken note of the exhortation of her uncle's Muse to 'look in thy heart, and write'.[42]

THE READING PLEASURES OF THE *URANIA*

The combination of a satirical attitude to romance with the use of Wroth's social experience as source material often produces witty, crackling dialogue far removed from Euphuistic rhetoric. We hear about a promiscuous lady: 'Is she beautifull sayd Steriamus; noe truly Sir replied the lady, what she hath she pays for, and itt is nott good neither' (*U2*, Book I, fo. 58v). When Pamphilia's country is attacked by Persia, Veralinda assures her that Amphilanthus will come to her aid: 'Thos days are past my deere Veralinda cride Pamphilia, and hee is changed, and proves a man,[43] hee was ever thought so sayd Veralinda' (*U2*, Book I, fo. 40r). Much affectionate teasing goes on among the intimate circle of Pamphilia, her best friend Urania and Urania's brother Amphilanthus. Amphilanthus interrupts a story Urania is telling, then, when her performance of a song is praised by Pamphilia, breaks in again: 'truly (said *Amphilanthus*) is this to be so much liked? but my cosin only doth it to please you. No in truth, said *Pamphilia*, it deserves in my judgement much liking; he smild on her, *Urania* going on, you seeme Brother, said she, a little willing to crosse me this day, but I will proceed in discourse' (*U1*, p. 212).

Pamphilia herself is often ready with a sardonic retort. In Book III of the 1621 *Urania*, Pamphilia and Urania are shipwrecked and see in the distance a sumptuous marble building. Urania has already been imprisoned by one enchantment from which Pamphilia freed her:

I feare this storme, and adventure said *Urania*, ever since I was carried to *Ciprus*; if it be an inchantment, woe be to us . . . Let it be what it will said *Pamphilia*, I will see the end of it . . . You may said *Urania*, having had such successe in the last, yet take heed, all adventures were not framed for you to finish. Nor for you to be enchanted in, answered shee. So they went on. (*U1*, p. 321)

Amphilanthus is most often the victim of Pamphilia's sharp tongue, tempering any sense that her constancy and melancholy in the face of his repeated betrayals is pitiful or abject. When she sees him fighting under new colours, she asks, 'But what colour shall wee have next: the last I saw was Crimson, now Watchet[44] and White; do you adde to your inconstancy, as fast as to your colours?' (*U1*, p. 138). On occasion the potency of her scorn renders Amphilanthus nervously deferential to her, as when they listen together to a shepherd's song abjuring love: 'The wiser man, said *Amphilanthus*. The liker to your mind, said *Pamphilia*, if hee love varities: hee looked upon her, but seeing shee smild, when shee spake itt, hee did so likewise' (*U1*, p. 483). The authorial narrator engages in the same affectionate, but nonetheless barbed mockery of her hero: '*Amphilanthus* I pittie thee . . . for inconstancy, was, and is the onely touch thou hast, yet can I not say, but thou art constant to love; for never art thou out of love' (*U1*, p. 312).

Pamphilia is skilled in exploiting the veil of irony, scoring points while superficially avoiding offence. She is visited by Nereana, who seeks to challenge her for the love of Steriamus, a love of no interest to Pamphilia anyway. Pamphilia tells her,

in truth I am sorry, that such a Lady should take so great and painefull a voyage, to so fond an end, being the first that ever I heard of, who take so Knight like a search in hand; men being us'd to follow scornefull Ladies, but you to wander after a passionate, or disdainefull Prince, it is great pitie for you.

However, she goes on to assure Nereana that she is welcome to Steriamus, since his love is

> what I will not accept, if offered me . . . These words were spoken so, as though proud *Nereana* were nettled with them, yet could she not in her judgement finde fault openly with them, but rather sufferd them with double force to bite, inwardly working upon her pride-fild heart, and that in her eyes she a little shewed, though she suffered her knees somewhat to bow in reverence to her. (*U1*, p. 163)

If adeptness at irony and sarcasm are among the characteristics which Pamphilia shared with her creator, it is not difficult to understand why Mary Wroth made enemies.

Another striking characteristic of Wroth's prose is her finely wrought and inventive imagery. The Queen of Bulgaria's pride kept her virtuous, 'and so by that meanes one of the greatest sinnes grew like a vertue, but no neerer being one, then the shadow of the purest Lilley in the water, is one; neither having colour or sweetenesse of the Lilley, only shape but blacke, and nothing of it selfe' (*U1*, p. 378). Amphilanthus, at a rare moment of complete fidelity to Pamphilia, becomes almost the personification of love itself,

> as neere as a round glasse made of the clearest temper, and fild full of the clearest water, turne it any way, you see thorow it, yet both seeme one colour, and cleerenesse in agreeing; so did the clearenesse of his love shew through him, or was it selfe onely love, and purely cleare, no vacant place, least turning of the glasse might make a bubble to appeare a change; no, he was round and true. (*U1*, p. 296)

Such intricate images are sometimes drawn by Wroth from close observation of domestic activities, such as gardening, spinning and housekeeping. As Antissia's personal resentments and plots secretly multiply, 'she remain'd like a Nettle, hardly scaping the weeders hand, but growing on, turnes to seede, and from thence springs hundreds as stinging' (*U1*, p. 313). A lamenting lady lapses into silence, 'but long continued she not so, like to women spinning, staid but to fasten the thread to begin againe to turne, and twine her sorrowes' (*U1*, p. 303). Three years after a marriage, 'other passions have crept in like Mothes into good stuffe' (p. 440). Perhaps most strikingly, the careworn Pamphilia suffers from 'continuall passions, which not utter'd did weare her spirits and waste them, as rich imbroyderies will spoyle one another, if laid without papers betweene them, fretting each other, as her thoughts and imaginations did her rich and incomprable minde' (*U1*, p. 423).

Such lively dialogue and original, vivid imagery enhance the vitality of the narrative. Its central strength, though, is the complexity of the relationship between Pamphilia and Amphilanthus. It is a potent combination of mutual attraction with mutual doubt, sexual magnetism with the comfortable intimacy of childhood friends. In the Newberry manuscript, as Amphilanthus begins to grow jealous of Rodomandro, Pamphilia retires to her chamber after a day's hunting where 'on her bed she found him layd' (*U2*, Book I, fo. 14r). Their longstanding companionship gives him privileged access to her private quarters, such that even as she dresses for her marriage to Rodomandro, Amphilanthus leans against the chimney beside her dressing table; and, after the wedding, visits her in her bedchamber to take his leave, and 'with deepe groanes stoped her mouth with kisses' (*U2*, Book II, fos. 22v, 25r).

The passion of this last scene is not unusual. Throughout the narrative, the pay-off for long periods of waiting in vain for Amphilanthus, for the reader as well as the heroine, is a cathartic release of pent-up emotion on the occasions when he returns and declares his love. In Book IV of the 1621 *Urania*, after Pamphilia witnesses Amphilanthus's triumph in a combat, they withdraw together,

> love expressing it selfe, not only lively but perfectly in their eyes: he tooke her hand, kiss'd it, beheld her earnestly, as amorously ready to make expression of what was expected and hoped for, she as yeelding fate ready to grant . . . his eyes fixt as they were, and shee observing his, he most lovingly, or rather passionately caught, (like a man drowning, catching at the next thing to him to save himselfe) the Queene in his armes, and as no offender, (except in boldnesse) embraced her. (*U1*, pp. 481–2)

Such rapturous moments may appear a little like Mills-and-Boon-type wish-fulfilment fantasies, but are given more depth and darkness by the insecurities and resentments which invariably underscore them. Immediately after this embrace Pamphilia doubts both Amphilanthus's fidelity and the ability of her fading beauty to sustain his desire, and chastises herself for having 'Wiped my eyes, and from him hid my sorrowes, to whom for my redresse they should have beene discovered' (*U1*, p. 482). The published *Urania* climaxes with another ecstatic reunion:

> the Queene lying among the flowres, and some bushes betweene, so as she could better see him, then he discerne her, especially not thinking of any there perceived; O what? nay what? her soule without her selfe, because in an other body returned, she quickly rose up, and as she parted so hoped to meete him, kind to her, she ranne unto him, forgiving, nay forgetting all

injuries, he seeing her threw downe his helme, with open armes received her, and withall unfained affection embraced her. (*U1*, p. 557)

Even here, though, Wroth cannot resist putting the knife in: 'and well might hee joyfully doe it, love thus exprest, besides a labour saved of asking pardon'.

In the Newberry manuscript, as each of them marries another partner and mistrusts multiply, reunions after long partings become even more fraught. At one point Amphilanthus and Pamphilia with their retinues happen to put in at the same harbour. He is wearing his beaver, or helmet, and she is wearing a veil. Their uncertainty yet suspicion as to one another's identity intensifies their uncertainty as to how each will receive the other and how they ought to conduct themselves towards one another:

the Emperour helpt his deerest lady ashoar, though trembling as if hee had bin in the water, and new come out to shake of such unfreindly coldenesses, she tooke his help, butt trembling to, her infinite passions beeing such and soe full as she feard the breaking of them . . . hee longed, butt durst nott adventur to bee certaine itt was she, his hart, not daring though assuredly hoping itt was she, till she pulled off her glove to lift up a great Vaile she had on, which beeing thick kept her close and hott . . . I pray Sir sayd she, if itt bee nott to unseemly an office for a knight to help the dressing of a lady to assiste mee in taking of this vaile . . . soe pulling off his gantletts, hee soe tenderly, and gently pulled of her vaile as if hee had bin bred in a lady's chamber. (*U2*, Book II, fo. 2r)

Wroth manages with great delicacy the gradual removal of layers of clothing as layers of self-concealment, formality and defensiveness are likewise peeled away. As Pamphilia recognises Amphilanthus's ungloved hand a flood of emotions is at last released; he collapses in a guilt-stricken faint and she bathes his face with her tears. The delay in expressing pent-up feelings not just leading up to the encounter, but within the encounter, makes that expression all the more cathartic when it finally comes.[45] Later again, Amphilanthus comes to Pamphilia incognito, but when he reveals his face casts them both into a paralysis of emotion and uncertainty: he 'stood gasing on her as in an exstasie of Joye, and fear; Pamphilia knew less what to doe' (*U2*, Book II, fo. 51r). Amphilanthus finally breaks the stasis with a profession of his love.

The generic category of 'romance' in the Renaissance is a vast one, and some romances could only barely or partly be described as love stories. There can be no doubt that the *Urania* is a love story.

Active desire, as an attribute of a heroine rather than a villainess, had been present in romances before, in some of Rich's heroines, in heroines of Iberian romance, in the Arcadian princesses, but Wroth gives it a new force, for the first time voicing female passion with an energy and profundity which bears comparison with more widely known nineteenth- and twentieth-century women writers.

Those of us who began our academic careers in a post-post-structuralist age, attuned to the play of text and the self-referentiality of literature, often feel anxious about praising a text for its depiction of lived experience. It is true that the *Urania* shows that Wroth was adept at literary games of allusion and self-consciousness. It is also true that we must avoid any reductive reading of her romance as autobiography: individuals from real life are often multiply shadowed by several different figures and sub-plots (Wroth herself, for instance, as Pamphilia, Lindamira, Bellamira, Limena and others) who represent different aspects and versions of their life stories.[46] Moreover, we must not discount an element of wish-fulfilment fantasy. When the Queen of Naples, who shadows the Countess of Pembroke, is shown encouraging Pamphilia to receive the already married Amphilanthus in private immediately after her marriage to Rodomandro, thereby apparently sanctioning the continuation of their adulterous relationship, this may indicate that Wroth wished for the approval of her aunt for her liaison with her cousin, but is far from proving that she received it (*U2*, Book II, fos. 22v–25r).[47] Amphilanthus is made to castigate himself for his loss of Pamphilia with the lament, 'she is just, she is pure, she is holy, she is immaculate . . . O for ever hated change, O for ever detested change, of all earthly ills, the wurst' (*U2*, Book I, fo. 65r). It would be rash to assume that the real William Herbert spoke these words, but not unlikely that Wroth relished making his fictional counterpart say them in the imaginary world which she controlled. At the same time, however, it is hard to avoid a conclusion that Wroth injects many kinds of verisimilitude into the *Urania* because of its relation to her lived experiences. These include realistic dialogue drawn from social observation, images drawn from domestic life and, not least, a voicing of female passion in a more intense and fervent register than is found in the romance before.

It is clear that in the Renaissance many kinds of writing were valued for the author's skill as an artificer. Examples include the many 1590s sonnet sequences in which the poet displays his ingenuity in reorganising a fairly fixed set of motifs and conventions, often involving formal patterning such as correlative verse, and may frankly admit that the immaculate mistress whom he supposedly addresses does not and need not exist. Giles Fletcher, for instance, asserted in the preface to *Licia* that 'a man may write of Love and not be in love', and explained, 'If thou muse, what my Licia is? Take her to be some Diana . . . It may be she is Learning's Image, or some heavenly wonder . . . it may be some College. It may be my conceit, and pretend nothing.'[48] There is also another order of writing in the period which points towards some kind of lived experience. Staying with sonnets for examples, one could adduce *Astrophil and Stella*, the second half of Spenser's *Amoretti* and of course Shakespeare's sonnets. In such cases the relation between text and life is always sophisticated and fluid, but the text takes on a charge from the sense both of glimpsed confessions, and of a cathartic release of griefs and joys strongly felt. Mary Wroth's sonnet sequence, *Pamphilia to Amphilanthus*, sits happily in this category, and so does her romance, the *Urania*. (One twist to this is that William Herbert, to whom her portrait of Amphilanthus refers, may also be the referent of the alluring young man in Shakespeare's sonnets; we may therefore think of him as the Muse of realism in Renaissance literature.) The *Urania* contains enough literary self-consciousness to satisfy both a cultivated Renaissance sensibility and a post-structuralist analysis, *and* combines this with reading pleasures of a less intellectually fashionable kind. Put simply, it is a passionate read.

Epilogue: the later seventeenth century

It is hard to know how many readers the *Urania* had in the seventeenth century. Although Wroth promised the Duke of Buckingham after the Denny scandal that she would attempt to recall copies, there is no evidence of whether this happened.[1] The fact that the work was never reprinted might suggest relative obscurity; but, on the other hand, twenty-nine copies are known to survive today,[2] which is not a bad number; only around twenty surviving copies are known of each of the 1590 and 1593 *Arcadia*s, for instance.[3] We do know of one woman who certainly owned and therefore probably read Wroth's romance: as mentioned before, one copy is three times inscribed 'Dorothy Long her booke'.[4] Another woman, herself an experimenter with the romance genre, at least knew about the row Wroth's publication caused. Lord Denny had directed Wroth to 'Work oth[er] Workes leave idle bookes alone / For wise and worthyer women have writte none'.[5] Margaret Cavendish, Duchess of Newcastle, in a preface to her own first publication, *Poems, and Fancies* (1653), complained that men

> hold *Books* as their *Crowne*, and the *Sword* as their *Scepter*, by which they rule, and governe. And very like they will say to me, as to the Lady that wrote the *Romancy*,
>
> *Work* Lady, *work, let writing* Books *alone,*
> *For surely* wiser Women *nere wrote one.*[6]

Cavendish takes up Denny's implication that women should 'work', that is, keep idle hands and minds safely busy with needlework, by converting her writing into a form of needlework, exploiting traditional metaphors of women's tale-telling as spinning or weaving:

> True it is, *Spinning* with the *Fingers* is more proper to our *Sexe*, then studying or writing *Poetry*, which is the *Spinning* with the *braine*: but I having no skill in the *Art* of the *first* . . . made me delight in the *latter* . . .; which made me

endeavour to Spin a *Garment* of *Memory*, to lapp up my *Name*, that it might grow to after *Ages*. (*Poems, and Fancies*, sig. A2r)

Her verses are 'like *Chast Penelope's Work*, for I wrote them in my *Husbands absence*, to delude *Melancholy Thoughts*, and avoid *Idle Time*' (*Poems, and Fancies*, p. 122). It is characteristic of Cavendish that she simultaneously lays claim to a model of feminine propriety (the spinning, weaving, dutiful woman) while subverting it with some aggression (the writing, and therefore transgressive, woman).

Denny's admonition to Wroth seems to have been much in Cavendish's mind as she published her own works, for she quotes it again in a preface to *Sociable Letters*, 1664. Addressing her husband, she remarks: 'My Lord, It may be said to me, as one said to a Lady, *Work Lady, Work, let writing Books alone, For surely Wiser women ne'er writ one*; But your Lordship never bid me to Work, nor leave Writing.' Again she interprets 'work' in a domestic sense, though now more broadly: 'the truth is, My Lord, I cannot Work, I mean such Works as Ladies use to pass their time withall . . . Needleworks, Spinning-works, Preserving-works, as also Baking, and Cooking-works, as making Cakes, Pyes, Puddings, and the like, all which I am Ignorant of'. Once more it is typical of Cavendish that she simultaneously apologises for her lack of proficiency in these domestic arts while making them sound far more mundane and insignificant than her art of writing, allying herself with the unnamed but almost mythologised Wroth as one who *must* write in spite of prohibitions.

Her attitude to romance is similarly ambivalent. To an extent she wished to dissociate her fictions from romance – understandably, considering the many decades of denigration of the genre. She announced that whenever she picked up a romance by mistake she threw it aside as 'an unprofitable study'. Romances contained 'little which ought to be practised, but rather shunned as foolish amorosities and desperate follies'. She claimed that her own tales, by contrast, inspired virtue and quenched 'amorous passions'.[7] Within one of these fictions, 'The Contract' (1656), the heroine's guardian 'never suffered her to read in Romancies, nor such light books'; while in another, 'Assaulted and Pursued Chastity' (also 1656) the heroine declines an offer of romances to read because 'their impossibilities makes them ridiculous to reason; and in youth they beget wanton desires, and amorous affections . . . pray give me play-books, or mathematical ones'.[8] Cavendish disdained women who read romances, 'wherein reading, they fall in love with the feigned heroes and carpet-knights, with whom their thoughts secretly commit adultery, and in their conversation and manner . . . they imitate the romancy-ladies'.[9] She is probably referring not only to the kinds of romances previously discussed in the present volume, but also to the most recent additions to the genre, the French heroic romances. Among the most popular were Madeleine de Scudéry's *Ibrahim* (four volumes, 1641), *Artamène, où le Grand Cyrus* (thirty volumes, 1649–53) and *Clélie* (ten volumes, 1654–61). These vast fictions claimed to depict personages from ancient history while dealing almost exclusively in matters of love, placing heroines and conventions of femininity very much in the foreground.[10] They were themselves in a line of descent from Sidney's *Arcadia*, which was very popular in France, and received an accolade unusual there for an English romance of translation, in two competing versions of 1624 and 1625.[11]

Despite Cavendish's professed contempt for the genre, a commendatory preface to her first publication, *Poems, and Fancies*, 1653, praised the author for her excellence in all genres including 'Poeticall Romances' (sig. B1v). The title page of *Nature's Pictures Drawn by Fancy's Pencil to the Life* (1656), also includes the 'Romancical' among the many genres of 'feigned Stories' on offer, and her husband's commendatory verses again praised her 'romancies'.[12] Reading further into her fictions confirms that romance is among the fictional modes being explored. In 'The Contract', one of the stories from *Nature's Pictures*, we encounter a heroine who has been brought up in pastoral innocence and in whom the power of love overcomes reason and duty to impel her to pursue the husband of her own choice.[13] As for the heroine of an Elizabethan romance, her feelings are explored through highly rhetorical interior monologue and self-debate. In another story in the same volume, 'Assaulted and Pursued Chastity', a sequence of shipwrecks, female-to-male cross-dressing, and the protective friendship of a fatherly sea-captain recall *Twelfth Night* and its romance sources.[14] Interspersed with this are the heroine's incarceration in a brothel, the attempts of an old female bawd to persuade her to vice and her conversion of her attempted deflowerer into an honourable lover, elements which echo the fates of Marina in *Pericles*, of the princesses imprisoned by Cecropia in the *Arcadia* and of some of Rich's heroines; and, behind these, the saints' lives with the same structure, such as the attempted corruption of St Agatha by Aphrodisia (see p. 126 above).[15] It is a narrative strand which can be traced forwards, too, to Richardson, especially when Cavendish's heroine finds herself falling irresistibly in love with her potential seducer even as she resists him.[16] Cavendish's *Blazing World* (1666), a hybrid work combining travel narrative, utopian fantasy, scientific speculation and philosophy, also opens in self-confessedly '*romancical*' vein with an elopement and a ship blown off course into strange territories (pp. 124–6).

Cavendish's recent editor, Kate Lilley, justly writes that Cavendish had a 'fascination with the possibilities of romance as the scene of a woman's heroic agency and successful negotiation of the theatres of power'.[17] Cavendish is interested in romance in so far as it gives her heroines scope for adventure and self-determination. Cross-dressing is a significant element in this in 'Assaulted and Pursued Chastity', as it is in several of Cavendish's plays.[18] Like previous romance heroines dressed as men, Affectionata, calling her/himself Travellia, inconveniently inspires the love of a woman, is revealed to her beloved on the battlefield and is obliged to defend the propriety of her disguise.[19] However, as a man she is also enabled to play the roles of political expert and military hero, and docs so with distinction (*Blazing World*, pp. 91, 96, 102).

A couple of decades on from Cavendish, Aphra Behn's fictions are also marked by the continuing influence of romance. Behn often styled herself Astrea, and indeed is registered in the burial record at Westminster Abbey as 'Astrea Behn', a name derived from the French pastoral romance *L'Astrée* (1607) by Honoré d'Urfé.[20] The courtship of the eponymous hero and Imoinda in *Oroonoko* (1688) follows romance conventions in its celebration of the wondrous powers of love. Like the heroine of an Iberian romance, Imoinda yields her virginity to Oroonoko when privately promised but not formally married to him, and this is represented as proving his virility but not impairing her virtue (p. 25). Oroonoko's slaying of a tigress while his female companions flee specifically recalls the vanquishing of the lion and the bear by the two heroes in the *Arcadia* (*Oroonoko*, p. 49; *NA*, pp. 176–8), while Imoinda emulates heroines of all kinds of romance in her unquestioning willingness to die for her beloved (*Oroonoko*, p. 67). Among other romance conventions in Behn's works, *The History of the Nun* (1689) presents a heroine who, in traditional romance fashion, thinks she is immune to love but then is conquered by it, and whose lost lover makes known his return by sending a ring which she gave him.[21] In *The Unfortunate Happy Lady*

(1696) we once more encounter a pious virgin who is left with an evil old bawd to be corrupted – the brothel is even ironically referred to as 'the old lady's enchanted castle'.[22] In time-honoured fashion the heroine converts her attempted seducer into a virtuous suitor, loses him by shipwreck and after long separation miraculously regains him.

This is not to say that Cavendish and Behn bring no innovations to romance – far from it. However, we should be cautious when assessing one of the principal areas in which late seventeenth-century fiction has often been seen as moving away from romance towards the novel: namely, new claims for the truthfulness of fiction, claims which, when applied to knowingly invented and untrue material, complicate the relationship between fact and fiction.[23] As we have seen, Elizabethan fiction often played sophisticatedly on the boundaries between fact and fiction, by means such as the references to historical figures in Painter and Nashe, the implied intimation of real private scandals in Gascoigne and Pettie, and the extensive representation of contemporary politics under the veil of romance in Sidney and Spenser. In Mary Wroth's *Urania* the relations between truth and fiction became especially complex, like a hall of mirrors in which life and art endlessly and multiply reflected back upon one another. Moreover, following John Barclay's *Argenis* in 1621, romance had been increasingly used through the Civil War period as political *roman à clef*, further enmeshing fantasy and factuality.[24] A sophisticated sense of fiction as a mode with both factual referents and liberating transformative powers may therefore be seen as integral to the romance tradition.

Cavendish continues this when, in the preface to *The Blazing World*, she asserts that 'The end of reason, is truth; the end of fancy, is fiction', only immediately to break down this distinction and affirm the value of combining fancy with reason and truth with fiction (p. 123). Thus the narrative which follows is at once a fantasy in which the Empress of the Blazing World enjoys 'making and dissolving several worlds in her own mind' (p. 188), and an account of how the Empress is taught to do this by the real-life Duchess of Newcastle. She travels not only through exotic and wondrous domains, but also to the English court and to the Newcastles' seat in Nottinghamshire (pp. 192–3).

Behn's first published fiction, *Love Letters Between a Nobleman and his Sister* (1684–7), was a *roman à clef* using romance conventions for both veiled depiction of a real-life scandal (the elopement of Lady Henrietta Berkeley with her brother-in-law, Lord Grey of Werke) and political comment (Werke was a supporter of the rebel Duke of Monmouth while the Berkeleys were Tories of the opposite camp).[25] This potential of romance for scandalous and political *roman à clef* was taken still further by another woman writer, Delarivier Manley, in works such as her *New Atalantis*.[26] Behn's *Oroonoko* turns instead to another factual/fantastical genre, the travel narrative of marvels encountered in far-flung territories. It incorporates both a romance-style love story as noted above, and emphatic truth-claims which have engendered longstanding scholarly debate as to the factual basis for the narrative:

> This is a true story . . . If there be anything that seems Romantic . . . consider these countries do, in all things, so far differ from ours, that they produce unconceivable wonders . . . What I have mentioned I have taken care should be truth . . . I do not pretend . . . to entertain my reader with the adventures of a feigned hero . . . I was myself an eye-witness to a great part of what you will find here set down. (*Oroonoko*, pp. 5–6)

The truth-claim becomes a formula in Behn's fictions. The dedication to *The Fair Jilt* (1688) states that 'I now desire to have it understood that this is reality, and matter of fact', and the story of a man claiming to be Prince Tarquin, a descendant of the last Roman kings, is indeed based upon factual sources.[27] *The History of the Nun* punctuates its sensational events of broken monastic vows, bigamy and double murder with topical reference when a character goes off to the real siege of Candia by the Turks from 1645 to 1669.[28]

Some of Behn's posthumously published fictions do perhaps illustrate some sort of development of recognisably novelistic principles in that topical, domestic, bourgeois frames of reference become increasingly prominent, though still not unleavened by romance. Thus *The Black Lady* (1696) depicts a pregnant girl who comes to town from Hampshire and seeks relatives and lodgings in Covent Garden and Soho. Her name, however, is given as 'Bellamora', very much a romance-type name. She is described as 'the fair innocent (I must not say foolish) one',[29] suggesting that in her search for assistance through the streets and lodging-houses of the metropolis she is a modern lady errant, but that to play the damsel-in-distress in a contemporary urban setting is unwise; yet her troubles are happily resolved by amazing coincidence. Similarly *The Unfortunate Happy Lady* combines all the romance conventions mentioned above with a solid setting amongst the English gentry, and makes almost journalistic claims of true misdeeds exposed on grounds of public interest: 'I cannot omit giving the world an account of the uncommon villainy of a gentleman of good family in England, practised upon his sister, which was attested to me by one who lived in the family and from whom I had the whole truth of the story' (Salzman, ed., *Seventeenth-Century Fiction*, p. 529).

For both Cavendish and Behn part of the play on the boundary between fact and fiction involves putting themselves into their fictions, just as had Philip Sidney and Mary Wroth before them. In Cavendish's *Blazing World*, just as we might have been thinking that the Empress was some sort of fictional projection of the author herself, she meets and forms a firm friendship with the Duchess of Newcastle, exploiting the hall-of-mirrors potential of fiction to create multiply reflexive images. Behn appears in *Oroonoko* as not merely an 'eye-witness' but a mentor and confidante to the hero. In a broader, more diffuse sense both authors may be said to be personally present throughout their fictions. Douglas Grant, Cavendish's biographer, maintains that all her tales have an element of autobiography, and Lilley agrees that in 'The Contract' and 'Assaulted and Pursued Chastity' she was 'rewriting the narrative of her own history as romance'.[30] In Behn's work the interventions of the knowing, engaging narrator coalesce such that 'in a way all the tales become part of a larger fictionalized autobiography of the author'.[31]

For both these authors the correlative of putting themselves into their fictions is a tendency to turn their lives into romances. In her 'True Relation, of my Birth, Breeding and Life', Cavendish represents her younger self as a bashful Cinderella heroine swept off her feet by her dashing older lover: 'though I did dread marriage, and shunned men's company as much as I could, yet I could not, nor had not the power to refuse him, by reason my affections were fixed on him, and he was the only person I ever was in love with'.[32] Her devotion to the Duke, through all the vicissitudes of the Civil War period, is fulsomely expressed in the romance terms of self-sacrifice: he is 'my Lord, with whom I had rather be as a poor beggar, than to be mistress of the world absented from him' (*The Life of William Cavendish*, p. 171). Even Cavendish's mother is rendered as a nobly enduring romance heroine, like Briana in *The Mirror of Knighthood* or Parthenia in the *Arcadia*, in her utter devotion to Cavendish's father even after his death. She refuses to countenance remarriage, instead 'mourning in sad complaints. She made her house her cloister, inclosing herself, as it were, therein . . . my mother was of an heroic spirit' (*The Life of William Cavendish*, p. 163). Cavendish's endeavours to play the romance heroine were recognised, even if with some amusement, by spectators: Pepys famously remarked that 'The whole story of this Lady is a romance, and all she doth is romantic.'[33]

While Cavendish used romance to assert her own heroism, Behn deployed hints at a romance-like shady and racy past to entice and engage the reader. Other women of the period also found in romance scope for exciting and empowering self-constructions, or at least frameworks for understanding their emotional experience. Dorothy Osborne, in her letters to Sir William Temple in 1653–4, not only discussed the characters and plots of the French heroic romances with the avid enthusiasm of a soap-opera addict, but also turned her life into romance. Sometimes this is to mock-heroic effect, as when she caricatures an unwelcome suitor:

> hee is resolved to bee a most Romance Squire and goe in quest of some inchanted Damzell, whome if hee likes, as to her person, (for fortunc is a thing below him and wee doe not reade in History that any knight, or squire, was ever soe discourtious as to inquire what portions theire Lady's had) then hee comes with the Power of the County to demande her.[34]

At other points romance was a means of celebrating, and imbuing with pathos, the thwarted affection between herself and Temple: 'can there be a more Romance Story then ours would make if the conclusion should prove happy [?]'.[35]

I mentioned on p. 8 above that two women of the early seventeenth century, Lady Elizabeth Southwell and Lady Arbella Stuart, acted out romance-roles in life by donning male clothes to elope. Later the abdicated Queen Christina of Sweden also played the cross-dressing romance heroine, although apparently not for love but in pursuit of a 'vagabond and wandering life . . . seeking Adventures in strange Lands', as recorded in *A Relation of the Life of Christina Queen of Sweden* (1656).[36] Mary Carleton, the adventuress and putative impostor known as the 'German Princess', in her 1663 autobiography expressed her admiration for Queen Christina as 'the onely Lady Errant in the World', and described her own story as 'this my (Errant-like) Adventure'.[37] She represented herself as well read in romances, and asserted that 'I might as well have given lustre to a Romance as any any any of those supposed *Heroina's*.'[38] Other seventeenth-century women who wrote autobiographical texts may also be seen as drawing upon romance for various kinds of self-fashioning, including Anne Halkett, Mary Rich and Anne Fanshawe.[39]

While such real seventeenth-century women seemed eager to view their lives as romances, it should also be conceded that in fiction, romance was being increasingly combined with elements which could be classified as realistic. Behn developed female protagonists with new degrees of moral ambiguity, such as Miranda in *The Fair Jilt*. She is guilty of false accusations, of plotting the death of her sister, of inciting her husband to crimes incurring the death sentence and, we learn in her final confession, of numerous lewd practices with both high and low persons. Yet she has an attractive vitality, and ends the story without divine retribution or poetic justice, penitent and in 'as perfect a state of happiness as this troublesome world can afford' (*Oroonoko*, p. 119). Isabella in *The History of the Nun* passes through widely varying emotional and moral states, as first a willingly cloistered nun of exceptional piety, then a passionate lover skilled at dissembling to gain her desires, then a dutiful wife, then an accidental bigamist, and finally the desperate yet Machiavellian murderer of both her husbands.

Cavendish's heroines have a spirit of enterprise which means that even when they find themselves in romance situations where convention dictates that they should suffer nobly, they may be more inclined to take action. Thus in 'Assaulted and Pursued Chastity', Affectionata in the brothel backs up her rhetorical efforts to convert her attempted seducer with more direct means: 'Stay, stay, said she, I will first build me a temple of fame upon your grave, where all young virgins shall come and offer at my shrine, and in the midst of these words shot him' (*Blazing World*, p. 53). There is also a new pragmatism about relationships and about the worldly implications and consequences of courtship and marriage. Cavendish's 'The Contract' subscribes to the romance ideology that love conquers all and that happiness lies in the achieved union of two destined lovers, but achieves this end by somewhat mundane legal ruses involving the reinstatement of a broken precontract. The heroine proves herself adept in legal technicalities:

> should you cast aside your canon law, most pious Judges, and judge it by the common law, my suit must needs be granted . . . should an heir, young, before he comes to years, run on the lender's score, though the lender had no law to plead against nonage, yet if his nature be so just to seal the bonds he made in nonage, when he comes to full years, he makes his former act

good, and fixes the law to a just grant . . . The like is my cause. (*Blazing World*, p. 38)

The strategic manipulation of the law to achieve a desired goal implies a lack of idealism, even a cynicism, slightly at odds with the romantic end being pursued. The betrothal of the King and Queen in 'Assaulted and Pursued Chastity' also does not pass without negotiation of a pre-nuptial contract (*Blazing World*, p. 114).

This pragmatism is developed further by Behn. The lovelorn Isabella in *The History of the Nun* takes to her bed not to write verses and descend into melancholy like a Pamphilia, but 'with a resolution to think over all she had to do and to consider how she should manage this great affair of her life' (*Oroonoko*, p. 165). Twice in her life she finds herself in Lucrece-like extremities when she considers suicide, and both times she dismisses the thought and comes up with other plans (pp. 166, 183). When she elopes with Henault, causing his disinheritance, we are made privy to Isabella's accounts – her mother has left her jewels worth two thousand pounds, and she has a further three or four hundred pounds in gold in case of emergency (p. 169) – and money remains a constant concern throughout their marriage. When Henault is reported killed in battle, Isabella runs out of money and for this reason marries again, accepting Villenoys not out of love but because 'she thought she could live better with [him] than any other' (p. 177). Her love for Henault, far from burning as an eternal flame, is gradually extinguished by the need to get on with life in the present. When, after eight years, Henault returns, transformed by travel and hardship, he finds that his Penelope is not chastely waiting for him but has moved on. Isabella's first thoughts are for her own public reputation and comfort:

She finds, by his return, she is not only exposed to all the shame imaginable, to all the upbraiding on his part when he shall know she is married to another, but all the fury and rage of Villenoys, and the scorn of the town, who will look on her as an adulteress. She sees Henault poor and knew she must fall from all the glory and tranquillity she had for five happy years triumphed in. (*Oroonoko*, p. 181)

If *The Unfortunate Happy Lady* is a romance in its plot – virgin in brothel reforms seducer, is separated from him by a shipwreck, then miraculously regains him – it differs from romance not only in its terse brevity and its contemporary London setting, but also in its obsessive interest in its characters' bank balances. The shipwreck causes the loss not only of Gracelove but of 'above twelve thousand pounds' of his estate (Salzman, ed., *Seventeenth-Century Fiction*, pp. 545, 546); Sir William Wilding, ne'er-do-well brother of the heroine, Philadelphia, spends eight thousand pounds in two years in France then contracts debts of above a hundred pounds over four months in England (p. 548); and Philadelphia's suitors are principally classified according to their financial status (p. 551). Philadelphia defeats her enemies and gains her beloved essentially by amassing more money than any of them. She does this by means of a crucial detail which Behn adds to the romance plot, the heroine's marriage to good old Counsellor Fairlaw, who stresses in his proposal to her that his widow 'would be worth above thirty thousand pounds in ready money, besides a thousand a year' (p. 547). Behn contrives to present Philadelphia's yielding to this courtship after a quarter of an hour as a deed of duty and piety rather than self-interest, the saintly heroine 'having mortified all her appetites to the enjoyments of this world' (p. 547). Fairlaw, of course, conveniently dies, after a mere four months, enabling Philadelphia to prove herself not merely a beacon of virtue but also a highly efficient book-keeper. In less than a year she 'had paid £25,000 and taken off the mortgages on £2,500 per annum of her brother's estate', and is on her way to make the final payment of £2,000 when she fortuitously encounters the returned Gracelove. The resounding climax of the narrative is marked not just by her betrothal to Gracelove and her stepdaughter Eugenia's tidy but extraordinarily willing accedence to marriage to Sir William. In the midst of the happy scene Philadelphia's steward sets before Sir William on the dinner table a covered serving dish: '"Come, Sir William," said his sister, "uncover it." He did so, and cried out: "O matchless goodness of a virtuous sister! Here are the mortgages of the best part of my estate. O, what a villain, what a monster have I been!" "No more, dear brother," said she, with tears in her eyes' (p. 553).

Dorothy Osborne had remarked that 'wee doe not reade in History that any knight, or squire, was ever soe discourtious as to inquire what portions theire Lady's had.'[40] By the end of the seventeenth century much had evidently changed. For Behn, herself writing for money, the happiness of her heroines consists not merely in fulfilling their destinies in love, but in financial security. The scene of fiction is shifting, not least because women authors are entering it; but to announce the death of romance would be extremely premature.

Notes

INTRODUCTION

1 Louis B. Wright, *Middle-Class Culture in Elizabethan England* (Chapel Hill: University of North Carolina Press, 1935), pp. 103, 110.
2 Suzanne W. Hull, *Chaste, Silent and Obedient: English Books for Women 1475–1640* (San Marino: Huntington Library, 1982), pp. 74–5.
3 See, for instance, Paul Salzman, *English Prose Fiction 1558–1700: A Critical History* (Oxford: Clarendon, 1985); Caroline Lucas, *Writing for Women: The Example of Woman as Reader in Elizabethan Romance* (Milton Keynes and Philadelphia: Open University Press, 1989); Lorna Hutson, *The Usurer's Daughter: Male Friendship and Fictions of Women in Sixteenth-Century England* (London and New York: Routledge, 1994); Constance C. Relihan (ed.), *Framing Elizabethan Fictions: Contemporary Approaches to Early Modern Narrative Prose* (Kent, OH: Kent State University Press, 1996); R. W. Maslen, *Elizabethan Fictions: Espionage, Counter-Espionage, and the Duplicity of Fiction in Early Elizabethan Prose Narratives* (Oxford: Clarendon, 1997).
4 For useful generic definitions of romance see Gillian Beer, *The Romance* (London: Methuen, 1970), pp. 1–10.
5 Robert Greene, *Pandosto. The Triumph of Time* (*c.*1585), in William Shakespeare, *The Winter's Tale*, ed. J. H. P. Pafford (1963; London: Routledge, 1988), appendix IV, pp. 206–7.
6 Henry Thomas, *Spanish and Portuguese Romances of Chivalry* (Cambridge: Cambridge University Press, 1920), pp. 65–77, 103–8.
7 Margaret Spufford, *Small Books and Pleasant Histories: Popular Fiction and its Readership in Seventeenth-Century England* (Cambridge: Cambridge University Press, 1985), p.234.
8 Linda Woodbridge, *Women and the English Renaissance: Literature and the Nature of Womankind, 1540–1620* (Brighton: Harvester, 1984), pp. 129, 116; see also pp. 114–17, 120.

1 THE READERSHIP OF RENAISSANCE ROMANCE

1 John Lyly, *Euphues: The Anatomy of Wit* (1578), and *Euphues and his England* (1580), eds. M. W. Croll and H. Clemons (London: Routledge, 1916), pp. 200–1.

2 Barnaby Rich, *Rich's Farewell to Military Profession* (1581), e
Mabry Cranfill (Austin: University of Texas Press, 1959), p. 1

3 Robert Greene, *Penelope's Web* (1587), in Alexander B. Gros
Life and Complete Works in Prose and Verse of Robert Greene, 12 vo
and Aylesbury: Huth Library/Hazell, Watson and Viney, 1881–3), vol. v, pp. 146–7.

4 Sir Thomas Overbury (attrib.), *New and Choise Characters of Severall Authors*, 6th edn (1615), sig.¶4v.

5 Thomas Powell, *Tom of All Trades. Or the Plaine Path-Way to Preferment* (1631), p. 47.

6 Tina Krontiris, 'Breaking Barriers of Genre and Gender: Margaret Tyler's Translation of *The Mirrour of Knighthood*', in Kirby Farrell, Elizabeth H. Hageman and Arthur F. Kinney (eds.), *Women in the Renaissance: Selections from 'English Literary Renaissance'* (Amherst: University of Massachusetts Press, 1990), p. 56.

7 David Cressy, *Literacy and the Social Order: Reading and Writing in Tudor and Stuart England* (Cambridge: Cambridge University Press, 1980), p. 176.

8 Keith Thomas, 'The Meaning of Literacy in Early Modern England', in Gerd Baumann (ed.), *The Written Word: Literacy in Transition* (Oxford: Clarendon, 1986), p. 130.

9 Paul Salzman, *English Prose Fiction 1558–1700: A Critical History* (Oxford: Clarendon, 1985), pp. 5–6.

10 Cressy, *Literacy and the Social Order*, p. 53.

11 Lady Margaret Hoby, *The Diary of Lady Margaret Hoby 1599–1605*, ed. Dorothy M. Meads (London: Routledge, 1930).

12 Rachel Weigall, 'An Elizabethan Gentlewoman: The Journal of Lady Mildmay, circa 1570–1617 (Unpublished)', *The Quarterly Review* 428 (July 1911), p. 121.

13 Jacqueline Pearson, 'Women Reading, Reading Women', in Helen Wilcox (ed.), *Women and Literature in Britain 1500–1700* (Cambridge: Cambridge University Press, 1996), p. 83.

14 Lady Anne Clifford, *The Diaries of Lady Anne Clifford*, ed. D. J. H. Clifford (1990; pbk., Stroud: Alan Sutton, 1992), pp. 48, 61.

15 Graham Parry, 'The Great Picture of Lady Anne Clifford', in David Howarth (ed.), *Art and Patronage in the Caroline Courts: Essays in Honour of Sir Oliver Millar* (Cambridge: Cambridge University Press, 1993), p. 210.

16 *Ibid.*, pp. 210, 217.

17 Bent Juel-Jensen, 'Sir Philip Sidney, 1554–1586: A Check-List of Early Editions of his Works', in Dennis Kay (ed.), *Sir Philip Sidney: An Anthology of Modern Criticism* (Oxford: Clarendon, 1987), pp. 294–5.

18 Sir Philip Sidney, *The Countess of Pembroke's Arcadia (The Old Arcadia)*, *c.*1580, ed. Katherine Duncan-Jones, World's Classics (1985; rev. edn, Oxford: Oxford University Press, 1994), p. 3.

19 Stephen Orgel, *Impersonations: The Performance of Gender in Shakespeare's England* (Cambridge: Cambridge University Press, 1996), pp. 112–15.

20 Lady Mary Wroth, *The First Part of The Countess of Montgomery's Urania*, ed. Josephine Roberts (Binghamton, NY: Mediaeval and Renaissance Texts and Studies, 1995), p. lxxxiii.
21 Parry, 'Great Picture', p. 213.
22 Dedicated to Margaret Clifford, Countess of Cumberland, and her sister Anne Dudley, Countess of Warwick, both Russells by birth.
23 Kate Clarke, 'The Russell Women as Literary Patrons, 1570–1620: A Reconsideration of the Role of Gender in the Kinds of Dedicated Works', *Women, Text and History* seminar, Merton College, Oxford University, 17 October 1989.
24 Lady Brilliana Harley, *Letters of the Lady Brilliana Harley*, ed. Thomas Taylor Lewis (London: Camden Society, 1854), pp. 13–14, letter dated 30 November 1638.
25 Sara Heller Mendelson, *The Mental World of Stuart Women: Three Studies* (Brighton: Harvester, 1987), p. 66.
26 Jennifer Lee Carrell, 'A Pack of Lies in a Looking Glass: Lady Mary Wroth's *Urania* and the Magic Mirror of Romance', *Studies in English Literature 1500–1900* 34 (1994), p. 82, p. 103 n.6.
27 Dorothy Osborne, *Letters to Sir William Temple*, ed. Kenneth Parker (London: Penguin, 1987), pp. 57, 59–60, 62, 67–8, 79, 97, 124–5, 131, 145–6, 150.
28 Margaret Cavendish, Duchess of Newcastle, *Sociable Letters*, p. 226, quoted in Heller Mendelson, *Mental World*, p. 35.
29 *DNB*, 'Mary I 1516–1558'.
30 Juan Luis Vives, *De Institutione Foeminae Christianae* (1524), trans. Richard Hyrde, *The Instruction of a Christian Woman*, c.1540, sigs. E4r–F1r.
31 Michael McKeon, *The Origins of the English Novel 1600–1740* (Baltimore and London: Johns Hopkins University Press, 1987), p. 52.
32 Paul J. Voss, 'Books for Sale: Advertising and Patronage in Late Elizabethan England', *Sixteenth-Century Journal* 29.3 (Fall 1998), pp. 733–56.
33 Lyly, *Euphues and his England*, p. 200.
34 Rich, *Rich's Farewell*, pp. 3–4.
35 Greene, *Penelope's Web*, pp. 144–5.
36 Maureen Quilligan, *Milton's Spenser: The Politics of Reading* (Ithaca and London: Cornell University Press, 1983), p. 180.
37 Sir Philip Sidney, *The Defence of Poesy*, in *The Oxford Authors: Sir Philip Sidney*, ed. Katherine Duncan-Jones (Oxford: Oxford University Press, 1989), p. 246.
38 Greene, *Penelope's Web*, pp. 152, 154, 162.
39 See Patricia Parker, *Literary Fat Ladies: Rhetoric, Gender, Property* (London and New York: Methuen, 1987), p. 26.
40 Ovid, *Metamorphoses*, Books I–VIII, trans. Frank Justus Miller (1916), rev. G. P. Goold, Loeb Classical Library, 3rd edn (Cambridge, MA: Harvard University Press, 1977), VI.401–674, I–145.
41 Corinne Saunders kindly shared with me her discussion of this topic in

her work-in-progress *Against Her Will: Rape and Ravishment in the Literature of Medieval England*. See also Jocelyn Catty, *Writing Rape, Writing Women in Early Modern England* (Houndmills: Macmillan, 1999).

42 Anthony Munday (trans.), *Amadis de Gaule* (1619) Book III, pp. 29–30; John J. O'Connor, *Amadis de Gaule and its Influence on Elizabethan Literature* (New Brunswick, NJ: Rutgers University Press, 1970), p. 135.

43 Christopher Marlowe, *Dr Faustus* (A-text, 1604), in David Bevington and Eric Rasmussen (eds.), *Dr Faustus and Other Plays*, World's Classics (Oxford: Oxford University Press, 1995), II.i.135.

44 Thomas Lodge, *Rosalynd* (1590), ed. Brian Nellist (Keele: Ryburn/Keele University Press, 1995), p. 93.

45 George Peele, *The Old Wives' Tale* (*c.*1593), ed. Patricia Binnie (Manchester: Manchester University Press, 1980), lines 85–93.

46 Spufford, *Small Books*, pp. 4–6, 12–13, 59, 62, 79–80, 172.

47 *Ibid.*, p.4.

48 See Hélène Cixous, 'Sorties: Out and Out: Attacks/Ways Out/Forays', trans. Betsy Wing, in Catherine Belsey and Jane Moore (eds.), *The Feminist Reader* (Houndmills: Macmillan, 1989), pp. 101–2.

49 Lisa Jardine, *Still Harping on Daughters: Women and Drama in the Age of Shakespeare* (1983; 2nd edn, Hemel Hempstead: Harvester Wheatsheaf, 1989), p. 6.

50 Nancy J. Vickers, 'Diana Described: Scattered Woman and Scattered Rhyme', in Elizabeth Abel (ed.), *Writing and Sexual Difference* (Brighton: Harvester, 1982), pp. 95–109; '"The Blazon of Sweet Beauty's Best": Shakespeare's *Lucrece*', in Patricia Parker and Geoffrey Hartman (eds.), *Shakespeare and the Question of Theory* (New York and London: Routledge, 1990), pp. 95–115; Woodbridge, *Women and the English Renaissance*; Eve Kosofsky Sedgwick, *Between Men: English Literature and Male Homosocial Desire* (New York: Cornell University Press, 1985); Parker, *Literary Fat Ladies*.

51 Vickers, 'Shakespeare's *Lucrece*', p. 112; Mary Jacobus, 'Is There a Woman in this Text?', *New Literary History* 14.1 (1982), pp. 117–41.

52 Roger Ascham, *The Scholemaster* (1570), p. 67; Stephen Gosson, *The Schoole of Abuse* (1579), in Arthur F. Kinney (ed.), *Markets of Bawdrie: The Dramatic Criticism of Stephen Gosson* (Salzburg: University of Salzburg Press, 1974), p. 77.

53 Parker, *Literary Fat Ladies*, chs. 2, 4.

54 Wendy Wall, *The Imprint of Gender: Authorship and Publication in the English Renaissance* (Ithaca and London: Cornell University Press, 1993), p. 6.

55 Lorna Hutson, *The Usurer's Daughter: Male Friendship and Fictions of Women in Sixteenth-Century England* (London and New York: Routledge, 1994), p. 89.

56 Lori Humphrey Newcomb, 'The Romance of Service: The Simple History of *Pandosto's* Servant Readers', in Constance C. Relihan (ed.), *Framing Elizabethan Fictions: Contemporary Approaches to Early Modern Narrative Prose* (Kent, OH: Kent State University Press, 1996), pp. 117–39.

2 RENAISSANCE ROMANCE AND MODERN ROMANCE

1 Francis Beaumont, *The Knight of the Burning Pestle* (1607), ed. Sheldon P. Zitner (Revels Plays, Manchester: Manchester University Press, 1984), p. 30.

2 David Margolies, *Novel and Society in Elizabethan England* (London and Sydney: Croom Helm, 1985), p. 2.

3 L. B. Wright, *Middle-Class Culture*, pp. 109–10.

4 A. C. Hamilton, 'Elizabethan Romance: The Example of Prose Fiction', *English Literary History* 49.2 (1982), p. 288.

5 George Eliot, 'Silly Novels by Lady Novelists', *Westminster Review*, October 1856, in A. S. Byatt and Nicholas Warren (eds.), *Selected Essays and Other Writings* (London: Penguin, 1990), pp. 140–63; Ian Watt, *The Rise of the Novel: Studies in Defoe, Richardson and Fielding* (1957; Harmondsworth: Penguin, 1963), pp. 170–4.

6 Arthur Kinney, *Humanist Poetics: Thought, Rhetoric and Fiction in Sixteenth-Century England* (Amherst: University of Massachusetts Press, 1986), p. xii.

7 Maslen, *Elizabethan Fictions*, pp. 18–19.

8 Francis Meres, *Palladis Tamia. Wits Treasury being the Secondpart of Wits Commonwealth* (1598), facs., introd. D. C. Allen (New York: Scholars' Facsmilies and Reprints, 1938), fo. 280.

9 Wye Saltonstall, *Picturae Loquentes. Or Pictures Drawne Forth in Characters. With a Poem of a Maid* (1631), sig. E6V.

10 William Prynne, *Histriomastix*, quoted in Annabel Patterson, *Censorship and Interpretation: The Conditions of Writing and Reading in Early Modern England* (Madison: University of Wisconsin Press, 1984), p. 171.

11 Thomas, *Spanish Romances*, pp. 257–61.

12 Sir John Harington (trans.), *Orlando Furioso* (1591), by Ludovico Ariosto, ed. Robert McNulty (Oxford: Clarendon, 1972), pp. xx–xxi, xxv.

13 Ann Rosalind Jones, 'Mills and Boon meets Feminism', in Jean Radford (ed.), *The Progress of Romance: The Politics of Popular Fiction* (London: Routledge, 1986), p. 199.

14 Ann Barr Snitow, 'Mass Market Romance: Pornography for Women is Different', in Ann Snitow, Christine Stansell, and Sharon Thompson (eds.), *Powers of Desire: The Politics of Sexuality* (New York: Monthly Review Press, 1983), pp. 245–63; Janet Batsleer, Tony Davies, Rebecca O'Rourke and Chris Weedon, *Rewriting English: Cultural Politics of Gender and Class* (London and New York: Methuen, 1985), p. 96.

15 See Margaret Patterson Hannay, *Philip's Phoenix: Mary Sidney, Countess of Pembroke* (Oxford: Oxford University Press, 1990), pp. 188–91; Clifford, *Diaries*, pp. xi–xii, 15–18.

16 Lawrence Stone, *The Family, Sex and Marriage in England, 1500–1800* (London: Weidenfeld and Nicolson, 1977), pp. 179–94; Ralph A. Houlbrooke, *The English Family 1450–1700* (London and New York:

Longman, 1984), pp. 68–73, 76–7. From literature, one might think of Juliet and Paris, or Katherina and Petruchio, among many others.

17 See Catherine Bates, *The Rhetoric of Courtship in Elizabethan Language and Literature* (Cambridge: Cambridge University Press, 1992).

18 See e.g. Arthur Marotti, '"Love is not Love": Elizabethan Sonnet Sequences and the Social Order', *English Literary History* 49 (1982), pp. 396–428; Ann Rosalind Jones and Peter Stallybrass, 'The Politics of *Astrophil and Stella*', *Studies in English Literature, 1500–1900* 24 (1984), pp. 53–68.

19 Anon., *The Treasury of Amadis of France* (1567), sig.¶3v; H. S. Bennett, *English Books and Readers 1558–1603* (Cambridge: Cambridge University Press, 1965), p. 257.

20 Hutson, *Usurer's Daughter*, pp. 96–7.

21 *Ibid.*, p. 89.

22 Krontiris, 'Breaking Barriers', p. 56.

23 Lucas, *Writing for Women*, p. 2, and cf. p. 26.

24 Overbury, *Characters* (1615), sig. ¶4v; and see p. 4 above.

25 Hull, *Chaste, Silent and Obedient*, p. 81.

26 Edmund Spenser, *The Faerie Queene* (1590–1609), ed. A. C. Hamilton (1977; London and New York: Longman, 1980), II.xii.81–3, III.xii, VI.viii.35–46.

27 Sir Philip Sidney, *The Countess of Pembroke's Arcadia (The New Arcadia)* (1593), ed. Maurice Evans (Harmondsworth: Penguin, 1977), pp. 528, 551–63.

28 Judith Fetterley, *The Resisting Reader: A Feminist Approach to American Fiction* (Bloomington, IL: 1978).

29 Lucas, *Writing for Women*, p. 2.

30 Maslen, *Elizabethan Fictions*, pp. 86, 108, 159, 245, 299–300.

31 Germaine Greer, *The Female Eunuch* (1970; London: Granada/Paladin, 1971), pp. 182, 180.

32 Tania Modleski, *Loving with a Vengeance: Mass-Produced Fantasies for Women* (1982; New York and London: Routledge, 1990); Janice A. Radway, *Reading the Romance: Women, Patriarchy and Popular Literature* (Chapel Hill and London: University of North Carolina Press, 1984); Alison Light, '"Returning to Manderley" – Romance Fiction, Female Sexuality, and Class', *Feminist Review* 16 (1984), excerpt reprinted in Mary Eagleton (ed.), *Feminist Literary Theory: A Reader* (Oxford: Blackwell, 1986), pp. 140–5.

33 Radway, *Reading the Romance*, ch. 3.

34 Snitow, 'Mass Market Romance', p. 252; Light, 'Returning to Manderley', p. 143.

35 Modleski, *Loving with a Vengeance*, p. 113.

36 Simon Shepherd (ed.), *The Women's Sharp Revenge: Five Women's Pamphlets from the Renaissance* (London: Fourth Estate, 1985), pp. 9–10.

37 See Margaret Patterson Hannay (ed.), *Silent But For the Word: Tudor*

Women as Patrons, Translators and Writers of Religious Works (Kent, OH: Kent State University Press, 1985).

38 Andrea Dworkin, *Intercourse* (London: Secker and Warburg, 1987), pp. 85, 94, 96.

39 Helen Hackett, *Virgin Mother, Maiden Queen: Elizabeth I and the Cult of the Virgin Mary* (Houndmills: Macmillan, 1995), pp. 15–18.

40 Jacobus de Voragine, *The Golden Legend: Readings on the Saints* (*c.*1260), trans. William Granger Ryan, 2 vols. (Princeton: Princeton University Press, 1993), vol. I, pp. 27–9, 101–4, 154–7; Thomas J. Heffernan, *Sacred Biography: Saints and Their Biographers in the Middle Ages* (Oxford: Oxford University Press, 1988), pp. 275, 281, 283; C. Saunders, *Against Her Will*, ch.4.

41 Hackett, *Virgin Mother*, pp. 151–3.

3 NOVELLAS OF THE 1560S AND 1570S

1 William Painter, *The Palace of Pleasure*, vol. I (1566), sigs. *3v, ¶¶2r.

2 Painter, *Palace of Pleasure*, vol. I, second, fourth, twenty-eighth and thirty-eighth novellas; vol. II, twenty-third and twenty-fifth novellas.

3 Anon., *The Institution of a Gentleman* (1555), sig. K3, quoted in Bennett, *English Books and Readers*, p. 18.

4 Geoffrey Fenton, *Certaine Tragicall Discourses Written oute of Frenche and Latin* (1567), sig. **i.r.

5 François de Belleforest, *The French Bandello: A Selection of the Original Text of Four of Belleforest's 'Histoires Tragiques'*, ed. Frank S. Hook (Columbia: University of Missouri Press, 1948), pp. 11, 13, 22–5, 36.

6 *Ibid.*, p. 36.

7 Geoffrey Fenton, *Actes of Conference in Religion* (trans.) (1571), STC 10790; *A Forme of Christian Pollicie*, trans. from Jean Talpin (1574), STC 10793a.

8 See Maslen, *Elizabethan Fictions*, p. 85.

9 No page number.

10 For more discussion of this episode see Maslen, *Elizabethan Fictions*, p. 109.

11 Belleforest, *French Bandello*, p. 27.

12 No page number.

13 Maslen, *Elizabethan Fictions*, pp. 82–3.

14 Edward Hake, *A Touchstone for this Time Present*, sig. C4, quoted in L. B. Wright, *Middle-Class Culture*, p. 105.

15 Maslen, *Elizabethan Fictions*, pp. 50–1.

16 George Gascoigne, *The Adventures of Master F.J.* (1573), in Paul Salzman (ed.), *An Anthology of Elizabethan Prose Fiction* (Oxford: Oxford University Press, 1987), p. 3.

17 See J. W. Saunders, 'The Stigma of Print: A Note on the Social Bases of Tudor Poetry', *Essays in Criticism* 1.2 (1951), pp. 139–64.

18 Painter, *Palace of Pleasure*, vol. I, forty-sixth and fifty-first novellas.

19 Salzman, *Elizabethan Prose Fiction*, p. xiii.

20 Gascoigne, *Adventures of Master F.J.*, Appendix, p. 81.

21 *Ibid.*, pp. 17–18, 40.
22 *Ibid.*,pp. 28, 40, 47, 50–2, 55.
23 Patterson, *Censorship and Interpretation*, p. 161.
24 Susan C. Staub, 'The Lady Frances did Watch: Gascoigne's Voyeuristic Narrative', in Relihan, *Framing Elizabethan Fictions*, p. 43.
25 George Pettie, *A Petite Pallace, of Pettie his Pleasure* (1576), sig. A3r. All further references are to this edition unless otherwise stated.
26 The last sentence is found in some but not all copies; see George Pettie, *A Petite Pallace of Pettie his Pleasure*, ed. Herbert Hartman (Oxford: Oxford University Press, 1938), p. 37.
27 Lucas, *Writing for Women*, pp. 53, 69.
28 *Ibid.*, p. 69.
29 Pettie, *Petite Pallace*, ed. Hartman, p. 41; Lucas, *Writing for Women*, p. 55.
30 Salzman, *English Prose Fiction*, p. 17.
31 Sharon Stockton, 'Making Men: Visions of Social Mobility in *A Petite Pallace of Pettie His Pleasure*', in Relihan, *Framing Elizabethan Fictions*, p. 63.
32 Lucas, *Writing for Women*, p. 62; Maslen, *Elizabethan Fictions*, pp. 186, 188.
33 Wall, *Imprint of Gender*, pp. 27–8.

4 SPANISH AND PORTUGUESE ROMANCES

1 Thomas, *Spanish Romances*, pp. 41–2, 85, 119.
2 *Ibid.*, pp. 65–77.
3 *Ibid.*, pp. 103–8.
4 O'Connor, *Amadis*, pp. 6–18; Thomas, *Spanish Romances*, pp. 85, 97–100, 119.
5 O'Connor, *Amadis*, p. 3.
6 Rosalind Coward, 'Come Back Miss Ellie: On Character and Narrative in Soap Operas', *Critical Quarterly* 28.1 and 2 (Spring and Summer 1986), p. 171; and see Modleski, *Loving with a Vengeance*, pp. 88–90, 104–6; Christine Geraghty, *Women and Soap Opera: A Study of Prime Time Soaps* (Cambridge: Polity Press, 1991), pp. 3, 11.
7 Geraghty, *Women and Soap Opera*, p. 13.
8 O'Connor, *Amadis*, pp. 107, 117.
9 *Ibid.*, p. 124; Thomas, *Spanish Romances*, pp. 70, 80–1.
10 Frank Kermode, *The Sense of an Ending: Studies in the Theory of Fiction* (Oxford: Oxford University Press, 1967); Peter Brooks, *Reading for the Plot: Design and Intention in Narrative* (Oxford: Clarendon, 1984).
11 M[argaret] T[yler] (trans.), *The Mirrour of Princely Deedes and Knighthood* (1578), trans. of Diego Ortuñez de Calahorra, *Espejo de Principes y Cavalleros* (1562), sig. A2r. All subsequent references are to this edition.
12 Sir Thomas Malory, *Works*, ed. Eugène Vinaver (Oxford: Oxford University Press, 1954), pp. 2–5.
13 See C. Saunders, *Against Her Will*, ch. 6.
14 See Celeste Turner Wright, 'The Amazons in Elizabethan Literature',

Studies in Philology 37.3 (July 1940), pp. 445–56; Antony Price (ed.), *A Midsummer Night's Dream*, Casebook (Houndmills: Macmillan, 1983), pp. 79–80; Peter Holland, 'Introduction', in William Shakespeare, *A Midsummer Night's Dream*, World's Classics (Oxford: Oxford University Press, 1995), pp. 49–51; Louis A. Montrose, '*A Midsummer Night's Dream* and the Shaping Fantasies of Elizabethan Culture: Gender, Power, Form', in Margaret W. Ferguson et al. (eds.), *Rewriting the Renaissance* (Chicago and London: University of Chicago Press, 1986), pp. 70–1; Winfried Schleiner, '"Divina Virago": Queen Elizabeth as an Amazon', *Studies in Philology* 75 (1978), pp. 163–80.

15 Reprinted in Betty Travitsky (ed.), *The Paradise of Women: Writings by Englishwomen of the Renaissance* (1981, New York: Columbia University Press, 1989), pp. 144–6.

16 See Anon., *The Second Part of the Myrror of Knighthood, Containing Two Severall Bookes*, trans. R. P[arry] (1583); Anon., *The Second Part of the First Booke of the Myrrour of Knighthood*, trans. R. P[arry] (1585; 2nd edn, 1599); Anon., *The Third Part of the First Booke of the Mirrour of Knighthood*, trans. R. P[arry] (1586?; 2nd edn, 1599?).

17 My emphasis, Anon., *Second Part of the Myrror of Knighthood*, sig. A2r–v.

18 Anon., *The Seventh Booke of the Myrrour of Knighthood, Being the Second of the Third Part*, trans. L.A. (1598), 'To the Friendly and Courteous Readers'.

19 The latter derived from a French translation of a Portuguese romance originally written in Spanish, and was unconnected with the *Palmerin* cycle despite its similar title; Thomas, *Spanish Romances*, pp. 131–2.

20 Anthony Munday (trans.), *Palmerin d'Oliva* (1588), epistle to the reader; *Palmendos* (1589), epistle to the reader; *The First Book of Amadis of Gaule*, (1590?), fo. 201v.

21 Munday, *Palmerin*, fo. 176r; *Palladine of England* (1588), fo. 92v; *Amadis* (1590?), fo. 201v.

22 Hull, *Chaste, Silent and Obedient*, pp. 191–2.

23 O'Connor, *Amadis*, pp. 49–53, 139.

24 *OED*, 'Quaint', *a*.I.2, 3; *n*.[1]

25 Sir Philip Sidney, *Defence of Poesy*, in *Oxford Authors: Sidney*, p. 227; Mary Patchell, *The Palmerin Romances in Elizabethan Prose Fiction* (New York: Columbia University Press, 1947), p. 99; O'Connor, *Amadis*, pp. 185, 187–8.

26 Roy C. Strong, 'Queen Elizabeth I as Oriana', *Studies in the Renaissance* 6 (1959), pp. 253, 255.

27 Bennett, *English Books and Readers*, pp. 62–3.

28 Francis Meres, *Palladis Tamia. Wits Treasury being the Secondpart of Wits Commonwealth* (1598), facs., introd. D. C. Allen, New York: Scholars' Facsimiles and Reprints, 1938, fo. 268r–v.

29 Moryson, *Itinerary* (1617), see Thomas, *Spanish Romances*, p. 268; Edward, First Lord Herbert of Cherbury, *The Life of Edward, First Lord Herbert of Cherbury, Written by Himself*, ed. J. M. Shuttleworth (Oxford: Oxford University Press, 1976), pp. 5, 38.

30 Strong, 'Elizabeth as Oriana', pp. 258–60.
31 William Vaughan, *The Golden Fleece* (1626), p. 11, quoted in Thomas, *Spanish Romances*, p. 267.
32 Ben Jonson, *The Alchemist*, in *The Alchemist and Other Plays*, ed. Gordon Campbell, World's Classics (Oxford: Oxford University Press, 1995), IV.vii.39–41.
33 Ben Jonson, *The New Inn*, ed. Michael Hattaway (Manchester: Manchester University Press, 1984), I.vi.124–30.
34 Robert Burton, *The Anatomy of Melancholy* (1632), eds. Thomas C. Faulkner, Nicolas K. Kiessling, and Rhonda L. Blair, 3 vols. (Oxford: Clarendon, 1989–94), I.II.iii.15, p. 321; II.II.iv.1, p. 90; III.II.ii.4, p. 113.
35 *Eastward Hoe* (1605) V.i; L. B. Wright, *The Middle-Class Culture*, p. 112.
36 Philip Massinger, *The Guardian* (1633), II.ii; quoted in L. B. Wright, *Middle-Class Culture*, p. 112.
37 William Browne, 'Fido: an Epistle to Fidelia', in Gillian Wright, 'A Commentary on and Edition of the Shorter Poems of William Browne of Tavistock in British Library MS Lansdowne 777' (PhD thesis, University of Glasgow, 1998), p. 238, ll.101–6.
38 Quoted in Geraghty, *Women and Soap Opera*, p. 2.
39 I.e. unnatural intercourse and wasting of seed.
40 Who features in *The Second Part*, 1583.
41 *Seventh Booke of the Myrrour of Knighthood* (1598), sig. B1r.
42 Anon., *The Ninth Part of the Mirrour of Knight-hood, Being the Fourth Booke of the Third Part Thereof*, trans. R. Parry? (1601), title page.
43 O'Connor, *Amadis*, pp. 30, 32–3.
44 Thomas, *Spanish Romances*, p. 125.
45 O'Connor, *Amadis*, pp. 32–3, 176, 238.
46 *Amadis* VIII.xv, cited in O'Connor, *Amadis*, pp. 56–7.
47 O'Connor, *Amadis*, pp. 52, 186–7.
48 Tyler, *Mirrour* (1578), fo. 88r; Munday, *Amadis* (1590?), fo. 71r.
49 Tyler, *Mirrour* (1578), fo. 111v.
50 Munday, *Amadis* (1590?), fo. 8v.
51 e.g. *ibid.*, fo. 78v.
52 *Ibid.*, fo. 146v.
53 Thomas, *Spanish Romances*, p. 47; O'Connor, *Amadis*, pp. 79–80.
54 Tyler, *Mirrour* (1578), fo. 20r.
55 *Ibid.*, fos. 99r, 177v.
56 *Ibid.*, fo. 128r.
57 Lady Mary Wroth, *The Countesse of Mountgomeries Urania* (1621), facs., introd. Josephine A. Roberts (Aldershot: Scolar, 1996), p. 73.
58 Munday, *Amadis* (1590?), fo. 7v.
59 Tyler, *Mirrour* (1578), fo. 19v.
60 *Ibid.*, fo. 118r.
61 Munday, *Amadis* (1590?), fo. 161r.

5 FICTIONS ADDRESSED TO WOMEN BY LYLY, RICH AND GREENE

1 John Lyly, *Euphues: The Anatomy of Wit* (1578) and *Euphues and his England* (1580), eds. M. W. Croll and H. Clemons (London: Routledge, 1916), p. 1. All subsequent references are to this edition.
2 *OED*, n.[1], 1a, 3a, 3c.
3 Also in Croll and Clemons (eds.), *Euphues*, pp. 191–204. All subsequent references are to this edition.
4 Kinney, *Humanist Poetics*, p. 232.
5 Richard Helgerson, *The Elizabethan Prodigals* (Berkeley: University of California Press, 1976).
6 *Ibid.*, pp. 70–1.
7 Maslen, *Elizabethan Fictions*, p. 245.
8 Thomas Middleton and William Rowley, *The Changeling* (1622), ed. Patricia Thomson (New Mermaids, 1964; London: A. and C. Black, 1987), II.ii.57–64.
9 John Webster, *The Duchess of Malfi* (1614), ed. René Weis, World's Classics (Oxford: Oxford University Press, 1996), II.i.33–4.
10 See Hackett, *Virgin Mother*, pp. 41, 50, 238–40.
11 See *ibid.*
12 John Marston, *The Dutch Courtezan* (1605), ed. M. L. Wine (London: Arnold, 1965), IV.i.30–48.
13 Barnaby Rich, *Rich's Farewell to Military Profession* (1581), ed. Thomas Mabry Cranfill (Austin: University of Texas Press, 1959), p. 8. All further references are to this edition.
14 Lyly, *Euphues*, pp. 338–9.
15 *Ibid.*, p. 6.
16 Juliet Fleming, 'The Ladies' Man and the Age of Elizabeth', in James Grantham Turner (ed.), *Sexuality and Gender in Early Modern Europe: Institutions, Texts, Images* (Cambridge: Cambridge University Press, 1993) p. 176.
17 Marina Warner, *Alone of All Her Sex: The Myth and the Cult of the Virgin Mary* (1976; London: Pan-Picador, 1985), pp. 197–9, pls. 30, 31.
18 Voragine, *Golden Legend*, vol. I, pp. 324–5, 365–8; vol. II, pp. 165–8, 230–4. See Michael Shapiro, *Gender in Play on the Shakespearean Stage: Boy Heroines and Female Pages* (1994; pbk., Ann Arbor: University of Michigan Press, 1996), pp. 207–9.
19 M. Shapiro, *Gender in Play*, p. 208.
20 Thomas Middleton, *Women Beware Women* (1621), ed. J. R. Mulryne (Manchester: Manchester University Press, 1975), I.ii.159–86.
21 Lyly, *Euphues*, pp. 107–9.
22 Hull, *Chaste, Silent and Obedient*, p. 80; Fleming, 'Ladies' Man', p. 167.
23 Thomas Nashe, *The Anatomie of Absurditie* (1589), sig. A2v.
24 R.B., *Greenes Funeralls* (1594), sig. B1, sonnet II; L. B. Wright, *Middle-Class Culture*, p. 115.

25 In G. A. Wilkes, C. H. Herford, P. Simpson, and E. Simpson (eds.), *The Complete Plays of Ben Jonson*, 4 vols. (Oxford: Clarendon, 1981), vol. I, II.iii.201–4; Lucas, *Writing for Women*, p. 75.
26 Salzman, *English Prose Fiction*, pp. 59, 68.
27 Newcomb, 'Romance of Service'.
28 Robert Greene, *Mamillia* parts I and II (1583?), in Alexander B. Grosart (ed.), *The Life and Complete Works in Prose and Verse of Robert Greene*, 12 vols. (London and Aylesbury: Huth Library/Hazell, Watson and Viney, 1881–3), vol. II, pp. 9–10. All further references are to this edition.
29 *Ibid.*, p. 54, and see p. 62.
30 *Ibid.*, pp. 76, 94–5, 102, 106–7, 134.
31 Robert Greene, *Penelope's Web* (1587), in Grosart, ed., vol. V, pp. 141–3. All further references are to this edition.
32 See Shepherd, *Women's Sharp Revenge.*
33 Helgerson, *Elizabethan Prodigals*, p. 95.
34 Robert Greene, *Menaphon* (1589), in Grosart (ed.), vol. VI, p. 13.
35 Spufford, *Small Books*, pp. 50–1.

6 THE *ARCADIA*: READERSHIP AND AUTHORSHIP

1 Katherine Duncan-Jones, *Sir Philip Sidney, Courtier Poet* (London: Hamish Hamilton, 1991), pp. 113–14, 174.
2 Sir Philip Sidney, *The Countess of Pembroke's Arcadia (The Old Arcadia)* (*c.*1580), ed. Katherine Duncan-Jones, World's Classics (1985, rev. edn, Oxford: Oxford University Press, 1994), p. 3. All further references to the *Old Arcadia* are to this edition (given as *OA*) unless otherwise stated.
3 See Wall, *Imprint of Gender*, p. 154.
4 Duncan-Jones, *Courtier Poet*, pp. 174–5.
5 *Ibid.*, p. 170.
6 *OA*, pp. vii–viii; *The Countess of Pembroke's Arcadia (The New Arcadia)* (1590), ed. Victor Skretkowicz (Oxford: Clarendon, 1987), pp. xliii, lviii. However, H. R. Woudhuysen has gathered conflicting evidence from the 1580s as to whether the *Old Arcadia* was 'common' or hard to get hold of: *Sir Philip Sidney and the Circulation of Manuscripts, 1558–1640* (Oxford: Clarendon, 1996), pp. 300–1.
7 For implied differences between female and male reading within the *Old Arcadia*, see Mary Ellen Lamb, *Gender and Authorship in the Sidney Circle* (Madison: University of Wisconsin Press, 1990), pp. 72–89.
8 *OA*, pp. 25, 26, 34, 36, 44, 46, 49, 152, 199, 211.
9 Duncan-Jones, *Courtier Poet*, p. 256.
10 John Buxton, *Elizabethan Taste* (London: Macmillan, 1963), pp. 250, 253, 256–7.
11 Blair Worden, *The Sound of Virtue: Philip Sidney's 'Arcadia' and Elizabethan Politics* (New Haven: Yale University Press, 1996), pp. 20, 311.
12 Woudhuysen, *Sidney and Circulation*, pp. 211, 219.

13 *Ibid.*, pp. 304–6, 312.

14 Sir Philip Sidney, *The Countess of Pembroke's Arcadia (The New Arcadia)* (1593), ed. Maurice Evans (Harmondsworth: Penguin, 1977), pp. 59–60. All further references to the *New Arcadia* are to this edition (given as *NA*), unless otherwise stated. Evans's edition of the *New Arcadia* may be regarded as less satisfactory than Skretkowicz's, since Evans's copy text is a 1907 modernised version based on the editions of 1638 and 1674. Nevertheless, I use Evans rather than Skretkowicz because Skretkowicz's copy text is the 1590 edition. Since Evans derives from the 1593 edition it is closer to what most readers read over the centuries.

15 Wall, *Imprint of Gender*, p. 155.

16 Hannay, *Philip's Phoenix*, pp. 74–7; Woudhuysen, *Sidney and Circulation*, p. 230.

17 Buxton, *Elizabethan Taste*, pp. 256–7.

18 Woudhuysen, *Sidney and Circulation*, p. 228.

19 Juel-Jensen, 'Check-List', pp. 291–308; Salzman, *English Prose Fiction*, pp. 131–3.

20 Thomas Dekker, *The Guls Horne-booke*, quoted in J. J. Jusserand, *The English Novel in the Time of Shakespeare*, trans. Elizabeth Lee, introd. Philip Brockbank (1890; London: Ernest Benn, 1966), p. 261.

21 Powell, *Tom of All Trades*, p. 47.

22 Wye Saltonstall, *Picturae Loquentes. Or Pictures Drawne Forth in Characters. With a Poem of a Maid* (1631), sig. E6v.

23 Buxton, *Elizabethan Taste*, p. 252.

24 Hull, *Chaste, Silent and Obedient*, p. 14.

25 Sidney, *New Arcadia*, ed. Skretkowicz, p. xliv.

26 Woudhuysen, *Sidney and Circulation*, pp. 326, 331; Folger MS H.b.I.

27 Lady Mary Wroth, *The Poems of Lady Mary Wroth*, ed. Josephine Roberts (Baton Rouge and London: Louisiana State University Press, 1983), pp. 31–5, 238–9.

28 Anna Weamys, *A Continuation of Sir Philip Sidney's Arcadia* (1651), ed. Patrick Colborn Cullen (Oxford: Oxford University Press, 1994), pp. xviii–xx.

29 *Ibid.*, pp. xxxvi–xxxviii.

30 *Ibid.*, pp. xxxviii–xxxix.

31 *Ibid.*, pp. xxxviii, lvi.

32 *Ibid.*, p. lii.

33 Salzman, *English Prose Fiction*, pp. 133–5.

34 Duncan-Jones, *Courtier Poet*, pp. 19, 37–8; Worden, *Sound of Virtue*, p. 328.

35 Mark Rose, 'Sidney's Womanish Man', *Review of English Studies* 15 (1964), p. 354.

36 Mary Ellen Lamb, 'Exhibiting Class and Displaying the Body in Sidney's *Countess of Pembroke's Arcadia*', *Studies in English Literature 1500–1900* 37.1 (Winter 1997), pp. 60–1; Worden, *Sound of Virtue*, pp. 243, 313–16.

37 Weamys, *Continuation*, pp. 166–7.
38 Sidney, *New Arcadia*, ed. Skretkowicz, p. xix.
39 Susan C. Shapiro, '"Yon Plumed Dandebrat": Male "Effeminacy" in English Satire and Criticism', *Review of English Studies* 39 (1988), pp. 400–12; Phyllis Rackin, 'Foreign Country: The Place of Women and Sexuality in Shakespeare's Historical World', in Richard Burt and John Michael Archer (eds.), *Enclosure Acts: Sexuality, Property and Culture in Early Modern England* (Ithaca and London: Cornell University Press, 1994), pp. 68–95.
40 Lamb, 'Exhibiting Class', pp. 62–7.
41 See Laura Mulvey, 'Visual Pleasure and Narrative Cinema', *Screen* 16.3 (1975), pp. 6–18; and E. Ann Kaplan, 'Is the Gaze Male?', in Snitow et al., *Powers of Desire*, pp. 309–27.

7 THE *ARCADIA*: HEROINES

1 See Mulvey, 'Visual Pleasure'; Vickers, 'Shakespeare's *Lucrece*'; Parker, *Literary Fat Ladies*, pp. 65–6, 126–54.
2 Vickers, 'Diana Described'.
3 Wall, *Imprint of Gender*, p. 213.
4 See Dennis Kay, '"She was a Queen, and Therefore Beautiful": Sidney, his Mother, and Queen Elizabeth', *Review of English Studies* n.s. 43 (February 1992), pp. 18–39.
5 *OA*, pp. 80–1, 99, 102–3, 107, 158ff., 185, 197.
6 *Ibid.*, p. 316, and pp. 240, 248, 317–18, 325.
7 *Ibid.*, pp. 96–7, 158–60, 174–6, 182, 185, 201–3; *NA*, pp. 241–2, 633–5, 650–2, 659–60, 662–3, 681–4.
8 Entered in Stationers' Register 1585, published 1592 (*STC*).
9 Lamb, *Gender and Authorship*, p. 106.
10 Dennis Kay, 'Introduction: Sidney – A Critical Heritage', in *Sidney: Modern Criticism*, pp. 31–2.
11 Voragine, *Golden Legend*, vol. 1, pp. 27–9, 101–4, 154–7; David Farmer, *The Oxford Dictionary of Saints* (1978; 4th edn, Oxford: Oxford University Press, 1997), pp. 311–12, 7–8, 6–7.
12 Voragine, *Golden Legend*, vol. 1, p. 28.
13 Caroline Walker Bynum, *Holy Feast and Holy Fast: The Religious Significance of Food to Mediaeval Women* (Berkeley: University of California Press, 1987), p. 212; *Fragmentation and Redemption: Essays on Gender and the Human Body in Mediaeval Religion* (New York: Zone, 1991), pp. 186–7.
14 There were ten editions between 1483 and 1527 (*STC*). See C. Saunders, *Against Her Will*, chapters 3 and 4; Voragine, *Golden Legend*, vol. 1, p. xiv.
15 Lucas, *Writing for Women*, p. 52.
16 Stephanie H. Jed, *Chaste Thinking: The Rape of Lucretia and the Birth of*

Humanism (Bloomington and Indianapolis: Indiana University Press, 1989), pp. 10, 13, 40–5; C. Saunders, *Against Her Will*, chapter 5.

17 Painter, *Palace of Pleasure*, vol. 1, fo. 6.

18 Lamb, *Gender and Authorship*, p. 103.

19 Elizabeth Hanson, 'Torture and Truth in Renaissance England', *Representations* 34 (Spring 1991), pp. 53–84; Elaine Scarry, *The Body in Pain* (Oxford: Oxford University Press, 1985).

20 See Helen Hackett, 'The Torture of Limena: Sex and Violence in Lady Mary Wroth's *Urania*', in Kate Chedgzoy, Melanie Hansen and Suzanne Trill (eds.), *Voicing Women: Gender and Sexuality in Early Modern Writing* (1996; pbk., Edinburgh: Edinburgh University Press, 1998), pp. 101–3.

21 Voragine, *Golden Legend*, vol. 1, p. 154.

22 Skretkowicz's *NA* gives 'rack' for 'wreck', p. 422.

23 C. Saunders, *Against Her Will*, chapter 5.

24 Voragine, *Golden Legend*, vol. 1, pp. 103, 156.

25 Heffernan, *Sacred Biography*, pp. 275, 281, 283; C. Saunders, *Against Her Will*, chapter 4.

26 See Lamb, *Gender and Authorship*, p. 109.

27 Lucas, *Writing for Women*, p. 38; Salzman, *English Prose Fiction*, pp. 268–9.

28 Emanuel Forde, *Parismus, The Renoumed Prince of Bohemia* (1598?), sigs. Y1vff., esp. Y4r–v.

29 Emanuel Forde, *The Most Pleasant History of Ornatus and Artesia* (1595?, 1634 edn.), chapter x, esp. sig. K2r.

8 THE FAERIE QUEENE

1 I proem 4. All references are to Edmund Spenser, *The Faerie Queene* (1590–1609), ed. A. C. Hamilton (1977; London and New York: Longman, 1980).

2 Montrose, 'Shaping Fantasies', p. 82; and see Helen Hackett, *A Midsummer Night's Dream*, Writers and Their Work (Plymouth: Northcote House, 1997), chapter 2.

3 Jonathan Goldberg, *Endlesse Worke: Spenser and the Structures of Discourse* (Baltimore: Johns Hopkins University Press, 1981).

4 Quilligan, *Milton's Spenser*, p. 202.

5 Spenser, *Faerie Queene*, p. 737.

6 Quilligan, *Milton's Spenser*, pp. 185–99.

7 *Ibid.*, p. 189.

8 See Schleiner, 'Divina Virago'.

9 Spenser, *Faerie Queene*, p. 303.

10 Quilligan, *Milton's Spenser*, p. 198.

11 *Ibid.*, p. 198.

12 Dorothy Stephens, 'Into Other Arms: Amoret's Evasion', in Jonathan Goldberg (ed.), *Queering the Renaissance* (Durham and London: Duke University Press, 1994), pp. 190–217.

9 SHAKESPEARE'S ROMANCE SOURCES

1 Barnaby Rich, *Rich's Farewell to Military Profession* (1581), ed. Thomas Mabry Cranfill (Austin: University of Texas Press, 1959), pp. lxiii–lxxiii. All further references are to this edition.
2 Salzman, *English Prose Fiction*, p. 60.
3 Voragine, *Golden Legend*, vol. I, pp. 324–5, 365–8; vol. II, pp. 165–8, 230–6.
4 Thomas Lodge, *Rosalynd* (1590), ed. Brian Nellist (Keele: Ryburn/Keele University Press, 1995), pp. 47–8. All further references are to this edition.
5 Sir Philip Sidney, *The Countess of Pembroke's Arcadia (The Old Arcadia)* (*c.*1580), ed. Jean Robertson (Oxford: Clarendon, 1973), p. xxxviii; Woudhuysen, *Sidney and Circulation*, pp. 302–3; Lodge, *Rosalynd*, Introduction, pp. 20–1.
6 E.g. Juliet Dusinberre, *Shakespeare and the Nature of Women* (London: Macmillan, 1975).
7 Jardine, *Still Harping*, chapter 1.
8 Kathleen McLuskie, *Renaissance Dramatists*, Feminist Readings (Hemel Hempstead: Harvester Wheatsheaf, 1989), chapter 5; Jean Howard, 'Crossdressing, the Theatre, and Gender Struggle in Early Modern England', *Shakespeare Quarterly* 39 (1988), pp. 418–40; M. Shapiro, *Gender in Play*, pp. 1–11, 41.
9 And cf. III.ii.227, III.iv.1–4.
10 M. Shapiro, *Gender in Play*, p. 7.
11 See William Shakespeare, *The Winter's Tale*, ed. Stephen Orgel (Oxford: Oxford University Press, 1996), pp. 2–3.
12 Thomas, *Spanish Romances*, pp. 275–83.
13 Stanley Wells, 'Shakespeare and Romance', in *Shakespeare's Later Comedies: An Anthology of Modern Criticism*, ed. D. J. Palmer (Harmondsworth: Penguin, 1971), pp. 121–2; Ben Jonson, 'Ode to Himself', line 21, in *The Complete Poems*, ed. George Parfitt (1975; Harmondsworth: Penguin, 1988), p. 283; see Leah Scragg, *Shakespeare's Mouldy Tales: Recurrent Plot Motifs in Shakespearian Drama* (London and New York: Longman, 1992).
14 Samuel Lee Wolff, *The Greek Romances in Elizabethan Prose Fiction* (New York: Burt Franklin, 1912), pp. 8–9.
15 O'Connor, *Amadis*, p. 109.
16 Salzman, *English Prose Fiction*, p. 62; Margaret Williamson, 'The Greek Romance', in Radford, *Progress of Romance*, p. 25.
17 Thomas Underdowne (trans.), *An Aethiopian Historie written in Greeke by Heliodorus* (1569), fo. 1r.
18 Wolff, *Greek Romances*, pp. 262–366.
19 *Ibid.*, pp. 316–17; Williamson, 'Greek Romance', p. 30.
20 Wolff, *Greek Romances*, pp. 420–5, 443.
21 *Ibid.*, pp. 452–5.

22 Williamson, 'Greek Romance', p. 25.

23 *Ibid.*, pp. 24, 36–7.

24 1556; *OED* winter, sb.[1], 5; and see examples at pp. 13–15 above.

25 B.L. Huth 50 (nos 33–6, 38), PB Mic.C.1185 or PB Mic.22563/A.10430.

26 *Ibid.*, nos 37, 39, 41–2.

27 Katherine Park, and Lorraine J. Daston, 'Unnatural Conceptions: The Study of Monsters in Sixteenth- and Seventeenth-Century France and England', *Past and Present* 92 (1981), pp. 20–54. I am grateful to the late Gareth Roberts for this reference.

28 See David Cressy, 'Purification, Thanksgiving and the Churching of Women in Post-Reformation England', *Past and Present* 141 (November 1993), pp. 106–46; Ulinka Rublack, 'Pregnancy, Childbirth and the Female Body in Early Modern Germany', *Past and Present* 150 (February 1996), pp. 84–110.

29 B. L. Huth 50, no.36.

30 Helen Wilcox, 'Gender and Genre in Shakespeare's Tragicomedies', in A. J. Hoenselaars (ed.), *Reclamations of Shakespeare, DQR Studies in Literature* 15 (Amsterdam: Rodopi, 1994), p. 137.

31 Walter Cohen, Introduction to *The Two Noble Kinsmen*, in *The Norton Shakespeare*, eds. Stephen Greenblatt et al. (New York and London: W. W. Norton, 1997), p. 3198.

32 I am grateful to Sarah Wintle for pointing this out to me.

33 Janet Adelman, *Suffocating Mothers: Fantasies of Maternal Origin in Shakespeare's Plays, 'Hamlet' to 'The Tempest'* (New York and London: Routledge, 1992), pp. 36–7.

34 Richard Wilson, 'Observations on English Bodies: Licensing Maternity in Shakespeare's Late Plays', in Burt and Archer, *Enclosure Acts*, pp. 121–50.

35 Danish giant fought by Guy of Warwick.

36 As used in Elizabeth I's coronation pageants; see Anon., *The Quenes Maiesties Passage through the Citie of London to Westminster the Day before her Coronacion* (1559), facs., ed. James M. Osborn, introd. Sir John Neale (New Haven: Yale University Press/Elizabethan Club, 1960), sigs. C2v–D1v.

37 Dennis Kay, '"To Hear the Rest Untold": Shakespeare's Postponed Endings', *Renaissance Quarterly* 37.2 (1984), pp. 207–77.

38 I am grateful to the late Gareth Roberts for pointing this out to me.

39 *The Norton Shakespeare* gives 'festivity'; but the 1623 Folio, the only source for *The Comedy of Errors*, gives 'nativity'. Editors have often felt a need to emend this because it repeats the last word of the last line but one. See William Shakespeare, *The Comedy of Errors*, ed. R. A. Foakes, *The Arden Shakespeare* (1962; London and New York: Routledge, 1988), v.i.406n.

40 Greene, *Pandosto*, p. 225.

10 LADY MARY WROTH'S *URANIA*

1 See, for example, Carolyn Ruth Swift, 'Female Identity in Lady Mary Wroth's Romance *Urania*', *English Literary Renaissance* 14.3 (Autumn 1984), pp. 328–46; Naomi J. Miller, '"Not Much to be Marked": Narrative of the Woman's Part in Lady Mary Wroth's *Urania*', *Studies in English Literature 1500–1900* 29 (1989), pp. 121–37; Amelia Zurcher, '"Dauncing in a Net": Representation in Lady Mary Wroth's *Urania*' (M.Phil. thesis, Oxford University, 1989); Lamb, *Gender and Authorship*, chapter 4 and Appendix; Naomi J. Miller and Gary Waller (eds.), *Reading Mary Wroth: Representing Alternatives in Early Modern England* (Knoxville: University of Tennessee Press, 1991); Gary Waller, *The Sidney Family Romance: Mary Wroth, William Herbert, and the Early Modern Construction of Gender* (Detroit: Wayne State University Press, 1993); Barbara Kiefer Lewalski, *Writing Women in Jacobean England* (Cambridge, MA: Harvard University Press, 1993), chapter 9; Wall, *Imprint of Gender*, chapter 5; and other works referred to through the present chapter.

2 Lady Mary Wroth, *The First Part of The Countess of Montgomery's Urania*, ed. Josephine Roberts (Binghamton, NY: Mediaeval and Renaissance Texts and Studies, 1995).

3 See Paul Salzman, 'Contemporary References in Mary Wroth's *Urania*', *Review of English Studies* n.s. 29 (1978), pp. 178–81; Lady Mary Wroth, *The Poems of Lady Mary Wroth*, ed. Josephine Roberts (Baton Rouge and London: Louisiana State University Press, 1983), pp. 28–36, 42–3; Wroth, *Urania*, ed. Roberts, pp. lxix–ciii.

4 Wroth, *Poems*, pp. 31–6, 236–42.

5 *Ibid.*, p. 236.

6 See Wroth, *Urania*, ed. Roberts, pp. lxix–ciii for identification of many of the major characters.

7 Wroth, *Poems*, p. 36.

8 This was a common proverbial phrase, denoting self-exposure under the delusion of concealment: compare Gascoigne, preface to *Master F.J.*: 'the fond devices of such as have enchained themselves in the golden fetters of fantasy, and having bewrayed themselves to the whole world do yet conjecture that they walk unseen in a net' (p. 3).

9 Jorge de Montemayor, *Diana*, trans. Bartholomew Yong (1598), in *A Critical Edition of Yong's Translation of George of Montemayor's 'Diana' and Gil Polo's 'Enamoured Diana'*, ed. Judith M. Kennedy (Oxford: Clarendon, 1968), p. 10.

10 Carrell, 'Pack of Lies', p. 87.

11 Lady Mary Wroth, *Urania* Part 2, Newberry Case MS fo. Y1565.W95, hereafter referred to as *U2*.

12 Wroth, *Poems*, p. 236.

13 *Ibid.*, p. 238.

14 Lady Mary Wroth, *The Countesse of Mountgomeries Urania* (1621), facs.,

introd. Josephine A. Roberts (Aldershot: Scolar, 1996), p. 325. All further references to the 1621 *Urania* are to this edition, designated as *U1*, unless otherwise stated.

15 Wroth, *Poems*, p. 33.

16 *Ibid.*, p. 30.

17 See elegy in Thomas Park and William Oldys (eds.), *The Harleian Miscellany*, 10 vols. (London: 1808–13), vol. x, p. 11.

18 George Puttenham, *The Arte of English Poesie* (1589), introd. Baxter Hathaway (Kent, OH: Kent State University Press, 1970), p. 53.

19 Wroth, *Urania*, ed. Roberts, pp. xxxix–liv.

20 See also *U1*, p. 555.

21 See Helen Hackett, 'Courtly Writing by Women', in Helen Wilcox (ed.), *Women and Literature in Britain 1500–1700* (Cambridge: Cambridge University Press, 1996), pp. 182–4; Jeff Masten, '"Shall I Turne Blabb?": Circulation, Gender, and Subjectivity in Mary Wroth's Sonnets', in Miller and Waller, *Reading Mary Wroth*, pp. 67–87; Nona Fienberg, 'Mary Wroth and the Invention of Female Poetic Subjectivity', in Miller and Waller, *Reading Mary Wroth*, pp. 175–90.

22 Kim Walker, *Women Writers of the English Renaissance* (New York: Twayne, 1996), p. 188.

23 Wroth, *Urania*, ed. Roberts, p. xvii.

24 Munday, *Amadis* (1590?), fo. 77r.

25 *Ibid.*, fos. 14r, 26r–v; *Palladine*, fos.91v–92r; Wroth, *Urania*, ed. Roberts, pp. xxvi–xxvii.

26 Wroth, *Urania*, ed. Roberts, pp. xxxviii–xxxix.

27 Munday, *Palmendos* (1589), title page.

28 On the structural relationship between romance narrative and the family, see Maureen Quilligan, 'Lady Mary Wroth: Female Authority and the Family Romance' in George M. Logan and Gordon Teskey (eds.), *Unfolded Tales: Essays on Renaissance Romance* (Ithaca, NY: Cornell University Press, 1989), pp. 257–80.

29 For Rosicleer's disguise see pp. 69–70 above.

30 *OA*, p. 85; *NA*, p. 239; see p. 121 above.

31 E.g. Amphilanthus's mistress Luceania, *U1*, p. 134; Nereana, *U1*, p. 163.

32 *U1*, p. 476 (numbered 486); Wroth, *Urania*, ed. Roberts, p. lxxxiii.

33 For a fuller discussion of Limena, see Hackett, 'Torture of Limena', pp. 93–110.

34 See Elaine V. Beilin, 'Heroic Virtue: Mary Wroth's *Urania* and *Pamphilia to Amphilanthus*', in *Redeeming Eve: Women Writers of the English Renaissance* (Princeton: Princeton University Press, 1987), pp. 208–43.

35 Tyler, *Mirrour*, fos. 169(i)r–169(ii)v (3 folios in a row are numbered 169).

36 See Quilligan, 'Family Romance', pp. 272–3; and 'The Constant Subject: Instability and Female Authority in Wroth's *Urania* Poems', in Elizabeth Harvey and Katherine Eisaman Maus (eds.), *Soliciting Interpret-*

ation: Literary Theory and Seventeenth-Century English Poetry (Chicago: University of Chicago Press, 1990), pp. 307–35.

37 Wroth, *Urania*, ed. Roberts, pp. xliii–xliv.

38 Other significances of the name Pamphilia include allusion to an ancient Roman woman writer, Pamphila, a historian (Wroth, *Urania*, ed. Roberts, p. xxxv). At the end of Munday's translation of *Palladine of England* the enchantress Orbiconte prophesies that Palladine's son Florano will be loved by '*Pamphilia* Daughter to the Emperor of Greece' (fos. 91v–92r).

39 See Quilligan, 'Family Romance', pp. 261–3.

40 Carrell, 'Pack of Lies', p. 100; Wroth, *Urania*, ed. Roberts, pp. xx–xxv.

41 Sidney, *Defence of Poesy*, p. 235.

42 Sir Philip Sidney, *Astrophil and Stella*, Sonnet 1, in *Oxford Authors: Sidney*, ed. Duncan-Jones, p. 153.

43 I.e. changeful, inconstant.

44 Light blue (*OED*).

45 For more discussion of this encounter, see Helen Hackett, '"A Book, and Solitariness": Melancholia, Gender and Literary Subjectivity in Mary Wroth's *Urania*', in Gordon McMullan (ed.), *Renaissance Configurations: Voices, Bodies, Spaces 1580–1690* (Houndmills: Macmillan, 1998), pp. 64–88.

46 For more on how Wroth breaks down boundaries between fact and fiction see Carrell, 'Pack of Lies'.

47 See Margaret P. Hannay, '"Your Vertuous and Learned Aunt": The Countess of Pembroke as Mentor to Mary Wroth', in Miller and Waller, *Reading Mary Wroth*, p. 25, for a more confident view that the *Urania* suggests that the Countess supported Wroth's view of herself as pledged to William Herbert; and see *Philip's Phoenix*, pp. 188–9, for evidence of the Countess's estrangement from her son at around the time of Wroth's and his marriages in 1604.

48 Giles Fletcher, *Licia*, in Sidney Lee (ed.), *An English Garner: Elizabethan Sonnets*, 2 vols. (Westminster: Constable, 1904), vol. II, pp. 28, 32.

EPILOGUE: THE LATER SEVENTEENTH CENTURY

1 Wroth, *Poems*, p. 236.

2 Wroth, *Urania*, ed. Roberts, pp. cix, 663–4.

3 Juel-Jensen, 'Check-List', pp. 291–2.

4 Carrell, 'Pack of Lies', p. 82, p. 103 n.6; see p. 9 above.

5 Wroth, *Poems*, p. 33; see pp. 108 and 162 above.

6 Margaret Cavendish, *Poems, and Fancies* (1653), facs. (Menston, Yorks.: Scolar, 1972), sig. A3v.

7 Quoted in Douglas Grant, *Margaret the First: A Biography of Margaret Cavendish 1623–1673* (London: Hart-Davis, 1957), p. 157.

8 Margaret Cavendish, *The Blazing World and Other Writings*, ed. Kate Lilley (1992; Harmondsworth: Penguin, 1994), pp. 5, 54–5.
9 Margaret Cavendish, *CCXI. Sociable Letters, Written by the Thrice Noble, Illustrious, and Excellent Princess, the Lady Marchioness of Newcastle* (1664), pp. 38–40.
10 See Ros Ballaster, *Seductive Forms: Women's Amatory Fiction from 1684 to 1740* (Oxford: Clarendon, 1992), pp. 42–9.
11 Jusserand, *English Novel*, pp. 275–83.
12 Grant, *Margaret the First*, pp. 151–2, 240.
13 Cavendish, *Blazing World*, pp. 41, 21.
14 *Ibid.*, pp. 48, 60–2.
15 *Ibid.*, pp. 48–50, 56–7; Voragine, *Golden Legend*, vol. I, p. 154.
16 Cavendish, *Blazing World*, p. 59.
17 *Ibid.*, p. xx.
18 See Sophie Tomlinson, '"My Brain the Stage": Margaret Cavendish and the Fantasy of Female Performance', in Clare Brant and Diane Purkiss (eds.), *Women, Texts and Histories 1575–1760* (London and New York: Routledge, 1992), pp. 134–63.
19 Cavendish, *Blazing World*, pp. 91, 95, 100, 115.
20 Aphra Behn, *Oroonoko and Other Writings*, ed. Paul Salzman, World's Classics (Oxford: Oxford University Press, 1994), p. ix.
21 *Ibid.*, pp. 153, 180.
22 In Paul Salzman (ed.), *An Anthology of Seventeenth-Century Fiction*, World's Classics (Oxford: Oxford University Press, 1991), p. 531.
23 See Lennard J. Davis, *Factual Fictions: The Origins of the English Novel* (New York: Columbia University Press, 1983).
24 See Annabel Patterson, 'The Royal Romance', in *Censorship and Interpretation*; Lois Potter, 'Genre as Code: Romance and Transgression', in *Secret Rites and Secret Writing: Royalist Literature, 1641–1660* (Cambridge: Cambridge University Press, 1989), chapter 3.
25 S. J. Wiseman, *Aphra Behn*, Writers and Their Work (Plymouth: Northcote House, 1996), pp. 71–84.
26 See Ballaster, *Seductive Forms*, chapter 4.
27 Behn, *Oroonoko*, pp. 74, xiv.
28 *Ibid.*, pp. 145, 276n.
29 *Ibid.*, p. 192.
30 Grant, *Margaret the First*, p. 154; Cavendish, *Blazing World*, p. xvii.
31 Janet Todd, *The Sign of Angellica: Women, Writing and Fiction 1660–1800* (London, Virago, 1989), p. 77.
32 In Margaret Cavendish, *The Life of William Cavendish Duke of Newcastle* (1667), ed. C. H. Firth (London: Routledge, 1906), p. 162.
33 Samuel Pepys, *Diary*, eds. Robert Latham and William Matthews, vol. VIII (London: Bell and Hyman, 1974), 11 April 1667, p. 163.
34 Osborne, *Letters*, p. 80, Letter 21, 14 or 15 May 1653.
35 *Ibid.*, p. 164, Letter 54, 14 January 1654.

36 Quoted in Hero Chalmers, '"The Person I Am, or What They Made Me to Be": The Construction of the Feminine Subject in the Autobiographies of Mary Carleton', in Brant and Purkiss, *Women, Texts and Histories*, p. 186.

37 *Ibid.*, pp. 186, 173.

38 *Ibid.*, p. 175.

39 Hero Chalmers, 'Seventeenth-Century Secular Women's Autobiographies', *Women, Text and History* seminar, Merton College, Oxford, 1 November 1989; 'The Feminine Subject in Women's Printed Writings, 1653–1689' (D.Phil. thesis, Oxford University, 1994).

40 Osborne, *Letters*, p. 80, Letter 21, 14 or 15 May 1653.

Bibliography

PRIMARY SOURCES

Place of publication for works earlier than 1900 is London unless otherwise stated.

Anon., *The Second Part of the Myrror of Knighthood, Containing Two Severall Bookes*, trans. R. P[arry], 1583.

Anon., *The Second Part of the First Booke of the Myrrour of Knighthood*, trans. R. P[arry], 1585; 2nd edn, 1599.

Anon., *The Third Part of the First Booke of the Mirrour of Knighthood*, trans. R. P[arry], 1586?; 2nd edn, 1599?

Anon., *The Seventh Booke of the Myrrour of Knighthood, Being the Second of the Third Part*, trans. L.A., 1598.

Anon., *The Eighth Booke of the Myrrour of Knighthood, Being the Third of the Third Part*, trans. L.A., 1599.

Anon., *The Ninth Part of the Mirrour of Knight-hood, Being the Fourth Booke of the Third Part thereof*, trans. R. Parry?, 1601.

Anon., *The Quenes Maiesties Passage Through the Citie of London to Westminster the Day Before her Coronacion* (1559), facs., ed. James M. Osborn, introd. Sir John Neale, New Haven: Yale University Press/Elizabethan Club, 1960.

Ascham, Roger, *Toxophilus*, 1545.

The Scholemaster, 1570.

Beaumont, Francis, *The Knight of the Burning Pestle* (1607), ed. Sheldon P. Zitner, Revels Plays, Manchester: Manchester University Press, 1984.

Behn, Aphra, *Oroonoko and Other Writings*, ed. Paul Salzman, World's Classics, Oxford: Oxford University Press, 1994.

The Unfortunate Happy Lady (1696), in Salzman (ed.), *Seventeenth-Century Fiction*, pp. 527–53.

Belleforest, François de, *The French Bandello: A Selection of the Original Text of Four of Belleforest's 'Histoires Tragiques'*, ed. Frank S. Hook, Columbia: University of Missouri Press, 1948.

B.L. Huth 50, PB Mic.C.1185 or PB Mic.22563/A.10430.

Brome, Richard, *The Weeding of the Covent-Garden* (1658), in *Five new Playes*, 1659.

Browne, William, 'Fido: an Epistle to Fidelia', in 'A Commentary on and Edition of the Shorter Poems of William Browne of Tavistock in British Library MS Lansdownc 777', cd. Gillian Wright, PhD thesis, University of Glasgow, 1998.

Bullinger, Heinrich, *The Christen State of Matrimonye*, trans. Miles Coverdale, 1541.

Burton, Robert, *The Anatomy of Melancholy* (1632), eds. Thomas C. Faulkner, Nicolas K. Kiessling, and Rhonda L. Blair, 3 vols., Oxford: Clarendon, 1989–94.

Cavendish, Margaret, Duchess of Newcastle, *The Blazing World and Other Writings*, ed. Kate Lilley, 1992; Harmondsworth: Penguin, 1994.

Poems, and Fancies (1653), facs., Menston, Yorks.: Scolar, 1972.

CCXI. Sociable Letters, Written by the Thrice Noble, Illustrious, and Excellent Princess, the Lady Marchioness of Newcastle, 1664.

'A True Relation, of my Birth, Breeding and Life', in *The Life of William Cavendish Duke of Newcastle* (1667), ed. C. H. Firth, London: Routledge, 1906, pp. 151–78.

Cervantes Saavedra, Miguel de, *The History of the Valorous and Wittie Knight-Errant, Don-Quixote Of the Mancha*, trans. Thomas Shelton, 1612.

Clifford, Lady Anne, *The Diaries of Lady Anne Clifford*, ed. D. J. H. Clifford, 1990; pbk., Stroud: Alan Sutton, 1992.

Fenton, Geoffrey, *Certaine Tragicall Discourses Written oute of Frenche and Latin*, 1567.

Fletcher, Giles, *Licia*, in Sidney Lee (ed.), *An English Garner: Elizabethan Sonnets*, 2 vols., Westminster: Constable, 1904, vol. II, pp. 23–74.

Fletcher, John, *The Wild-Goose Chase* (1652), ed. Fredson Bowers, in Fredson Bowers (gen. ed.), *The Dramatic Works in the Beaumont and Fletcher Canon*, Cambridge: Cambridge University Press, 1985.

Forde, Emanuel, *The Most Pleasant History of Ornatus and Artesia*, 1595?; 1634 edn.

Parismus, The Renoumed Prince of Bohemia, 1598?

Gascoigne, George, *The Adventures of Master F.J.* (1573), in Salzman (ed.), *Elizabethan Prose Fiction*, pp. 1–81.

Gosson, Stephen, *The Schoole of Abuse* (1579), in Arthur F. Kinney (ed.), *Markets of Bawdrie: The Dramatic Criticism of Stephen Gosson*, Salzburg, University of Salzburg, 1974.

Greene, Robert, *Mamillia* parts I and II (1583?), in Alexander B. Grosart (ed.), *The Life and Complete Works in Prose and Verse of Robert Greene*, 12 vols., London and Aylesbury: Huth Library/Hazell, Watson and Viney, 1881–3, vol. II.

Menaphon (1589), in Grosart, *Life and Works*, vol. VI, pp. 1–146.

Pandosto. The Triumph of Time (*c*.1585), in William Shakespeare, *The Winter's Tale*, ed. J. H. P. Pafford, 1963; London: Routledge, 1988, Appendix IV, pp. 181–225.

Penelope's Web (1587), in Grosart, *Life and Works*, vol. V, pp. 137–234.

Harington, Sir John (trans.), *Orlando Furioso* (1591), by Ludovico Ariosto, ed. Robert McNulty, Oxford: Clarendon, 1972.

Harley, Lady Brilliana, *Letters of the Lady Brilliana Harley*, ed. Thomas Taylor Lewis, London: Camden Society, 1854.

Herbert of Cherbury, Edward, First Lord, *The Life of Edward, First Lord Herbert of Cherbury, Written by Himself*, ed. J. M. Shuttleworth, Oxford: Oxford University Press, 1976.

Hoby, Lady Margaret, *The Diary of Lady Margaret Hoby 1599–1605*, ed. Dorothy M. Meads, London: Routledge, 1930.

Jonson, Ben, *The Alchemist* (1612), in Gordon Campbell (ed.), *The Alchemist and Other Plays*, World's Classics, Oxford: Oxford University Press, 1995.

The Complete Poems, ed. George Parfitt, 1975; Harmondsworth: Penguin, 1988.

Epicene (1616), in Campbell, *Alchemist.*

Every Man Out of His Humour (1599), in G. A. Wilkes, C. H. Herford, P. Simpson, and E. Simpson (eds.), *The Complete Plays of Ben Jonson*, 4 vols., Oxford: Clarendon, 1981, vol. I.

The New Inn, ed. Michael Hattaway, Manchester: Manchester University Press, 1984.

Lodge, Thomas, *A Margarite of America* (1596), with Robert Greene, *Menaphon* (1589), ed. G. B. Harrison, Oxford: Blackwell, 1927.

Rosalynd (1590), ed. Brian Nellist, Keele: Ryburn/Keele University Press, 1995.

Lyly, John, *Euphues: The Anatomy of Wit* (1578), and *Euphues and his England* (1580), eds. M.W. Croll and H. Clemons, London: Routledge, 1916.

Malory, Sir Thomas, *Works*, ed. Eugène Vinaver, Oxford: Oxford University Press, 1954.

Marlowe, Christopher, *Dr Faustus* (A-text, 1604), in David Bevington and Eric Rasmussen (eds.), *Dr Faustus and Other Plays*, World's Classics, Oxford: Oxford University Press, 1995.

Marston, John, *The Dutch Courtezan* (1605), ed. M. L. Wine, London: Arnold, 1965.

Meres, Francis, *Palladis Tamia. Wits Treasury being the Secondpart of Wits Commonwealth* (1598), facs., introd. D. C. Allen, New York: Scholars' Facsimiles and Reprints, 1938.

Middleton, Thomas, *Women Beware Women* (1621), ed. J. R. Mulryne, Manchester: Manchester University Press, 1975.

Middleton, Thomas and Rowley, William, *The Changeling* (1622), ed. Patricia Thomson, New Mermaids, 1964, London: A. and C. Black, 1987.

Montemayor, Jorge de, *Diana*, trans. Bartholomew Yong (1598), in *A Critical Edition of Yong's Translation of George of Montemayor's 'Diana' and Gil Polo's 'Enamoured Diana'*, ed. Judith M. Kennedy, Oxford: Clarendon, 1968.

Munday, Anthony (trans.), *The First Book of Amadis of Gaule*, 1590?

(trans.), *The Ancient, Famous, and Honourable History of Amadis of Gaule*, Books I–IV, 1619.

(trans.), *Palladine of England*, 1588.

(trans.), *Palmendos*, 1589.

(trans.), *Palmerin d'Oliva*, 1588.

(trans.), *The Seconde Part of . . . Palmerin of England*, 1596.

Nashe, Thomas, *The Anatomie of Absurditie*, 1589.

The Unfortunate Traveller (1594), in Salzman, *Elizabethan Prose Fiction*, pp. 205–309.

Osborne, Dorothy, *Letters to Sir William Temple*, ed. Kenneth Parker, London: Penguin, 1987.

Overbury, Sir Thomas (attrib.), *New and Choise Characters of Severall Authors*, 6th edn, 1615.

Ovid, *Metamorphoses*, Books I–VIII, trans. Frank Justus Miller (1916), rev. G. P. Goold, Loeb Classical Library, 3rd edn, Cambridge, MA: Harvard University Press, 1977.

Painter, William, *The Palace of Pleasure*, vol. I, 1566.

The Second Tome of the Palace of Pleasure, Conteyning Store of Goodly Histories, Tragicall Matters, and Other Morall Argument, Very Requisite for Delighte and Profit, 1567.

Park, Thomas, and William Oldys (eds.), *The Harleian Miscellany*, 10 vols., London: 1808–13, vol. X.

Peele, George, *The Old Wives' Tale* (*c*.1593), ed. Patricia Binnie, Manchester: Manchester University Press, 1980.

Pepys, Samuel, *Diary*, eds. Robert Latham and William Matthews, vol. VIII, London: Bell and Hyman, 1974.

Pettie, George, *A Petite Pallace, of Pettie his Pleasure*, 1576.

A Petite Pallace of Pettie his Pleasure, ed. Herbert Hartman, Oxford: Oxford University Press, 1938.

Powell, Thomas, *Tom of All Trades. Or the Plaine Path-Way to Preferment*, 1631.

Puttenham, George, *The Arte of English Poesie* (1589), introd. Baxter Hathaway, Kent, OH: Kent State University Press, 1970.

Rich, Barnaby, *Rich's Farewell to Military Profession* (1581), ed. Thomas Mabry Cranfill, Austin: University of Texas Press, 1959.

Saltonstall, Wye, *Picturae Loquentes. Or Pictures Drawne Forth in Characters. With a Poeme of a Maid*, 1631.

Salzman, Paul (ed.), *An Anthology of Elizabethan Prose Fiction*, World's Classics, Oxford: Oxford University Press, 1987.

(ed.), *An Anthology of Seventeenth-Century Fiction*, World's Classics, Oxford: Oxford University Press, 1991.

Shakespeare, William, *The Comedy of Errors*, ed. R. A. Foakes, The Arden Shakespeare, 1962; London and New York: Routledge, 1988.

The Norton Shakespeare, eds. Stephen Greenblatt et al., New York and London: W. W. Norton, 1997.

The Winter's Tale, ed. Stephen Orgel, Oxford: Oxford University Press, 1996.

Shepherd, Simon, ed., *The Women's Sharp Revenge: Five Women's Pamphlets from the Renaissance*, London: Fourth Estate, 1985.

Sidney, Sir Philip, *The Countess of Pembroke's Arcadia (The Old Arcadia)* (*c*.1580), ed. Jean Robertson, Oxford: Clarendon, 1973.

The Countess of Pembroke's Arcadia (The Old Arcadia) (*c*.1580), ed. Katherine Duncan-Jones, World's Classics, 1985; rev. edn, Oxford: Oxford University Press, 1994.

The Countess of Pembroke's Arcadia (The New Arcadia) (1593), ed. Maurice Evans, Harmondsworth: Penguin, 1977.

The Countess of Pembroke's Arcadia (The New Arcadia) (1590), ed. Victor Skretkowicz, Oxford: Clarendon, 1987.

The Oxford Authors: Sir Philip Sidney, ed. Katherine Duncan-Jones, Oxford: Oxford University Press, 1989.

Spenser, Edmund, *The Faerie Queene* (1590–1609), ed. A. C. Hamilton, 1977; London and New York: Longman, 1980.

Stubbes, Phillip, *The Anatomie of Abuses*, 1583.

Travitsky, Betty (ed.), *The Paradise of Women: Writings by Englishwomen of the Renaissance*, 1981; New York: Columbia University Press, 1989.

T[yler], M[argaret] (trans.), *The Mirrour of Princely Deedes and Knighthood* (1578); trans. of Diego Ortuñez de Calahorra, *Espejo de Principes y Cavalleros* (1562).

Underdowne, Thomas (trans.), *An Aethiopian Historie written in Greeke by Heliodorus*, 1569.

Vives, Juan Luis, *De Institutione Foeminae Christianae* (1524), trans. Richard Hyrde, *The Instruction of a Christian Woman*, *c*.1540.

Voragine, Jacobus de, *The Golden Legend: Readings on the Saints* (*c*.1260), trans. William Granger Ryan, 2 vols., Princeton: Princeton University Press, 1993.

Weamys, Anna, *A Continuation of Sir Philip Sidney's Arcadia* (1651), ed. Patrick Colborn Cullen, Oxford: Oxford University Press, 1994.

Webster, John, *The Duchess of Malfi* (1614), ed. René Weis, World's Classics, Oxford University Press, 1996.

Wroth, Lady Mary, *The Poems of Lady Mary Wroth*, ed. Josephine Roberts, Baton Rouge and London: Louisiana State University Press, 1983.

Urania, Book 1, in Salzman (ed.), *Seventeenth-Century Fiction*, pp. 3–208.

The Countesse of Mountgomeries Urania (1621), facs., introd. Josephine A. Roberts, Aldershot: Scolar, 1996.

The First Part of The Countess of Montgomery's Urania (1621), ed. Josephine Roberts, Binghamton, NY: Mediaeval and Renaissance Texts and Studies, 1995.

Urania Part 2, Newberry Case MS f. Y1565.W95.

SECONDARY SOURCES

Adelman, Janet, *Suffocating Mothers: Fantasies of Maternal Origin in Shakespeare's Plays, 'Hamlet' to 'The Tempest'*, New York and London: Routledge, 1992.

Ballaster, Ros, *Seductive Forms: Women's Amatory Fiction from 1684 to 1740*, Oxford: Clarendon, 1992.

Barbour, Reid, *Deciphering Elizabethan Fiction*, Newark: University of Delaware Press, 1993.

Bates, Catherine, *The Rhetoric of Courtship in Elizabethan Language and Literature*, Cambridge: Cambridge University Press, 1992.

Batsleer, Janet; Davies, Tony; O'Rourke, Rebecca; and Weedon, Chris, *Rewriting English: Cultural Politics of Gender and Class*, London and New York: Methuen, 1985.

Beer, Gillian, *The Romance*, London: Methuen, 1970.

Beilin, Elaine V., 'Heroic Virtue: Mary Wroth's *Urania* and *Pamphilia to Amphilanthus*', in *Redeeming Eve: Women Writers of the English Renaissance*, Princeton: Princeton University Press, 1987, pp. 208–43.

Bennett, H. S., *English Books and Readers 1558–1603*, Cambridge: Cambridge University Press, 1965.

Brant, Clare and Purkiss, Diane (eds.), *Women, Texts and Histories 1575–1760*, London and New York: Routledge, 1992.

Brooks, Peter, *Reading for the Plot: Design and Intention in Narrative*, Oxford: Clarendon, 1984.

Burt, Richard and Archer, John Michael (eds.), *Enclosure Acts: Sexuality, Property and Culture in Early Modern England*, Ithaca and London: Cornell University Press, 1994.

Buxton, John, *Elizabethan Taste*, London: Macmillan, 1963.

Bynum, Caroline Walker, *Holy Feast and Holy Fast: The Religious Significance of Food to Mediaeval Women*, Berkeley: University of California Press, 1987.

Fragmentation and Redemption: Essays on Gender and the Human Body in Mediaeval Religion, New York: Zone, 1991.

Carrell, Jennifer Lee, 'A Pack of Lies in a Looking Glass: Lady Mary Wroth's *Urania* and the Magic Mirror of Romance', *Studies in English Literature 1500–1900* 34 (1994), pp. 79–107.

Carver, Robert H. F., '"Transformed in Show": The Rhetoric of Transvestism in Sidney's *Arcadia*', *English Literary History* 28.3 (Autumn 1998), pp. 323–52.

Catty, Jocelyn, *Writing Rape, Writing Women in Early Modern England*, Houndmills: Macmillan, 1999.

Chalmers, Hero, 'The Feminine Subject in Women's Printed Writings, 1653–1689', D.Phil. thesis, Oxford University, 1994.

'"The Person I Am, or What They Made Me to Be": The Construction of the Feminine Subject in the Autobiographies of Mary Carleton', in Brant and Purkiss, *Women, Texts and Histories*, pp. 164–94.

'Seventeenth-Century Secular Women's Autobiographies', *Women, Text and History* seminar, Merton College, Oxford, 1 November 1989.

Cixous, Hélène, 'Sorties: Out and Out: Attacks/Ways Out/Forays', trans. Betsy Wing, in Catherine Belsey and Jane Moore (eds.), *The Feminist Reader*, Houndmills: Macmillan, 1989, pp. 101–16.

Clarke, Kate, 'The Russell Women as Literary Patrons, 1570–1620: A Reconsideration of the Role of Gender in the Kinds of Dedicated Works', *Women, Text and History* seminar, Merton College, Oxford University, 17 October 1989.

Coquet, Anne, and Georges Paizis, 'The Romantic Novel in France, Britain, and the US: The Object, its Production, its Consumption', *Opium of the People or Heart of a Heartless World? Class and Gender in Popular Culture*, conference, University of London Institute of Romance Studies/Centre for English Studies, 4 February 1994.

Coward, Rosalind, 'Come Back Miss Ellie: On Character and Narrative in Soap Operas', *Critical Quarterly* 28.1 and 2 (Spring and Summer 1986), pp. 171–8.

Cressy, David, *Literacy and the Social Order: Reading and Writing in Tudor and Stuart England*, Cambridge: Cambridge University Press, 1980.

'Purification, Thanksgiving and the Churching of Women in Post-Reformation England', *Past and Present* 141 (November 1993), pp. 106–46.

Davis, Lennard J., *Factual Fictions: The Origins of the English Novel*, New York: Columbia University Press, 1983.

Duncan-Jones, Katherine, *Sir Philip Sidney, Courtier Poet*, London: Hamish Hamilton, 1991.

Dusinberre, Juliet, *Shakespeare and the Nature of Women*, London: Macmillan, 1975.

Dworkin, Andrea, *Intercourse*, London: Secker and Warburg: 1987.

Eliot, George, 'Silly Novels by Lady Novelists', *Westminster Review*, October 1856, in A. S. Byatt and Nicholas Warren (eds.), *Selected Essays and Other Writings*, London: Penguin, 1990, pp. 140–63.

Farmer, David, *The Oxford Dictionary of Saints*, 1978; 4th edn, Oxford: Oxford University Press, 1997.

Fetterley, Judith, *The Resisting Reader: A Feminist Approach to American Fiction*, Bloomington, IL: 1978.

Fienberg, Nona, 'Mary Wroth and the Invention of Female Poetic Subjectivity', in Miller and Waller, *Reading Mary Wroth*, pp. 175–90.

Fleming, Juliet, 'The Ladies' Man and the Age of Elizabeth', in James Grantham Turner (ed.), *Sexuality and Gender in Early Modern Europe: Institutions, Texts, Images*, Cambridge: Cambridge University Press, 1993, pp. 158–81.

Geraghty, Christine, *Women and Soap Opera: A Study of Prime Time Soaps*, Cambridge: Polity Press, 1991.

Goldberg, Jonathan, *Endlesse Worke: Spenser and the Structures of Discourse*, Baltimore: Johns Hopkins University Press, 1981.

Grant, Douglas, *Margaret the First: A Biography of Margaret Cavendish 1623–1673*, London: Hart-Davis, 1957.

Greer, Germaine, *The Female Eunuch*, 1970; London: Granada/Paladin, 1971.

Hackett, Helen, '"A Book, and Solitariness": Melancholia, Gender and Literary Subjectivity in Mary Wroth's *Urania*', in Gordon McMullan (ed.), *Renaissance Configurations: Voices, Bodies, Spaces 1580–1690*, Houndmills: Macmillan, 1998, pp. 64–88.

'Courtly Writing by Women', in Wilcox, *Women and Literature*, pp. 169–89.

A Midsummer Night's Dream, Writers and Their Work, Plymouth: Northcote House, 1997.

'The Torture of Limena: Sex and Violence in Lady Mary Wroth's *Urania*', in Kate Chedgzoy, Melanie Hansen and Suzanne Trill (eds.), *Voicing Women: Gender and Sexuality in Early Modern Writing*, 1996; pbk., Edinburgh University Press, 1998, pp. 93–110.

Virgin Mother, Maiden Queen: Elizabeth I and the Cult of the Virgin Mary, Houndmills: Macmillan, 1995.

'"Yet Tell me Some Such Fiction": Lady Mary Wroth's *Urania* and the "Femininity" of Romance', in Brant and Purkiss, *Women, Texts and Histories*, pp. 39–68.

Hamilton, A. C., 'Elizabethan Romance: The Example of Prose Fiction', *English Literary History* 49.2 (1982), pp. 287–99.

Hannay, Margaret Patterson, *Philip's Phoenix: Mary Sidney, Countess of Pembroke*, Oxford: Oxford University Press, 1990.

'"Your Vertuous and Learned Aunt": The Countess of Pembroke as Mentor to Mary Wroth', in Miller and Waller, *Reading Mary Wroth*, pp. 15–34.

Hannay, Margaret Patterson (ed.), *Silent But For the Word: Tudor Women as Patrons, Translators and Writers of Religious Works*, Kent, OH: Kent State University Press, 1985.

Hanson, Elizabeth, 'Torture and Truth in Renaissance England', *Representations* 34 (Spring 1991), pp. 53–84.

Heffernan, Thomas J., *Sacred Biography: Saints and Their Biographers in the Middle Ages*, Oxford: Oxford University Press, 1988.

Helgerson, Richard, *The Elizabethan Prodigals*, Berkeley: University of California Press, 1976.

Holland, Peter, 'Introduction', in William Shakespeare, *A Midsummer Night's Dream*, World's Classics, Oxford: Oxford University Press, 1995.

Houlbrooke, Ralph A., *The English Family 1450–1700*, London and New York: Longman, 1984.

Howard, Jean, 'Crossdressing, the Theatre, and Gender Struggle in Early Modern England', *Shakespeare Quarterly* 39 (1988), pp. 418–40.

Hull, Suzanne W., *Chaste, Silent and Obedient: English Books for Women 1475–1640*, San Marino: Huntington Library, 1982.

Hutson, Lorna, *The Usurer's Daughter: Male Friendship and Fictions of Women in Sixteenth-Century England*, London and New York: Routledge, 1994.

Jacobus, Mary, 'Is There a Woman in this Text?', *New Literary History* 14.1 (1982), pp. 117–41.

Jardine, Lisa, *Still Harping on Daughters: Women and Drama in the Age of Shakespeare*, 1983; 2nd edn, Hemel Hempstead: Harvester Wheatsheaf, 1989.

Jed, Stephanie H., *Chaste Thinking: The Rape of Lucretia and the Birth of Humanism*, Bloomington and Indianapolis: Indiana University Press, 1989.

Jones, Ann Rosalind, 'Mills and Boon Meets Feminism', in Radford, *Progress of Romance*, pp. 195–220.

Jones, Ann Rosalind and Stallybrass, Peter, 'The Politics of *Astrophil and Stella*', *Studies in English Literature, 1500–1900* 24 (1984), pp. 53–68.

Jordan, Constance, *Renaissance Feminism: Literary Texts and Political Models*, Ithaca and London: Cornell University Press, 1990.

Juel-Jensen, Bent, 'Sir Philip Sidney, 1554–1586: A Check-List of Early Editions of his Works', in Kay, *Sidney: Modern Criticism*, pp. 289–314.

Jusserand, J. J., *The English Novel in the Time of Shakespeare*, trans. Elizabeth Lee, introd. Philip Brockbank, 1890; London: Ernest Benn, 1966.

Kaplan, E. Ann, 'Is the Gaze Male?', in Snitow et al., *Powers of Desire*, pp. 309–27.

Kay, Dennis, ' "She was a Queen, and Therefore Beautiful": Sidney, his Mother, and Queen Elizabeth', *Review of English Studies* n.s. 43 (February 1992), pp. 18–39.

' "To Hear the Rest Untold": Shakespeare's Postponed Endings', *Renaissance Quarterly* 37.2 (1984), pp. 207–77.

Kay, Dennis (ed.), *Sir Philip Sidney: An Anthology of Modern Criticism*, Oxford: Clarendon, 1987.

Kelso, Ruth, *Doctrine for the Lady of the Renaissance*, Urbana: University of Illinois Press, 1956.

Kermode, Frank, *The Sense of an Ending: Studies in the Theory of Fiction*, Oxford: Oxford University Press, 1967.

Kinney, Arthur F., *Humanist Poetics: Thought, Rhetoric and Fiction in Sixteenth-Century England*, Amherst: University of Massachusetts Press, 1986.

Krontiris, Tina, 'Breaking Barriers of Genre and Gender: Margaret Tyler's Translation of *The Mirrour of Knighthood*', in Kirby Farrell, Elizabeth H. Hageman, and Arthur F. Kinney (eds.), *Women in the Renaissance: Selections from 'English Literary Renaissance'*, Amherst: University of Massachusetts Press, 1990, pp. 48–68.

Lamb, Mary Ellen, 'Exhibiting Class and Displaying the Body in Sidney's *Countess of Pembroke's Arcadia*', *Studies in English Literature 1500–1900* 37.1 (Winter 1997), pp. 55–72.

Gender and Authorship in the Sidney Circle, Madison: University of Wisconsin Press, 1990.

Lewalski, Barbara Kiefer, *Writing Women in Jacobean England*, Cambridge, MA: Harvard University Press, 1993.

Light, Alison, ' "Returning to Manderley" – Romance Fiction, Female Sexuality, and Class', *Feminist Review* 16 (1984), excerpt reprinted in

Mary Eagleton (ed.), *Feminist Literary Theory: A Reader*, Oxford: Blackwell, 1986, pp. 140–5.

Lucas, Caroline, *Writing for Women: The Example of Woman as Reader in Elizabethan Romance*, Milton Keynes and Philadelphia: Open University Press, 1989.

McKeon, Michael, *The Origins of the English Novel 1600–1740*, Baltimore and London: Johns Hopkins University Press, 1987.

McLuskie, Kathleen, *Renaissance Dramatists*, Feminist Readings, Hemel Hempstead: Harvester Wheatsheaf, 1989.

Margolies, David, *Novel and Society in Elizabethan England*, London and Sydney: Croom Helm, 1985.

Marotti, Arthur, '"Love is not Love": Elizabethan Sonnet Sequences and the Social Order', *English Literary History* 49 (1982), pp. 396–428.

Maslen, R. W., *Elizabethan Fictions: Espionage, Counter-Espionage, and the Duplicity of Fiction in Early Elizabethan Prose Narratives*, Oxford: Clarendon, 1997.

Masten, Jeff, '"Shall I Turne Blabb?": Circulation, Gender, and Subjectivity in Mary Wroth's Sonnets', in Miller and Waller, *Reading Mary Wroth*, pp. 67–87.

Mendelson, Sara Heller, *The Mental World of Stuart Women: Three Studies*, Brighton: Harvester, 1987.

Miller, Naomi J., '"Not Much to be Marked": Narrative of the Woman's Part in Lady Mary Wroth's *Urania*', *Studies in English Literature 1500–1900* 29 (1989), pp. 121–37.

Miller, Naomi J. and Waller, Gary (eds.), *Reading Mary Wroth: Representing Alternatives in Early Modern England*, Knoxville: University of Tennessee Press, 1991.

Modleski, Tania, *Loving with a Vengeance: Mass-Produced Fantasies for Women*, 1982; New York and London: Routledge, 1990.

Montrose, Louis A., '*A Midsummer Night's Dream* and the Shaping Fantasies of Elizabethan Culture: Gender, Power, Form', in Margaret W. Ferguson et al. (eds.), *Rewriting the Renaissance*, Chicago and London: University of Chicago Press, 1986, pp. 65–87.

Mulvey, Laura, 'Visual Pleasure and Narrative Cinema', *Screen* 16.3 (1975), pp. 6–18.

Newcomb, Lori Humphrey, 'The Romance of Service: The Simple History of *Pandosto*'s Servant Readers', in Relihan, *Framing Elizabethan Fictions*, pp. 117–39.

O'Connor, John J., *Amadis de Gaule and its Influence on Elizabethan Literature*, New Brunswick, NJ: Rutgers University Press, 1970.

Orgel, Stephen, *Impersonations: The Performance of Gender in Shakespeare's England*, Cambridge: Cambridge University Press, 1996.

Park, Katherine, and Daston, Lorraine J., 'Unnatural Conceptions: The Study of Monsters in Sixteenth- and Seventeenth-Century France and England', *Past and Present* 92 (1981), pp. 20–54.

Parker, Patricia, *Literary Fat Ladies: Rhetoric, Gender, Property*, London and New York: Methuen, 1987.

Parry, Graham, 'The Great Picture of Lady Anne Clifford', in David Howarth (ed.), *Art and Patronage in the Caroline Courts: Essays in Honour of Sir Oliver Millar*, Cambridge: Cambridge University Press, 1993, pp. 202–19.

Patchell, Mary, *The Palmerin Romances in Elizabethan Prose Fiction*, New York: Columbia University Press, 1947.

Patterson, Annabel, *Censorship and Interpretation: The Conditions of Writing and Reading in Early Modern England*, Madison: University of Wisconsin Press, 1984.

Pearson, Jacqueline, 'Women Reading, Reading Women', in Wilcox, *Women and Literature*, pp. 80–99.

Potter, Lois, *Secret Rites and Secret Writing: Royalist Literature, 1641–1660*, Cambridge: Cambridge University Press, 1989.

Price, Antony (ed.), *A Midsummer Night's Dream*, Casebook, Houndmills: Macmillan, 1983.

Quilligan, Maureen, 'The Constant Subject: Instability and Female Authority in Wroth's *Urania* Poems', in Elizabeth Harvey and Katherine Eisaman Maus (eds.), *Soliciting Interpretation: Literary Theory and Seventeenth-Century English Poetry*, Chicago: University of Chicago Press, 1990, pp. 307–35.

'Lady Mary Wroth: Female Authority and the Family Romance' in George M. Logan and Gordon Teskey (eds.), *Unfolded Tales: Essays on Renaissance Romance*, Ithaca, NY: Cornell University Press, 1989, pp. 257–80.

Milton's Spenser: The Politics of Reading, Ithaca and London: Cornell University Press, 1983.

Rackin, Phyllis, 'Foreign Country: The Place of Women and Sexuality in Shakespeare's Historical World', in Burt and Archer (eds.), *Enclosure Acts*, pp. 68–95.

Radford, Jean (ed.), *The Progress of Romance: The Politics of Popular Fiction*, London: Routledge, 1986.

Radway, Janice A., *Reading the Romance: Women, Patriarchy and Popular Literature*, Chapel Hill and London: University of North Carolina Press, 1984.

Relihan, Constance C. (ed.), *Framing Elizabethan Fictions: Contemporary Approaches to Early Modern Narrative Prose*, Kent, OH: Kent State University Press, 1996.

Rose, Mark, 'Sidney's Womanish Man', *Review of English Studies* 15 (1964), pp. 353–63.

Rubin, Gayle, 'The Traffic in Women: Notes on the "Political Economy" of Sex', in Rayna R. Reiter (ed.), *Towards an Anthropology of Women*, New York and London: Monthly Review Press, 1975, pp. 157–210.

Rublack, Ulinka, 'Pregnancy, Childbirth and the Female Body in Early Modern Germany', *Past and Present* 150 (February 1996), pp. 84–110.

Salzman, Paul, 'Contemporary References in Mary Wroth's *Urania*', *Review of English Studies* n.s. 29 (1978), pp. 178–81.

English Prose Fiction 1558–1700: A Critical History, Oxford: Clarendon, 1985.

Saunders, Corinne, *Against Her Will: Rape and Ravishment in the Literature of Medieval England*, forthcoming.

Saunders, J. W. 'The Stigma of Print: A Note on the Social Bases of Tudor Poetry', *Essays in Criticism* 1.2 (1951), pp. 139–64.

Scarry, Elaine, *The Body in Pain*, Oxford: Oxford University Press, 1985.

Schleiner, Winfried, '"Divina Virago": Queen Elizabeth as an Amazon', *Studies in Philology* 75 (1978), pp. 163–80.

Scragg, Leah, *Shakespeare's Mouldy Tales: Recurrent Plot Motifs in Shakespearian Drama*, London and New York: Longman, 1992.

Sedgwick, Eve Kosofsky, *Between Men: English Literature and Male Homosocial Desire*, New York: Cornell University Press, 1985.

Shapiro, Michael, *Gender in Play on the Shakespearean Stage: Boy Heroines and Female Pages*, 1994; pbk., Ann Arbor: University of Michigan Press, 1996.

Shapiro, Susan C., '"Yon Plumed Dandebrat": Male "Effeminacy" in English Satire and Criticism', *Review of English Studies* 39 (1988), pp. 400–12.

Shepherd, Simon (ed.), *The Women's Sharp Revenge: Five Women's Pamphlets from the Renaissance*, London: Fourth Estate, 1985.

Snitow, Ann Barr, 'Mass Market Romance: Pornography for Women is Different', in Snitow et al., *Powers of Desire*, pp. 245–63.

Snitow, Ann Barr; Stansell, Christine; and Thompson, Sharon (eds.), *Powers of Desire: The Politics of Sexuality*, New York: Monthly Review Press, 1983.

Spufford, Margaret, *Small Books and Pleasant Histories: Popular Fiction and its Readership in Seventeenth-Century England*, Cambridge: Cambridge University Press, 1985.

Staub, Susan C., 'The Lady Frances did Watch: Gascoigne's Voyeuristic Narrative', in Relihan, *Framing Elizabethan Fictions*, pp. 41–54.

Stephens, Dorothy, 'Into Other Arms: Amoret's Evasion', in Jonathan Goldberg (ed.), *Queering the Renaissance*, Durham and London: Duke University Press, 1994, pp. 190–217.

Stockton, Sharon, 'Making Men: Visions of Social Mobility in *A Petite Pallace of Pettie His Pleasure*', in Relihan, *Framing Elizabethan Fictions*, pp. 55–72.

Stone, Lawrence, *The Family, Sex and Marriage in England, 1500–1800*, London: Weidenfeld and Nicolson, 1977.

Strong, Roy C., 'Queen Elizabeth I as Oriana', *Studies in the Renaissance* 6 (1959), pp. 251–60.

Swift, Carolyn Ruth, 'Female Identity in Lady Mary Wroth's Romance *Urania*', *English Literary Renaissance* 14.3 (Autumn 1984), pp. 328–46.

Thomas, Henry, *Spanish and Portuguese Romances of Chivalry*, Cambridge: Cambridge University Press, 1920.

Thomas, Keith, 'The Meaning of Literacy in Early Modern England', in Gerd Baumann (ed.), *The Written Word: Literacy in Transition*, Oxford: Clarendon, 1986, pp. 97–131.

Todd, Janet, *The Sign of Angellica: Women, Writing and Fiction 1660–1800*, London, Virago, 1989.

Tomlinson, Sophie, '"My Brain the Stage": Margaret Cavendish and the Fantasy of Female Performance', in Brant and Purkiss, *Women, Texts and Histories*, pp. 134–63.

Vickers, Nancy J., '"The Blazon of Sweet Beauty's Best": Shakespeare's *Lucrece*', in Patricia Parker and Geoffrey Hartman (eds.), *Shakespeare and the Question of Theory*, New York and London: Routledge, 1990, pp. 95–115.

'Diana Described: Scattered Woman and Scattered Rhyme', in Elizabeth Abel (ed.), *Writing and Sexual Difference*, Brighton: Harvester, 1982, pp. 95–109.

Voss, Paul J., 'Books for Sale: Advertising and Patronage in Late Elizabethan England', *Sixteenth-Century Journal* 29.3 (Fall 1998), pp. 733–56.

Walker, Kim, *Women Writers of the English Renaissance*, New York: Twayne, 1996.

Wall, Wendy, *The Imprint of Gender: Authorship and Publication in the English Renaissance*, Ithaca and London: Cornell University Press, 1993.

Waller, Gary, *The Sidney Family Romance: Mary Wroth, William Herbert, and the Early Modern Construction of Gender*, Detroit: Wayne State University Press, 1993.

Warner, Marina, *Alone of All Her Sex: The Myth and the Cult of the Virgin Mary*, 1976; London: Pan-Picador, 1985.

Watt, Ian, *The Rise of the Novel: Studies in Defoe, Richardson and Fielding*, 1957; Harmondsworth: Penguin, 1963.

Weigall, Rachel, 'An Elizabethan Gentlewoman: The Journal of Lady Mildmay, circa 1570–1617 (Unpublished)', *The Quarterly Review* 428 (July 1911), pp. 119–38.

Wells, Stanley, 'Shakespeare and Romance', in D. J. Palmer (ed.), *Shakespeare's Later Comedies: An Anthology of Modern Criticism*, Harmondsworth: Penguin, 1971, pp. 117–42.

Wilcox, Helen, 'Gender and Genre in Shakespeare's Tragicomedies', in A. J. Hoenselaars (ed.), *Reclamations of Shakespeare, DQR Studies in Literature* 15, Amsterdam: Rodopi, 1994, pp. 129–38.

Wilcox, Helen (ed.), *Women and Literature in Britain 1500–1700*, Cambridge: Cambridge University Press, 1996, pp. 80–99.

Williamson, Margaret, 'The Greek Romance', in Radford, *Progress of Romance*, pp. 23–45.

Wilson, Richard, 'Observations on English Bodies: Licensing Maternity in Shakespeare's Late Plays', in Burt and Archer, *Enclosure Acts*, pp. 121–50.

Wiseman, S. J., *Aphra Behn*, Writers and Their Work, Plymouth: Northcote House, 1996.

Wolff, Samuel Lee, *The Greek Romances in Elizabethan Prose Fiction*, New York: Burt Franklin, 1912.

Woodbridge, Linda, *Women and the English Renaissance: Literature and the Nature of Womankind, 1540–1620*, Brighton: Harvester, 1984.

Worden, Blair, *The Sound of Virtue: Philip Sidney's 'Arcadia' and Elizabethan Politics*, New Haven: Yale University Press, 1996.

Woudhuysen, H. R., *Sir Philip Sidney and the Circulation of Manuscripts, 1558–1640*, Oxford: Clarendon, 1996.

Wright, Celeste Turner, 'The Amazons in Elizabethan Literature', *Studies in Philology* 37.3 (July 1940), pp. 433–56.

Wright, Louis B., *Middle-Class Culture in Elizabethan England*, Chapel Hill: University of North Carolina Press, 1935.

Zurcher, Amelia, ' "Dauncing in a Net": Representation in Lady Mary Wroth's "Urania" ', M.Phil. thesis, Oxford University, 1989.

Index